"Having taught through Köstenberger's *The Jesus of the Gospels* for both church and college audiences, I am excited that *Introducing Jesus* offers a streamlined version for high school students along with anyone interested in meeting Jesus for the first time. This book hits that coveted balance of accessibility and substantive content as it walks readers through what is historically referred to as 'the fourfold Gospel.' By closely following each account's storyline and theological emphasis, along with various points of application, *Introducing Jesus* offers more than a mere study of an extraordinary life; it summons the reader to action—follow Jesus and become more like him. Furthering the call are various suggested resources from Köstenberger at the book's end, tools proven to equip readers in what it means to follow the Jesus of the fourfold Gospel in a world hostile to him."

—Cory M. Marsh,
Professor of New Testament, Southern California Seminary;
Scholar-in-Residence, Revolve Bible Church

"*Introducing Jesus* makes the Gospels come alive in a way that is both accessible and deeply enriching. Drawing on the distinctive voices of the evangelists, Dr. Köstenberger beautifully unifies their narratives, offering readers a comprehensive and engaging introduction to Jesus's life and teachings. This book is not only a valuable resource for students and educators, but also a reflection of Dr. Köstenberger's profound insight and dedication to making spiritual knowledge approachable for all. I highly recommend it for believers and nonbelievers alike!"

—Jordan Raynor,
Author of *The Sacredness of Secular Work* and *Redeeming Your Time*

"Whether you're new to the Bible or have been reading it your whole life, *Introducing Jesus* will serve as a reliable companion to your reading. Providing a helpful mixture of explanations of terms and events, insights on Old Testament background, and overviews on how each gospel is arranged, this book will serve to broaden and deepen your understanding of who Jesus is and what his ministry and message is all about."

—Nancy Guthrie,
Bible teacher;
Author, *Saints & Scoundrels in the Story of Jesus*

"While we have many books about Jesus and the Gospels, we have very few that do what Andreas Köstenberger's does. Here, finally, is a volume that is introductory and accessible, but without sacrificing scholarly depth and up-to-date research. Such a combination will be a great benefit to college-aged students and to any Christian looking for a jargon-free overview of the Gospels."

—Michael J. Kruger,
President, Reformed Theological Seminary

"This work is a succinct overview of the four evangelists' individual accounts of the life of Christ. Köstenberger is the guide you want for this pilgrimage through the four Gospels. Landmarks and contours are pointed out, light is shone on some of the more difficult texts, and there is even a plan to tour the four books in thirty days. Those who are journeying this terrain anew will be aided to know Jesus and to acknowledge the Gospels as the good news—the best news ever!"

—Abraham Kuruvilla,
Carl E. Bates Professor of Christian Preaching, The Southern Theological Seminary

"Andreas Köstenberger, one of the experts on the Gospels in our day, provides an accessible and heartwarming introduction to the Jesus of the Gospels. A wonderful resource for students and for all who wish to encounter Jesus Christ."

—Thomas R. Schreiner,
Professor and Associate Dean, The Southern Baptist Theological Seminary

"In this helpful introduction to the Jesus of the canonical Gospels, Andreas Köstenberger helps us all to appreciate that Jesus was far too complex a historical and religious figure for one portrait to do him justice. We should be thankful that we have four, each of which contribute something to our overall understanding of our Savior. Portraits are not like bare photographs; they are inherently interpretative in their very nature, and so what we actually have in the New Testament are four distinct—yet compatible—portraits of the real Jesus of both history and faith, which help us 'see him more clearly, love him more dearly, and follow him more nearly, day by day.' Highly recommended!"

—Ben Witherington III,
Professor of New Testament for Doctoral Studies, Asbury Theological Seminary

"Köstenberger's *Introducing Jesus* is intended to be an introduction to the four Gospels for high school and college students and, very intentionally, as an introduction to Jesus. The consistent focus on the biblical text ensures that the life and message of Jesus is indeed the center of the book. The fruit of many years of careful scholarship, this fine, easily accessible introduction is highly recommended for Christians and non-Christians alike."

—Eckhard J. Schnabel,
Emeritus Professor of New Testament, Gordon-Conwell Theological Seminary

"Books on this subject may be so technical that only scholars can make sense of them. Not so here. The author makes wonderfully plain what the Gospel writers were convinced of—that Jesus is Lord, and that his life, teachings, self-sacrifice, and resurrection are not dead tales of the past. Rather, they are truths that remain life-changing right now. Read each gospel with this book as a guide. It will give you fresh eyes for Jesus's meaning on the vast stage of first-century Jewish expectation and Roman history. And it will open up avenues for the informed personal commitment to Jesus now that all four Gospels commend."

—Robert W. Yarbrough,
Professor of New Testament, Covenant Theological Seminary

"I have always longed for a work that helps us read the Gospels well, not merely to understand what happened but also to grasp their theological import. Success at that task is no small endeavor; it requires facility in historical context, literary structure, exegesis, and theology. In *Introducing Jesus*, Köstenberger has brought all these qualities together in clear exposition so that we have a companion that walks us through the Gospel accounts, explaining the significance of each event the way the gospel writer desired us to see them. This volume is an invaluable resource and a must-have for all those who yearn to know our Lord's life the way the biblical authors fully intended."

—Abner Chou,
President and John F. MacArthur Endowed Fellow, The Master's University and Seminary

"It is sometimes claimed that today's students know comparatively less about the Bible than past generations. Whatever the status of such comments, this new textbook by Andreas Köstenberger, *Introducing Jesus*, does something that very few recent publications even attempt. It was designed to fill a gap that is primarily aimed toward high school students, homeschoolers, or anyone else who desires a basic treatment of who Jesus is, including his teachings and actions that made him utterly unlike anyone else who ever lived. Here is a reliable guide to pursue along with the Gospels, either in personal or group settings. This solid work of research, wisdom, and application marks just such a readable text that is much needed today."

—Gary R. Habermas,
Distinguished Research Professor, Liberty University

"This book is a treasure! My colleague Andreas Köstenberger has brought his seasoned scholarship, his decades-long engagement with Scripture, and his love for Jesus to bring us a remarkable book! It is accessible and informative, easy to follow, and a pleasure to read. And it's a book for *everyone*—for all Christians (including pastors, Bible-study leaders, and campus ministers) as well as for those wanting to know more about the person who not only changed history, but also transformed the lives of his contemporaries and continues to do so today."

—Paul Copan,
Pledger Family Chair of Philosophy and Ethics, Palm Beach Atlantic University;
Author of *Is God a Vindictive Bully?* and *An Introduction to Biblical Ethics*

"In *Introducing Jesus*, Andreas Köstenberger supplies a much-needed resource for an often neglected audience: college students. You get first-rate, up-to-date scholarship without getting bogged down in overly technical detours suitable only for doctoral students. In a clear, engaging, and inspiring way, Köstenberger centers on the most important questions and issues confronting students when they study the life of Jesus. As a well-respected and established evangelical scholar, Köstenberger offers a thorough treatment of Matthew, Mark, Luke, and John without losing sight of the one, fourfold gospel. Brilliantly done! I highly recommend *Introducing Jesus*."

—J. Scott Duvall,
J. C. and Mae Fuller Professor of New Testament, Ouachita Baptist University

INTRODUCING

Jesus

THE

FOURFOLD

GOSPEL

Andreas J. Köstenberger

Introducing Jesus: The Fourfold Gospel

Published by Kregel Academic, an imprint of Kregel Publications, 2450 Oak Industrial Dr. NE, Grand Rapids, MI 49505-6020

Cataloging-in-Publication Data is available from the Library of Congress.

ISBN 978-0-8254-4812-6

Printed in the United States of America

25 26 27 28 29 / 5 4 3 2 1

For all seekers of truth:
"I am the way, and the truth, and the life.
No one comes to the Father except through me" (John 14:6).

And to my sons-in-law:
John and Dan, thank you for loving
our daughters so well. We love you!

CONTENTS

AUTHOR'S NOTE

This book is an abridgment and adaptation of my book *Jesus of the Gospels*. It is primarily meant as an introduction to Jesus for seekers, new Christians, and high school or college students, but could also be of interest to anyone interested in the story of Jesus.

Please note that for teachers of classes on the Gospels, I have divided the material into fourteen chapters—four chapters each for Matthew, Luke, and John; and two for Mark. In addition, I have posted various teaching resources on my website, https://biblicalfoundations.org.

Thanks are due to Andy Chung for encouraging this project and David Trower for his help with introductory paragraphs for Matthew, Mark, and Luke. I am also grateful to editors Brandon Benziger and Stephanie Juliot for their help in making this book more readable and enjoyable.

By far the best way to know Jesus is through the four Gospels in our New Testament. It is my hope and prayer that all of you who read this simple and humble book will trust in Jesus and follow him. He is so worthy and will never let you down!

PROLOGUE

Before delving into the story of Jesus in each of the four biblical Gospels, let me start by telling you a bit of my own story. The turning point came when I met an opera student, who shared her Christian faith with me on a train. When I heard God's Word that day, I didn't immediately drop everything and follow Jesus. That initial encounter with Jesus was just the beginning of what would turn out to be a life-changing relationship. I first had to come to terms with my inner corruption and brokenness and my need for someone who could reconcile me to my Creator and remove my guilt before him for all the wrong things I had done and for the self-centered, critical, unloving person I was.

It took six months, twice reading through the Bible, and the convicting work of the Holy Spirit to bring me to the point where I was willing to confess that I was a rebel, a transgressor of God's law, a sinner who continually missed the mark and robbed God of the glory that was rightfully his. As Paul writes in the book of Romans, "all have sinned and fall short of the glory of God" (3:23)—and that "all," I now realized, included me. It's not just that I fell short of my divinely created potential, sad and tragic as that was; I fell "short of the glory of God"—that is, I didn't bring God the glory he so richly deserved.

When I prayed to receive Christ, angels rejoiced in heaven but nothing tangible or visible happened that very moment. Spiritually, however, everything changed: I received the Spirit—God's continual, life-changing presence—into my heart, and my desire changed from pleasing myself to loving God and following Christ. There was a purity of desire I'd never known before. Over the next few months, I bore witness to my family and friends about the life-changing experience I'd had with Christ. And I resolved to strive for purity and integrity in my relationships with others and made things right wherever possible.

Also, by following Christ, I had joined a new family: the family of God, which became increasingly precious to me—my fathers and mothers, brothers and sisters in Christ. In a very real sense, they replaced my natural family, who didn't (yet) know Christ the way I'd come to know him. I craved spiritual fellowship with my new brothers and sisters and met with them for worship, Bible study, and prayer. We shared meals together and laughed and cried together. Everything changed, and I've never been the same—ask those who knew me before I became a Christian! As Paul writes, "I have been crucified with Christ. It is no longer I who live, but Christ who lives in me. And the life I now live in the flesh I live by faith in the Son of God, who loved me and gave himself for me" (Gal. 2:20).

I've written this book to introduce you to the person I love the most in this world, the person I'm infinitely grateful to for saving me from my sins, and the person with whom I'll spend eternity. It's my desire that you get to know him the way I've come to know him. As Jesus says, "You are my friends if you do what I command you" (John 15:14). As you walk with him and talk with him, and as you obey his Word, you'll increasingly come to know him as your best friend, as one who offers you a supernatural yet very real friendship that far exceeds any depth of relationship the world has to offer.

As you're getting ready to read this book, let me ask you: Do you know Jesus? If you don't, why don't you resolve to get to know him? You won't regret it. Or if you know him already, why don't you make knowing him your first priority? There's so much more he can do in and through you if you yield your life unreservedly to him. As Jesus says, "For what will it profit a man if he gains the whole world and forfeits his soul? Or what shall a man give in return for his soul?" (Matt. 16:26; cf. Mark 8:36–37; Luke 9:25). Thank you so much for joining me on this journey. God bless you as you seek and serve him.

INTRODUCTION

GETTING TO KNOW JESUS THROUGH THE GOSPELS

"The very best 'Life of Christ' is the four gospels. We read them with delight."
—Charles Haddon Spurgeon[1]

WHO DO PEOPLE SAY THAT I AM?

Oxford professor and Christian apologist C. S. Lewis once argued that Jesus is either a liar, a lunatic, or Lord. If he is a liar or lunatic, then of course we can readily dismiss him as a fraud or self-deluded. Yet is this really the most credible conclusion to draw from reading the primary sources we have about Jesus—the four New Testament gospels? To find out, we need to read these gospels and do so with an open mind and a sound strategy.

If Jesus is Lord and has supreme authority over the universe and all of humanity, then you and I shouldn't approach him merely with interested curiosity but with a readiness to obey and an eagerness to follow him. As

1. Charles Haddon Spurgeon, "Faith's Sure Foundation," in *The Metropolitan Tabernacle Pulpit* (Pasadena, TX: Pilgrim, 1878), 24:459.

Jesus tells his disciples, "If anyone would come after me, let him deny himself and take up his cross daily and follow me" (Luke 9:23).

At a critical juncture during his time on earth, Jesus takes his closest followers aside and asks them, "Who do people say that I am?" (Mark 8:27). After his disciples report a variety of responses to him, he poses an even more pointed, deeply personal question: "But who do *you* say that I am?" (Mark 8:29, emphasis added).

So who do *you* say Jesus is? Before I became a Christian, I spent much of my time trying to solve the world's (i.e., everybody else's!) problems—quick to diagnose what was wrong with those around me while being slow to find fault with myself. But when I encountered Jesus, I came to realize that he called me to decide: Who do *I* think he is? How should *I* respond to the one who died for me on the cross to offer me forgiveness and salvation out of sheer love and grace? By his mercy, I realized that I desperately needed what he had to offer and chose to follow him.

Of course, I was not the first to encounter Jesus, and many of you have had similar journeys of faith. So who did people over the past few centuries say Jesus is? And what can we learn from their quest for Jesus as we read the Gospels today?

LIVES OF JESUS AND GOSPEL HARMONIES

The centuries following the age of the Enlightenment (1500s and later) saw the production of numerous "lives of Jesus." These were accounts of Jesus's earthly journey that typically owed more to the imagination of their authors than to the actual Jesus, the first-century Palestinian Jew depicted in the Gospels.

Albert Schweitzer (1875–1965), a biblical scholar and later medical doctor, humanitarian, and Nobel Peace Prize winner, chronicled this phenomenon in *The Quest of the Historical Jesus* (1906). Schweitzer shows how writers sought to rediscover the "Jesus of history" by peeling off layers of human tradition. In that pursuit, Schweitzer discovered that each individual created Jesus in keeping with his own character and imagination.

In thinking about writing this book, I had to ask myself the question: How am I going to do any better than those scholars? What makes me think I can escape the tendency to recreate Jesus in my own image? The answer, I concluded, lies in sticking closely to the available sources—the gospels of Matthew, Mark, Luke, and John.

It's true that the Gospels don't cover Jesus's life exhaustively. John, for example, candidly acknowledges that he was highly selective (20:30–31; 21:25). But that doesn't mean we need to be skeptical. As we'll see, we have every reason to believe that the gospel accounts of Jesus's life and ministry are reliable, since they were written by eyewitnesses or based on their accounts.

What's more, the manuscript evidence indicates that the text of the Gospels has been faithfully preserved and transmitted since their composition by the original authors. So we can have a high degree of confidence that the gospels in our Bibles—faithful translations of the originals—are accurate representations of what the evangelists wrote.

What this means, then, is that in our quest to know Jesus, we can trust the Gospels as reliable witnesses to the life of Jesus. For some of us, this will be a big step. It can be unsettling to think that our knowledge of Jesus boils down to trust, but the Scriptures reassure us that the information the four gospels provide about Jesus is rock solid and backed up by firsthand personal experience.

READING THE GOSPELS

How, then, should you read these trustworthy accounts of Jesus's life? Let me suggest four ways of reading the Gospels that will help you get to know Jesus better: as a unified witness, as eyewitness testimony, as narratives, and one at a time.

As a Unified Witness

In keeping with the early church's understanding, we should view the individual gospels as unified documents within the larger framework of the fourfold gospel. When you look at your English Bible, you'll notice that the actual titles of the individual gospels are *not* "The Gospel of Matthew," "The Gospel of Mark," and so forth, but "The Gospel *According to* Matthew," "The Gospel *According to* Mark," and so on.

In a sense, therefore, we don't have *four* gospels but *one* gospel according to four witnesses—Matthew, Mark, Luke, and John. It's very important for us to let the implications of this insight sink in. The church doesn't have four gospels; it proclaims *one unified gospel.* We should never lose sight of the fact that the one gospel, given to us in the form of a fourfold witness, is unified.

What's more, the Gospels exhibit not merely a *literary* unity; they are also unified *historically* and *theologically.* That is, they attest to the same historical set of events and teachings in the life of Jesus and reflect unified convictions expressed by Jesus, the biblical authors, and the early church. And while the titles of the four gospels are not themselves part of these texts, they were affixed to them at a very early stage.

As Eyewitness Testimony

From the vantage point of *history*, we should read the Gospels as eyewitness testimony. Matthew and Mark followed accepted conventions for history writing in the first century. Luke too claims in his preface that his account is based on eyewitness testimony (Luke 1:1–4). While he himself was not an eyewitness, as a good historian Luke carefully researched his subject matter by drawing on eyewitness accounts. John, for his part, stakes a strong claim to being an eyewitness (John 19:35; 21:24).

The eyewitness nature of the testimony contained in the four gospels also accounts for the diversity of perspectives they convey. Eyewitnesses of, say, a traffic accident who testify in court, or different reporters covering the same event, might highlight different things about that event. Their accounts complement one another and give us a better understanding of the event. Similarly, the four gospels provide us with complementary perspectives of the life and ministry of Jesus that enrich our knowledge and understanding of what Jesus said and did.

Thus, we find in the Gospels a remarkable unity in diversity. The unity is evident in the close similarity between the gospels according to Matthew, Mark, and Luke, which are often called "the Synoptic Gospels" (from *syn*, "together," and *optic*, "look"). If you look at these gospels in a gospel harmony in parallel columns, you will detect a striking similarity among them, most likely because one or two of them used the other(s) in composing their gospel. The diversity finds expression in some thematic emphases, while John's gospel blazes its own trail.

As Narratives

From a *literary* vantage point, we should read the Gospels as narratives. This means that we appreciate them as self-contained works, consisting of literary units and subunits (called pericopes). This point is vital, since this is the form in which information regarding the life of Jesus has come down to us. Respecting Scripture, therefore, also means respecting the literary boundaries and characteristics of the respective gospel accounts.

Recent literary scholarship has given us valuable tools for reading the Gospels. In the past few decades, people have increasingly come to recognize that the gospel accounts display a large variety of literary features that can be studied with great profit by students of Scripture. This includes their overarching plotline, characterization, setting, various literary structures, and other devices.

Without imposing modern categories onto the biblical text, we can benefit from reading the gospels as literary wholes. This type of reading will also enable us to keep the literary and theological diversity of the four gospels in concert with their underlying unity. Reading all four accounts in relation to one another will provide us with a theological richness that is unattainable by reading one gospel alone.

One at a Time

To get the most out of our study of Scripture, it's best to read the gospels *one at a time*, vertically. Track each one's plotlines and the ways in which they characterize their one main character, Jesus, with regard to what he did (his actions) and what he said (his teachings). All of this is part of the biblical portrait of Jesus's messianic mission, which in turn is rooted in a long stream of prophetic predictions that, in Jesus, have come to fulfillment.

READING THIS BOOK

Our account *about* the accounts of Jesus has five fundamental assumptions:

1. God gave us four inspired gospels, and the church recognized this by including them in her collection of sacred books (the "canon"). In fact, the church fathers insisted there could be only four gospels. The New Testament doesn't include a harmony (a consolidated account) of the life of Jesus.
2. Each of the gospels provides an accurate and distinctive account. The Gospels are complementary, not contradictory. We should appreciate the historical, literary, and theological insights they offer without pitting them against each other, as if different perspectives on one life necessarily is a problem.
3. We should read all four gospels rather than preferring one over the others. Among other things, this means that we should affirm the

historical value of each of these gospels and read all four accounts to derive the maximum benefit when learning about the canonical witness to the life of Jesus.

4. Out of respect for the New Testament, it's best to discuss the Gospels in their canonical order: Matthew, Mark, Luke, and John. This is true regardless of the order in which the Gospels were written. Mark may have been first, but the Bibles we have put Matthew first, and this is how we should proceed as well.
5. We should affirm, as the early church did, that the four canonical gospels are "the fourfold gospel"—*one* gospel according to *four* witnesses. This attests to the essential unity among the Gospels regarding the key events in Jesus's life, particularly his crucifixion, burial, and resurrection.

This book is not meant to be a substitute for reading the Gospels. Rather, it is to serve as a companion, helping you to understand better what you're reading. It's meant to be a resource for reading the four gospels by closely tracking with their respective storylines and theological emphases.

In addition to explanations, I've suggested some proper points of application. The life of Jesus is not primarily a life to be contemplated or even admired; it is a call to response and action. We don't merely read the Gospels to understand *history*; we read them to find our place in *his story*. The life of Jesus is a summons to follow him and become more like him, both in our own character and in the way we relate to others.

This approach will also help us develop a better grasp of how the gospel of salvation in Jesus Christ is central to the fourfold gospel witness. What's more, not only will we recognize Jesus as Savior and Lord but we will also join him on mission. We'll take up our cross daily and identify with him in a world that desperately needs to see that "God so loved the world, that he gave his only Son, that whoever believes in him should not perish but have eternal life" (John 3:16).

DISCUSSION QUESTIONS

1. Who do you think Jesus is: liar, lunatic, lord, legend, or something else, and why?

2. Do you think it's true that we tend to recreate Jesus in our own image?

3. Do you like having four Gospels or would you rather just have one, and why?

4. What is your favorite book, novel, or Bible story, and why? Or, what's the last book you've read?

When Jesus came to the region of Caesarea Philippi, he asked his disciples, "Who do people say the Son of Man is?" They replied, "Some say John the Baptist; others say Elijah; and still others, Jeremiah or one of the prophets." "But what about you?" he asked. "Who do you say I am?" Simon Peter answered, "You are the Messiah, the Son of the living God."

—Matthew 16:13–16 NIV

What do you think about Jesus? In this volume, you'll be working through precious eyewitness testimony from those who knew him best. It's moving to see that Jesus cared what Simon Peter and the other disciples thought of him. While they knew there was a range of opinions regarding Jesus, they had made up their minds, and Peter spoke for all of them when he stated boldly that Jesus was the Messiah, the Son of the living God. Without Christ, there is no Christianity. There is no salvation, no forgiveness, no gospel. With Christ, there is life, because he is the Son of the living God, and he came to give life, eternal life, to those who put their trust wholeheartedly in him.

PART 1

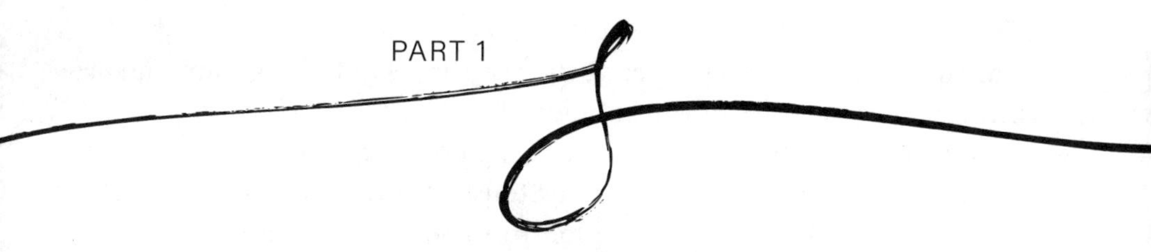

THE GOSPEL ACCORDING TO MATTHEW: JESUS, THE JEWISH MESSIAH

WHO WAS MATTHEW?

Matthew, called Levi in the other gospels, was one of the twelve apostles (Matt. 9:9; cf. Mark 2:14; Luke 5:27). He records his own call as follows: "As Jesus passed on from there, he saw a man called Matthew sitting at the tax booth, and he said to him, 'Follow me.' And he rose and followed him." After this, Jesus has dinner at Matthew's house with many other tax collectors and "sinners." When the Pharisees object, Jesus says that he has come to call sinners, not the righteous (Matt. 9:9–13).

Shortly after this, "Matthew the tax collector" is mentioned as one of the twelve apostles Jesus appoints (10:3). Matthew's background and special interest in tax-related issues are occasionally highlighted, such as when he alone includes the account of Jesus and Peter paying the temple tax or discusses paying taxes to Caesar (17:24–27; 22:15–22). Like John, Matthew wrote as a member of the twelve apostles and an eyewitness of the earthly mission of Jesus.

WHAT IS DISTINCTIVE ABOUT MATTHEW'S GOSPEL?

For the most part, Matthew tells the story of Jesus in *chronological* order, moving from his virgin birth and infancy to his public ministry, culminating in Jesus's crucifixion, burial, and resurrection. Jesus's ministry proceeds *geographically* from Galilee—where Jesus is shown to engage in multiple cycles of ministry—to Judea and, from there, to the capital city of Jerusalem.

Matthew organizes Jesus's teaching in five major "books of Jesus," similar to the five books of Moses and the Psalms. In these books, Matthew portrays Jesus as the "new Moses" who gives a new law (the Sermon on the Mount), as the messianic shepherd who gathers a Jewish remnant—the Twelve—to preach the gospel of God's kingdom, and as the teacher of parables of the kingdom.

Matthew sets off each of these teaching portions with a version of the concluding formula "And when Jesus finished these sayings . . ." (7:28; 11:1; 13:53; 19:1; 26:1). In addition to these teaching units, Matthew, throughout his gospel, alternates between teaching and narrative portions, portraying Jesus as the Jewish Messiah in both word and deed.

WHAT ARE SOME OF MATTHEW'S MAJOR EMPHASES?

Matthew presents Jesus as the long-awaited Messiah predicted across a broad spectrum of passages in Scripture. He styles his gospel as a continuation of God's relationship with Israel, and cites numerous Old Testament passages to highlight the identity of Jesus as the Jewish Messiah.

Matthew's close connection with the Old Testament is further reinforced by the placement of his gospel in the New Testament. The fact that Matthew alone starts with a genealogy of Jesus makes his gospel the perfect starting point for the New Testament and a fitting first gospel in the canon.

In many ways, therefore, Matthew introduces both the fourfold gospel canon and the entire New Testament. As we read his narrative, we'll do well to keep one finger in the pages of the Old Testament—Israel's Scriptures. In the introduction alone, Matthew presents Jesus as fulfilling as many as six Old Testament prophecies.

For those of us who are Gentiles (non-Jews)—probably the majority of those reading this—we may legitimately ask: What's the relevance of a gospel that distinctly presents Jesus as the Jewish Messiah? There are at least two answers:

1. Even for us Gentiles, it's important to realize that our Christian faith is firmly rooted in Jewish soil, in the history of God's relationship with Israel, culminating in Jesus's coming—in keeping with Old Testament promises.
2. While Matthew portrays Jesus as the Messiah in the line of Abraham and David, in the course of the gospel the scope of salvation gradually widens from Jews to Gentiles until the risen Jesus commissions his followers—a Jewish believing remnant—to go and make disciples of all nations. This shows that Matthew's gospel is relevant for all—Gentiles as well as Jews.

CHAPTER 1—MATTHEW

SETTING THE STAGE

JESUS, THE MESSIAH, DESCENDANT OF ABRAHAM AND DAVID (1:1–4:16)
The Genealogy (1:1–17)
The Virgin Birth (1:18–25)
The Wise Men's Worship (2:1–12)
The Escape to Egypt, Herod's Rage, and the Return to Nazareth (2:13–23)
The Ministry of John the Baptist (3:1–12)
The Baptism by John (3:13–17)
The Temptation (4:1–11)
The Beginning of Jesus's Public Ministry (4:12–16)

JESUS, THE MESSIAH, DESCENDANT OF ABRAHAM AND DAVID (1:1–4:16)

Identity is a big part of the world now. People are constantly trying to be something, whether they define themselves by their relationships, success, popularity, or even by their biology or gender. Who was Jesus? What was his identity? The Bible says Christians are "in Christ." So who

Jesus is—Jesus's identity—has tremendous implications for us as his followers. Who does Matthew say Jesus is?

Matthew sets out to provide a thorough account of Jesus's ministry and teaching. He is very diligent and starts at the beginning, with a family tree. After this, he records Jesus's birth and subsequent events during Jesus's boyhood. But Matthew is not primarily interested in Jesus's growing-up years. He fast-tracks to the ministry of Jesus's forerunner, John the Baptist, who announces the arrival of God's kingdom in the person of Jesus, the Messiah. We read about Jesus's baptism by John, and then about Jesus's temptation by the devil. The present section closes with a reference to John's arrest and Jesus taking up residence in the bustling town of Capernaum on the shores of the Sea of Galilee.

The Genealogy (1:1–17)

The opening phrase of Matthew's gospel, "The book of the genealogy," mirrors the language used to introduce both the creation account and the genealogy of Adam (Gen. 2:4; 5:1). Matthew isn't telling a new story; he's providing an account with deep roots in God's creation and the covenants God established with his people Israel, as recorded in the Scriptures—the Messiah's "genesis"!

Matthew is one of two evangelists (the other being Luke) who includes a genealogy, yet there are several notable differences:

1. Matthew puts his genealogy at the very *beginning*, as an introduction to Jesus's messianic birth in Bethlehem in keeping with prophetic prediction, while Luke puts his genealogy right before Jesus's public ministry (Luke 3:23–38).
2. Matthew traces Jesus's ancestry back to *Abraham*, the father of the Jewish nation, accentuating Jesus's Jewishness; Luke traces it back all the way to *Adam*, stressing more broadly Jesus's humanity.
3. Matthew presents his genealogy in *ascending* order, starting with Abraham and moving forward to end with Jesus, while Luke presents his genealogy in *descending* order, starting with Jesus and moving backward to end with Adam.
4. Counting Mary, the mother of Jesus, Matthew includes five women in Jesus's genealogy, which is highly unusual, especially considering which women are included:

- Tamar, Judah's daughter-in-law, who posed as a harlot (Gen. 38);
- Rahab, a former Jericho prostitute (Josh. 2);
- Ruth, a Moabite woman and great-grandmother of David (Ruth);
- "Uriah's wife"—Bathsheba—later David's wife and mother of Solomon (2 Sam. 11); and
- Mary, the mother of Jesus.

Most likely, Matthew includes these women as part of his argument for the plausibility of the virgin birth. The presence of these women in Jesus's genealogy shows that the appearance (or reality) of scandal was not unprecedented in Jewish history. Since Jews widely believed God acted consistently in history, this would have added persuasiveness to Matthew's account of the virgin birth.

5. The phrase "became the father of" leaves open whether a given ancestor was a biological father or a legal father through adoption.
6. Matthew and Luke organize their genealogies differently (though both are selective about which ancestors they highlight). Matthew organizes Jesus's ancestry in the form of fourteen generations, from Abraham to David, from David to the Babylonian exile, and from there to Jesus.
7. The genealogies begin to diverge after arriving at king David, where Matthew continues to trace Jesus's ancestry through Solomon (Matt. 1:6–7) while Luke continues with Nathan, Solomon's brother (Luke 3:31). (The numerical value of the name "David" in Hebrew is fourteen.)

Finally, there's an interesting twist toward the end. While the repeated phrase throughout is "X was the father of Y," at the end the familiar pattern breaks off. Rather than say, "Joseph *the father of Jesus*," the text says, "Joseph *the husband of Mary*, of whom Jesus was born, who is called Christ" (Matt. 1:16, emphasis added). Jesus was born "of Mary," his *mother*, but Joseph, while being Mary's husband, was not Jesus's *biological father*! Rather, he was Jesus's adoptive, legal father; Jesus's actual father was God. In this way, the end of Matthew's genealogy anticipates the account of the virgin conception and birth of Jesus.

The Virgin Birth (1:18–25)

Matthew's depiction of Jesus's virgin conception, Bethlehem birth, and early boyhood shows Jesus's uniqueness and connects his coming with God's promises to his people Israel. A young virgin named Mary is pregnant—not by Joseph, her fiancé, but by the Holy Spirit (1:18, 20). While greatly distressed by Mary's pregnancy, Joseph, "being a just man," resolves to divorce her quietly (v. 19). (In that day, dissolving an engagement required a certificate of divorce, which shows that first-century Jews considered betrothal binding, akin to marriage.) Yet before Joseph can do so, an angel appears to him in a dream, addressing him as "son of David" and directing him to take Mary as his wife (v. 20).

What's more, the angel reveals the gender and name of the child growing in Mary's womb: a son named Jesus—which in Hebrew means "Yahweh (God) saves"—"for he will save his people from their sins" (v. 21). In keeping with Isaiah's prophecy, the Messiah will be born of a young woman, a virgin (v. 23a; cf. Isa. 7:14). In addition to "Jesus," he will also be called "Immanuel"—which means "God with us." God would be continually present with his people in fulfillment of the new covenant Jesus would establish with the believing remnant of Israel at the Last Supper (Matt. 1:23b; cf. 26:26–29).

The Wise Men's Worship (2:1–12)

At Jesus's birth in Bethlehem, a group of wise men—Gentiles—makes the long trek from the far East to the Holy Land, following the path of a star in search of the "king of the Jews" (2:2). Numerous legends have grown around this story, such as that these wise men were "kings from the Orient" and that there were three of them. However, more important than their occupation is their role in Matthew's gospel: representatives of the non-Jewish world impacted by Jesus.

Coming first to Jerusalem, the wise men find an anxious King Herod ("the Great"), who professes a desire to worship the baby but in truth sees him as a threat to his own power. Herod asks the Jewish high priests and scribes where the Messiah is to be born, and they reply, without a moment's hesitation, "In Bethlehem of Judea" (v. 5; cf. Mic. 5:2). At this, Herod tells the wise men to go to Bethlehem to "search diligently for the child," feigning a desire to worship him (Matt. 2:8).

The wise men follow the star to Bethlehem in search for the infant king. Most likely, they arrive sometime after Jesus's birth, since Jesus seems to be no longer in a manger but in a "house" and is no longer an infant but a "child" (v. 11). They bow in worship and present their gifts: gold (a gift for royalty), frankincense (a priestly item), and myrrh (conveying the grief associated with Jesus's suffering). In this, the wise men starkly contrast with Herod as Gentiles who approach Jesus in a reverent fashion. Having been warned in a dream by an angel, they don't go back to Herod but return to their country by another route.

The Escape to Egypt, Herod's Rage, and the Return to Nazareth (2:13–23)

The following events reveal God's sovereign hand in protecting Jesus from the murderous designs of King Herod. Having been warned by the angel of the Lord in a dream (similar to the wise men earlier), Joseph takes his young family to Egypt to remain there until Herod's death. The escape of Jesus's family to Egypt echoes the escape of Moses. It also fulfills Hosea's words, "Out of Egypt I called my son" (Hos. 11:1). Just as God called Israel, "his son," out of Egypt into the Promised Land, so he calls Jesus, "his Son," out of Egypt back into the Holy Land.

Discovering that the infant Messiah has eluded his grasp, Herod is enraged and orders all male children two years old and under in Bethlehem and the vicinity to be killed, unwittingly fulfilling Jeremiah's prophecy (Jer. 31:15). Mercifully, since Bethlehem was a small village, the mad king's edict may have applied to no more than one or two dozen children. Matthew's portrayal of Jesus begins to paint the picture of Jesus as the new Moses, who delivers and instructs God's people and who will shortly give his inaugural address, the Sermon on the Mount.

In response to another angelic vision, Joseph brings his family to Nazareth, a city in Galilee, where Jesus will live for the remainder of his childhood. This too happens in keeping with Old Testament prophecy, which establishes a connection between the messianic "root" (*nezer* in Hebrew) of King David's father Jesse and the city of Nazareth (Isa. 11:1, 10). In all these ways—the Messiah's birthplace, the escape to Egypt, the slaughter of infant boys, and Jesus's boyhood in Nazareth—Jesus fulfills messianic expectations.

The Ministry of John the Baptist (3:1–12)

The narrative now shifts to the ministry of John the Baptist, who appears in the Judean wilderness urging the Jewish people to "repent, for the kingdom of heaven is at hand" (Matt. 3:2). That a prophet calls God's people to repentance is nothing new; yet the announcement that "the kingdom of heaven" has almost arrived is momentous. In keeping with Isaiah's prophecy, John identifies himself as a "voice of one crying in the wilderness: 'Prepare the way of the Lord'" (v. 3; cf. Isa. 40:3). What John is announcing is that the Messiah will lead a new exodus by which God will deliver his people, and they should prepare by way of repentance. John's attire resembles that of the Old Testament prophet Elijah, who likewise "wore a garment of [camel] hair, with a belt of leather about his waist" (2 Kings 1:8).

John's preaching meets with a huge response among the ordinary people, but when the Jewish leaders come to him, he denounces them in harsh terms; their appeal to Abraham won't save them. For them, there'll be only judgment, for "God is able from these stones to raise up children for Abraham" (Matt. 3:9). God doesn't need them to populate his messianic community; he can start over from scratch! Unless they repent and put their trust in the Messiah, their Jewish heritage isn't going to save them. That said, John's baptizing activity is only the beginning; one mightier than him will follow after him, and he will baptize not with mere water but with "the Holy Spirit and fire" (v. 11).

The Baptism by John (3:13–17)

That figure who is infinitely mightier than John the Baptist now appears on the scene: Jesus, the Messiah. He comes to the Jordan River to be baptized by John. John voices the question that is on everybody's mind: "I need to be baptized by you, and do you come to me?" (v. 14). Typically, the lesser is baptized by the greater. What's more, isn't John's a baptism of repentance? If Jesus is baptized by John, wouldn't that indicate that he is a sinner? This may be a plausible way of reasoning in human terms, but Jesus brushes all such concerns aside, reassuring John that he should go ahead with the baptism so as "to fulfill all righteousness" (v. 15); this is part of Jesus's identification with sinners, without implying that Jesus is a sinner himself (cf. Rom. 8:3–4).

When Jesus is baptized, as soon as he emerges from the water, heaven opens and the Spirit of God descends and rests on him like a dove, conveying the notion of a new creation, as the Spirit of God hovered above the waters at the original creation (Gen. 1:2). Also, a voice from heaven—God the Father—declares, "This is my beloved Son, with whom I am well pleased" (Matt. 3:17). This declaration is reminiscent of Old Testament messianic passages in which the Messiah or the suffering Servant provides forgiveness for sinners by sacrificing his life for them (Ps. 2:7; Isa. 42:1). The Father's commendation of his Son makes clear that Jesus isn't a self-proclaimed Messiah; he is the Son of God who does the will of the Father.

The Temptation (4:1–11)

The scene of the narrative shifts once again, as Jesus is "led up by the Spirit into the wilderness to be tempted by the devil" (Matt. 4:1). Again, the wilderness reference connects Jesus's experience with Israel's during the exodus (cf. 3:1–3). Jesus's forty days of temptation show that he has truly come to "fulfill all righteousness" (cf. 3:15; on the theme of righteousness, see 5:6, 20; 6:33). Where the Israelites failed to be faithful to God during their forty years of wandering in the wilderness, Jesus remains faithful and demonstrates his identity as the true Son of God. The connection with Moses, wilderness Israel, and the exodus is reinforced by the fact that all three Old Testament passages Jesus quotes in response to Satan's temptations come from Deuteronomy 6–8, Moses's address to the Israelites before entering the Promised Land. All these were lessons that the Israelites should have learned:

1. "Man shall not live by bread alone, but by every word that comes from the mouth of God" (Matt. 4:4; cf. Deut. 8:3);
2. "You shall not put the Lord your God to the test" (Matt. 4:7; cf. Deut. 6:16); and
3. "You shall worship the Lord your God and him only shall you serve" (Matt. 4:10; cf. Deut. 6:13).

At Jesus's baptism, we saw that Jesus has come to "play by the rules," being committed to fulfilling "all righteousness." In fact, he goes beyond what could reasonably have been expected when he, the sinless Son of God, submits to baptism. Here, at the temptation, we see that once again Jesus refuses to succumb to Satan's lie that Jesus, as the Messiah, can write his own ticket.

1. When hungry, Jesus, if he wanted to, could turn stones into bread, but he refuses to take matters into his own hands. He is committed to trusting in God's provision rather than acting independently, as Adam and Eve had done in the garden. How often are we tempted to take matters into our own hands rather than trusting God?

2. When the devil dares him to jump off the pinnacle of the temple—even quoting Scripture—Jesus doesn't take the bait but refuses to put God to the test. Jesus has angels at his command who could soften his fall, but calling on them to do so would have been to claim special status when Jesus had chosen to empty himself of his divine prerogatives (Phil. 2:6–7).
3. Finally, when Satan offers to give Jesus all the kingdoms of the world "and their glory," Jesus rebukes him, saying, "Be gone, Satan!" (Matt. 4:8, 10). As the true Israelite, he'd worship none other than God alone (even though he himself, as the Son of God, could have commanded worship). How much less should we seek fame or fortune! We must beware of gaining the world but forfeiting our souls (Matt. 16:26; Mark 8:36; Luke 9:25).

At these temptations, Jesus shows his humility and obedience to God's will. At the very beginning of his public ministry, therefore, he is revealed as the true Israel. Here, we see his identification with both Israel and humanity in general, as well as a marked contrast with Israel's wilderness experience. Where Israel was disobedient, Jesus obeys.

Where the wilderness generation failed to enter the Promised Land because of unbelief and inability to conquer the land completely, this "Son of God" will succeed and bring about a new exodus. He will effect permanent deliverance from sin through his death on a cross and bring believers into their eternal rest. At the end of the temptation, the devil withdraws, and angels come and attend to Jesus (Matt. 4:11–12).

The Beginning of Jesus's Public Ministry (4:12–16)

Upon hearing that John the Baptist has been arrested (cf. 14:1–12), Jesus withdraws to Galilee, where he had been before his baptism. He moves from Nazareth, where he had grown up (cf. 2:23), to Capernaum "by the sea" (i.e., the Sea of Galilee).

At this, Matthew introduces the setting in which Jesus will begin his public ministry. Again in keeping with Old Testament prophecy, Jesus begins his ministry in Galilee, declaring the arrival of God's kingdom in terms identical to those of John the Baptist: "Repent, for the kingdom of heaven is at hand" (4:17; cf. 3:2; see Isa. 9:1–2). John's and Jesus's messages are one and the same, yet whereas John has merely heralded Jesus's arrival, Jesus is the King who has come to inaugurate God's kingdom.

DISCUSSION QUESTIONS

1. How would Matthew's background (tax collector) have made it difficult for him to follow Jesus?

2. What would be a modern-day equivalent to tax collector?

3. What makes Matthew a suitable first gospel in the New Testament?

4. Why would Matthew present Jesus in relation to, and continuity with, Abraham, Moses, and David?

As Jesus was walking beside the Sea of Galilee, he saw two brothers, Simon called Peter and his brother Andrew. They were casting a net into the lake, for they were fishermen. "Come, follow me," Jesus said, "and I will send you out to fish for people." At once they left their nets and followed him. Going on from there, he saw two other brothers, James son of Zebedee and his brother John. They were in a boat with their father Zebedee, preparing their nets. Jesus called them, and immediately they left the boat and their father and followed him.

—Matthew 4:18–22 NIV

The first thing Jesus does when he embarks on his mission is call two pairs of brothers, all Galilean fishermen, to follow him. From John's gospel we learn that these men had already heard about Jesus from John the Baptist, so their decision to follow Jesus was not quite as abrupt as it might seem. But when Jesus calls them to follow, they leave their nets, boat—and in James and John's case, their father Zebedee—and "at once" go with Jesus. What Jesus promises those who follow him is that he'll transform their natural vocation into a spiritual calling. In these men's case, no longer would they fish for fish; Jesus would send them out "to fish for people." Will you allow Jesus to transform your natural vocation?

CHAPTER 2—MATTHEW

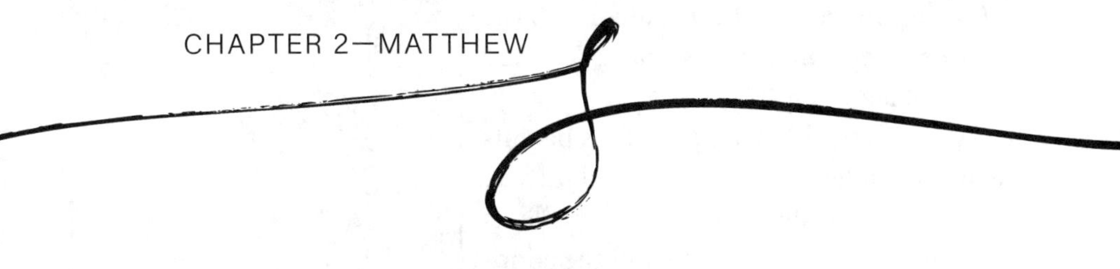

CASTING THE VISION

MINISTRY IN GALILEE (4:17–10:42)
Initial Ministry, Calling the First Disciples (4:17–25)
Book 1: The Sermon on the Mount (5:1–7:29)
Healing Many, Raising Laborers for the Harvest (8:1–9:38)
Book 2: The Commissioning of the Twelve (10:1–42)

MINISTRY IN GALILEE (4:17–10:42)

After setting the stage in the opening chapters, Matthew now shows how Jesus starts his ministry in earnest. Like John, Jesus announces the arrival of God's kingdom—God's authoritative rule among people. In the chapters that follow, Matthew skillfully switches back and forth between what Jesus *does* and what he *teaches*. This storytelling method shows that Jesus is the Messiah in word and deed: he didn't merely talk the talk; he also walked the walk and followed through on his teaching with actions that proved his authority as the Messiah.

In keeping with Old Testament prediction, Jesus begins his ministry in Galilee, a province north of Judea. While he is born in Bethlehem in Judea, he starts his public ministry in the Galilean north, underscoring his status as an outsider in opposition to the Jewish religious establishment in Jerusalem. While he will occasionally travel to Jerusalem for major religious festivals, such as the Passover, Jesus is based in Galilee. In fact, all the apostles (with the possible exception of Judas, the traitor) are from Galilee.

When Jesus is a young boy, his parents establish residence in Nazareth, southwest of the Sea of Galilee. This is where Jesus grows up as the son of Mary and the adoptive son of Joseph, a carpenter, from whom he learns the same trade. Joseph likely died prior to Jesus's public ministry, as he is never mentioned in the Gospels as still living. This means that Jesus, as Mary's oldest son, is responsible for her and the family. Later, the adult Jesus establishes a residence at Capernaum (his "own city"; 9:1) on the north shore of the Sea of Galilee.

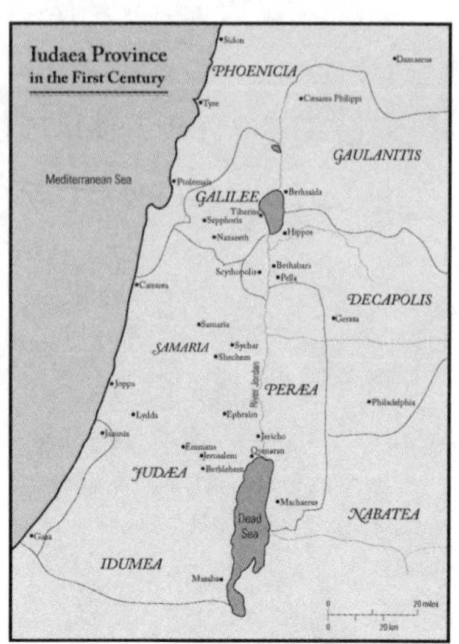

First-century Palestine

Initial Ministry, Calling the First Disciples (4:17–25)

Jesus begins his public ministry by calling his first followers: Simon Peter and Andrew, as well as James and John, the sons of Zebedee—two pairs of Galilean brothers. He promises these disciples—all of whom are fishermen—that if they follow him, he will make them "fishers of people." At Jesus's call, these four men "immediately" leave their nets and boats (and, in James and John's case, also their father) and follow Jesus. Their willingness to leave their occupation—and temporarily even their families—in order to attach themselves to Jesus shows that entering into a committed relationship with Jesus is more important than family ties. Jesus often highlights this truth in the course of his teaching, especially when prospective disciples approach him.

While Matthew's gospel focuses primarily on *Jesus*, from this point on the *disciples* emerge as significant characters as well. While they've been called by Jesus to follow him, they've only begun their journey of discovering who Jesus really is and of exploring the call he has extended to them. At this point in the narrative, Matthew presents a concluding statement that aptly sums up Jesus's ministry in Galilee. His message consists in "teaching . . . and proclaiming the gospel of the kingdom," while his deeds consist in "healing every disease and every affliction among the people"

(4:23). As Jesus declares the arrival of God's kingdom and provides living proof that in him the kingdom has already arrived, his reputation continues to grow, and large crowds follow him wherever he goes.

Book 1: The Sermon on the Mount (5:1–7:29)

The Sermon on the Mount, a body of ethical teaching that has indelibly shaped Western civilization, makes up the first of five "books of Jesus" in Matthew's gospel containing Jesus's teaching on the kingdom. These units provide the framework for the remainder of the narrative, as Matthew alternates between Jesus's teachings (speeches) and actions (healings, exorcisms, nature miracles, etc.).

The sermon centers on the radically new lifestyle demanded of Jesus's followers, who form a Christian counterculture. It provides Jesus's instruction as to how his followers are to live and relate to one another and to the world in light of their citizenship in God's kingdom. What a powerful vision undergirding Jesus's messianic mission!

Introduction (5:1–16)

Setting (5:1–2). Matthew's description of the setting of the sermon parallels the setting of comparable events in Scripture. Throughout the Old Testament, mountains are sites of divine revelation. Jesus's ascent of the mountain to speak to his disciples harks back to Moses's ascent of Mount Sinai to receive the law to give to Israel (Exod. 19:3). The setting of the sermon thus depicts Jesus as the greater Moses, a characterization that Matthew sustains throughout the sermon and his entire gospel.

The Beatitudes (5:3–12). At the very outset, Jesus extols virtuous characteristics of the inhabitants of God's kingdom (the Beatitudes, from Latin *beatus*, "happy" or "blessed"). In turn, Jesus pronounces blessings on

- the poor in spirit,
- those who mourn,
- the meek,
- those who hunger and thirst for righteousness,
- the merciful,
- the pure in heart,
- the peacemakers, and
- those who are persecuted for the sake of righteousness.

Jesus doesn't specifically mention the need for grace or the empowerment of the Holy Spirit. Rather than focus on outward characteristics, Jesus zeroes in on people's hearts. It is those who are humble, meek, merciful, pure in heart, and peaceful who will inherit and inhabit God's kingdom. Clearly, we can't be those kinds of people apart from the enablement of God's Spirit. The Beatitudes give us ideals for which to aim, and the impossibility of attaining these kinds of characteristics on our own will drive us closer to God and help us realize our dependence on him.

Salt and Light (5:13–16). Next, Jesus turns to his followers' relationship with the world around them. He likens the desired nature of their relationship to salt and light. "Salt" means that Christ's followers should give flavor to the world in which they live. They should be distinct and spiritually set apart, and thus give a distinctive taste of what it's like to be Christ's followers rather than being indistinguishable from the world, as the church so often is today.

"Light" means that Christians should set a high moral standard—not through self-effort but in the power of the Spirit. Rather than adding to the world's moral darkness, they should be a source of light to those around them. The twin images of salt and light underscore the countercultural identity of Jesus's followers, whose lives are to be marked by the kind of purity and integrity that will lead others to see their good works and give glory to their heavenly Father.

Kingdom Values (5:17–7:12)

Greater Righteousness (5:17–20). Anticipating his listeners' question as to the relationship between his teaching and the Law and the Prophets (the Old Testament Scriptures), Jesus states emphatically that he hasn't come to abolish the Scriptures but rather to fulfill them. By doing so, Jesus *does* in a sense abolish the law. For example, Jesus's followers no longer need to keep Old Testament food laws. But this doesn't mean they're free to do anything they want! Rather, Jesus introduces them to a deeper understanding of God and his righteous requirements. God's character, which found earlier expression in the law, is now expressed in Jesus in an even deeper way.

Predictably, Jesus's teaching and practice (e.g., healing on the Sabbath) are going to prove offensive to those who rigidly adhere to the law. Yet what Jesus's detractors fail to realize is that the law is not an end in itself; rather, it points to Christ (the prophetic dimension of the law) and was given to hold people accountable to the righteous standards of a holy God. When Jesus describes himself as the fulfillment of the Law and the Prophets, this is perfectly in keeping with his role as the Messiah, who fulfills countless Old Testament promises and predictions.

Obedience to the Law (5:21–48). Jesus's fulfillment of the Law and the Prophets doesn't absolve his disciples from their responsibility to live righteous lives; in fact, it increases it: "unless your righteousness exceeds that of the scribes and Pharisees, you will never enter the kingdom of heaven" (Matt. 5:20). Jesus's call to righteous living is vastly different from the external compliance with the law with which the scribes and Pharisees are concerned; rather, his call is to heartfelt obedience lived out in daily actions. Just as the Old Testament law has commanded, disciples of Jesus are to do the following:

- *Control their anger.* Hatred is spiritual murder. Before you worship, be reconciled to your brother (vv. 21–26).
- *Pursue sexual purity.* Lust is spiritual adultery. Be radical in dealing with what causes you to sin (vv. 27–30).
- *Honor the covenant of marriage.* Don't divorce your spouse, except for sexual immorality (vv. 31–32).
- *Speak with honesty and integrity.* Don't swear any oaths. Simply be a person of your word (vv. 33–37).
- *Resist the temptation to take their own revenge.* Don't resist evil. Rather, go the extra mile (vv. 38–42).
- *Love their enemies and pray for those who persecute them.* Otherwise, they're no better than pagans, who love those who already love them (vv. 43–47).

While general wisdom can be found in many times and places, the teaching of the Sermon on the Mount is unique. Even unbelievers can subscribe to the ideals enunciated in Jesus's teaching; yet only believers will be able to live consistently and in a heartfelt way in keeping with these principles. What's needed is nothing less than inner transformation and divine enablement. Only regenerate believers can truly love, consistently refrain from lust, control their desire for revenge, and love their enemies.

Loving one's enemy doesn't come naturally. Yet this is what Jesus requires of his followers. He doesn't merely demand what's hard; he demands the impossible! And yet he doesn't lower his standards just to make his expectations more easily attainable. To the contrary he insists, "You therefore must be perfect, as your heavenly Father is perfect" (v. 48). And just because on this side of eternity perfection is impossible, this doesn't mean we should stop trying—with God's help.

Avoiding Hypocrisy (6:1–18). Continuing on the topic of righteousness, Jesus now addresses the question of how his followers should practice their righteousness before others. He had previously told his disciples that unless their righteousness exceeded that of the Pharisees—who were known to be scrupulous with regard to keeping even the most minute matters in the law—they would never enter God's kingdom. Those with a reputation for righteousness in Jesus's day thought they were OK if they didn't break the Ten Commandments, but Jesus held his followers to a much higher standard.

At this, Jesus turns to the so-called three pillars of Judaism: prayer, fasting, and almsgiving—pious acts that identify someone as a righteous person before others. Jesus's underlying concern, once again, is a person's motivation: Why do people pray, fast, or give alms in public in the first place? Is it because they truly love God? Or is it merely to impress others with their piety? If their motive truly is to honor God, Jesus argues, they would be content to perform their good works in secret; after all, God sees everything, so he knows what we're doing, and he will reward us on the last day.

When giving, then, people shouldn't "let [their] left hand know what [their] right hand is doing" (6:3). Giving should be discreet. If our trust is in God and our giving is ultimately to him, we won't give merely so others can see how generous we are. When we pray, no flowery language is required. Nor do God's people need to utter lengthy prayers. We can just talk to God, our heavenly Father, who already knows what we need before we ask. Such an exemplary prayer—the "Lord's Prayer"—puts God first: the honor of his name, the arrival of his kingdom, and the accomplishment of his will.

A Disciple's Priorities (6:19–34). Next, Jesus moves beyond "practicing one's righteousness" to the underlying values he seeks to instill in his followers. Above all, his disciples should "seek first the kingdom of God and his righteousness" (v. 33). In many ways, this command sums up the ethos of the entire sermon. Rather than putting their own interests and concerns first, Jesus wants his followers to trust God to provide for their needs.

In this vein, Jesus urges his disciples to value what is eternal and spiritual rather than what is merely temporary and material. Rather than seeking treasure on earth, Jesus's followers are to store up treasure in heaven: "For where your treasure is, there your heart will be also" (v. 21). Thus, Jesus's followers "cannot serve God and money" (v. 24). Our interests shouldn't be divided; we should put God first—wholeheartedly and unreservedly.

At this, Jesus anticipates a predictable objection: What about our need for daily necessities—food, clothing, and shelter? He responds with a challenge: If believers are anxious about material provisions, how are they different from unbelievers? His followers should trust in *God's* ability to provide for their daily needs and let *his* priorities shape their values. They should seek *God's* kingdom and *his* righteousness.

Relationships (7:1–12). Jesus also speaks out against hypocritical judgment of others. He is *not* saying that we should practice spineless tolerance, condoning the sins of others. Rather, he is warning us that we must apply the same standard to ourselves that we use when judging others. Otherwise, we'll be like a man who tries to remove a tiny piece of wood from another person's eye while failing to take care of a huge log in his own. How ironic—and yet how true!

In what follows, Jesus continues to try to instill confidence in answered prayer in his followers. God is good! So like trusting children, we should never hesitate to approach God in prayer with our needs and requests. In an argument from the lesser to the greater, Jesus says, "If you then, who are evil, know how to give good gifts to your children, how much more will your Father who is in heaven give good things to those who ask him!" (7:11).

Not only should Jesus's followers ask so they can receive; they should also do good to others, following the maxim "Whatever you wish that others would do to you, do also to them" (v. 12). This "Golden Rule" sums up the tenor of the entire Scriptures.

Conclusion (7:13–29)

Two Roads and Gates (7:13–14). As he moves toward a conclusion, Jesus issues several cautions. First, he observes that the gate to salvation is narrow and hard to find, while the gate to destruction is wide and well traveled. Only a few will choose the path of discipleship; most will be too attached to this world to willingly put God first. While this may be unsettling, it helps manage expectations. Even in one's own family, there will often be those who refuse to follow Jesus's teaching. Yet Jesus's disciples must follow him no matter what others do.

Two Trees and Fruits (7:15–20). Second, Jesus warns his followers against "wolves in sheep's clothing," false prophets who are out to wreak havoc in other people's lives. Jesus's advice is simple: look at the (rotten) fruit in the lives of these deceivers and pretenders! By a simple yet irrefutable natural law, good trees bear good fruit, while bad trees bear bad fruit. Similarly, if anyone leaves destruction and misery in their wake, they can't be a good teacher or true prophet.

Two Confessions (7:21–23). Third, Jesus tells his followers to be discerning about two confessions: While many claim to be his disciples, not all are genuine followers. Many who call Jesus "Lord," professing allegiance to him and even doing many things in his name, have no true knowledge of him, and as a result, he will disavow them on Judgment Day. So don't be fooled by false professions of faith! Also, don't be self-deceived: you can't be a follower of Jesus without being Spirit-born and a genuine citizen of his kingdom.

Two Hearers and Builders (7:24–27). Jesus closes the sermon with an illustration about two hearers and builders. The first builds his house on rock, and when storms and floods come the house stands firm. The other builds his house on sand, and when the elements rage against that house it promptly collapses. The timeless lesson is that mere hearing is not enough; we must put Jesus's teaching into practice. Then, when challenges come, our lives will be weatherproof and rock solid because they're built on the unshakeable truth of God's Word.

Response (7:28–29). Jesus's teaching leaves the crowds amazed, for he has instructed them "as one who had authority, and not as their scribes" (7:29). There's no question—the Sermon on the Mount is one of the greatest ethical discourses of all time. In this powerful message, Jesus addresses himself to those who are willing to leave behind the attachments and affections of this world in order to follow the one who has been sent to earth by his heavenly Father—the Messiah and Son of God.

Healing Many, Raising Laborers for the Harvest (8:1–9:38)

The narrative following the Sermon on the Mount presents a representative sample of Jesus's ministry. In fact, half of Jesus's miracles recorded in Matthew's gospel are found in this section. The scope of Jesus's authority is breathtaking, encompassing the demonic world, sickness, the natural realm, and even death. Specifically, we see Jesus

- cleanse a leper,
- heal the paralyzed servant of a Roman centurion,
- heal the sickness of Simon Peter's mother-in-law,
- calm a powerful storm on the Sea of Galilee by his mere word, and
- deliver two Gadarene men from demon possession.

After this, in Capernaum Jesus

- heals a paralytic,
- raises a synagogue ruler's daughter from the dead and stops a woman's twelve-year-long discharge of blood,
- gives sight to two blind men, and
- opens the mouth of a demon-possessed mute man.

In the midst of this section, Matthew cites the Old Testament once again, showing that Jesus's miracles serve to identify him as the Servant of the Lord who takes up our infirmities and bears our diseases (8:17; cf. Isa. 53:4). Jesus's healing ministry thus foreshadows the cross.

What's more, what Jesus says and does is grounded in who he is. (Remember, identity is important!) He is the Messiah, who alone has the power to open the eyes of the blind, to unstop the ears of the deaf, to make the lame leap like a deer, and to loosen the tongue of the mute (Isa. 35:5–6).

In addition, Jesus's compassion extends to non-Jews. The Gentile centurion is commended for his faith, in contrast to the disciples who have "little faith" and the hardened Pharisees who attribute Jesus's power to Satan (Matt. 8:10, 26; 9:34). Jesus is not only the Jewish Messiah; his messianic authority extends to Gentiles as well.

The call of Matthew sees the first evangelist join those whom Jesus has already called, such as Peter, Andrew, James, and John, just before Jesus appoints his twelve apostles (cf. 10:1–4).

The unit closes with a summary of Jesus's ministry thus far ("teaching," "proclaiming the gospel of the kingdom," and "healing"; 9:35). Jesus's description of the crowds as "harassed and helpless, like sheep without a shepherd" echoes Moses's words during the leadership transition from him to Joshua, indicting the Jewish leaders as faithless shepherds (v. 36; cf. Num. 27:17; Ezek. 34:5).

Book 2: The Commissioning of the Twelve (10:1–42)

The narrative now gives way to the second discourse featured in Matthew's gospel, the commissioning of the Twelve. There is a certain historical uniqueness to this unit at this juncture in Jesus's ministry. Not everything that is said here applies directly to the church today (e.g., the limitation to Israel), though on a principial level, there is much we can learn about what it means to follow Jesus.

The Sending (10:1–4)

The disciples become the first answer to their own prayers for additional workers to reap the rich spiritual harvest that lies ahead (cf. Matt. 9:37–38). Jesus appoints twelve "apostles"—messengers or emissaries—who constitute the core of his new messianic community.

Instructions (10:5–15)

Jesus sends out the Twelve with the following instructions. To begin, they are to focus exclusively on the "lost sheep of the house of Israel" (10:6). Jesus's mission is first and foremost to the Jewish people, since it has been God's purpose to bless all the families of the earth through Abraham and Jesus, his descendant (Gen. 12:1–3).

The message the Twelve are given to proclaim is the same as that preached by John the Baptist and Jesus himself: "The kingdom of heaven is at hand" (Matt. 10:7; cf. 3:2; 4:17). Their work is an extension of Jesus's. Like their Master, they are to "heal the sick, raise the dead, cleanse lepers, [and] cast out demons" (10:8). They are to do their work free of charge and take only minimal supplies on their journey. When entering a city, they are to seek out the hospitality of worthy individuals and lodge there for the duration of their stay. If rejected, they should move on to another place. God's judgment will surely be upon those who reject them.

Persecution (10:16–33)

As they embark on their mission, Jesus's followers should have realistic expectations. Not everyone will receive them with open arms. They must be "wise as serpents and innocent as doves" (v. 16). Just as hostility has begun to mount against Jesus, so his followers will suffer persecution for his sake. They will be dragged into court and flogged in synagogues, but they needn't be anxious, because "the Spirit of [their] Father" will speak through them (v. 20).

In fact, opposition will arise even within their own families, and they'll be "hated by all" for his name's sake (v. 22). Yet this chilling prospect shouldn't discourage them, because it's a sure sign that they're following in their Master's footsteps. What's more, they should view such opposition as a sobering call to fear God rather than people, resting in his provision and looking to him for vindication. The most precious assurance Jesus can give is that on Judgment Day, he'll acknowledge them before his heavenly Father.

The Cost of Discipleship (10:34–42)

The closing portion of Jesus's instructions to the Twelve brings into even sharper focus the cost of discipleship for those who choose to follow him. Jesus has "not come to bring peace, but a sword" (v. 34). Rather than a person's life improving, their decision to follow Jesus may in fact make matters worse, at least initially. In fact, a person's enemies will be the members of his own household (v. 36; cf. Mic. 7:6).

One has to admire Jesus for not sugarcoating his call to discipleship. No one could ever say they didn't know what they were getting themselves into when following Jesus! Yet Jesus is worthy of being followed. He will give his life for his followers so they can be forgiven and saved and spend eternity with him in God's presence. Following Jesus will have many rewards both in this life and in the life to come.

DISCUSSION QUESTIONS

1. In the Sermon on the Mount, Jesus calls on his followers to love their enemies. What is your response to this command?

2. How can Christians be salt and light in today's culture?

3. Why would Matthew alternate Jesus's teaching and healing narratives?

4. Why would Jesus try to impress on prospective followers the cost of discipleship?

You are the salt of the earth. But if the salt loses its saltiness, how can it be made salty again? It is no longer good for anything, except to be thrown out and trampled underfoot. You are the light of the world. A town built on a hill cannot be hidden. Neither do people light a lamp and put it under a bowl. Instead they put it on its stand, and it gives light to everyone in the house. In the same way, let your light shine before others, that they may see your good deeds and glorify your Father in heaven.

—Matthew 5:13–16 NIV

In his inaugural address, the famous Sermon on the Mount, Jesus described the status and identity of his followers by using two simple metaphors: salt and light. Notice that he doesn't say they *should be* salt and light; he said, "You *are* the salt of the earth" and "You *are* the light of the world." They are fundamentally different than people in the world and in a position to provide seasoning and illumination, but only if they remain salty (i.e., grace- and Spirit-filled) and allow their good works to shine for all to see. Jesus's words here presuppose the Spirit's work in regeneration and sanctification. So, remember: If you're a follower of Christ, you *are* spiritual salt and spiritual light; just don't dim the light through sin or disobedience.

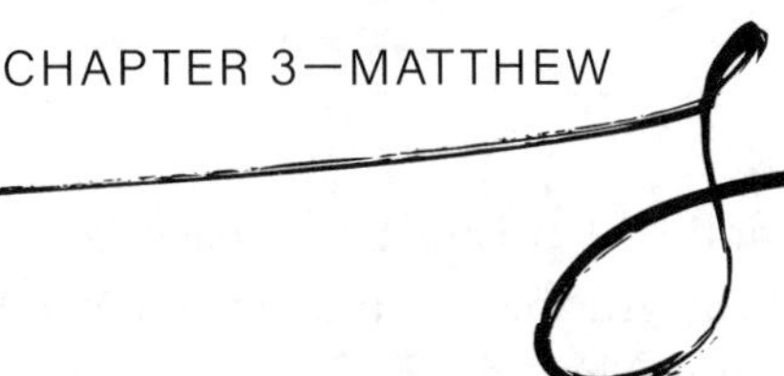

CHAPTER 3—MATTHEW

HERALDING GOD'S KINGDOM

MINISTRY IN GALILEE (11:1–18:35)
Blasphemy Against the Spirit, the Sign of Jonah (11:1–12:50)
Book 3: Kingdom Parables, Mostly from the Realm of Agriculture (13:1–53)
Farther North: Feeding Thousands, Walking on Water, Transfiguration (13:54–17:27)
Book 4: More Kingdom Parables: On Shepherds and Servants (18:1–35)

MINISTRY IN GALILEE (11:1–18:35)

We are now in the middle section of Matthew's gospel and of Jesus's ministry. Matthew continues his pattern of alternating between Jesus's actions and his teaching. In his ministry, Jesus continues to act the part of the Messiah, especially by healing countless people. In his teaching, he illustrates the coming of God's kingdom by numerous parables—made-up comparisons or even full-fledged stories designed to help people understand what God's rule is like. As Jesus moves further and further north, he never tires of telling more stories about his Father's kingdom.

Blasphemy Against the Spirit, the Sign of Jonah (11:1–12:50)

Matthew now moves on to the third cycle of Jesus's ministry in Galilee. While this section is less clearly defined and includes a mixture of

Jesus's words *and* actions, a main theme that emerges is varying responses to Jesus.

The Baptist's Query (11:1–19)

The opening reference to John in prison harks back to Matthew's earlier comment, "Now when he heard that John had been arrested," just prior to the Sermon on the Mount (Matt. 4:12). Now, the scene shifts to John in prison. Apparently, John, who at first had boldly proclaimed that Jesus was the Messiah, is now plagued by doubt and so sends his followers to Jesus to inquire whether he truly is "the one who is to come"—the Messiah (11:3). Rather than giving a direct answer, Jesus points John and his disciples to his *actions*, painting a composite picture of various messianic passages in Isaiah (Isa. 26:19; 29:18–19; 35:5; 42:7, 18; 61:1; see the quote of Isa. 53:4 at Matt. 8:17).

At this, Jesus goes and tells the crowds that John is not only a prophet but "more than a prophet" (11:9). He is the "messenger" whose coming the prophet Malachi had announced, the one who would come to prepare the way of the Messiah (v. 10; cf. Mal. 3:1). In fact, Jesus asserts, "among those born of women there has arisen no one greater than John the Baptist" (Matt. 11:11). This emphatically underscores John's vital role as the Messiah's forerunner. As Jesus points out, John is the capstone of "all the Prophets and the Law" (v. 13).

Rightly understood, therefore, John is Elijah—not literally, of course, which he has rightly denied, but the end-time figure who would powerfully testify to the coming Messiah. Yet "this generation," Jesus laments, is like children who can't agree on which game to play (vv. 16–17). John is too austere, while Jesus is too permissive—a glutton and drunkard, a friend of tax collectors and "sinners" (vv. 18–19)! Again, Jesus shows himself to be an astute observer of human nature and points out with masterful irony that people's unbelief isn't due to lacking messianic manifestations on his part but rather to inaccurate expectations on theirs.

The Denunciation of Unbelief and Invitation to Learn from Jesus (11:20–30)

Jesus proceeds to denounce the cities where he has performed most of his miracles yet that haven't repented, declaring that God's judgment on them will be exceedingly severe. He goes on to praise his heavenly Father for hiding "these things" (Jesus's messianic identity) from the worldly-wise but revealing them to little children.

In a statement containing "Father-Son" language reminiscent of John's gospel, Jesus declares, "All things have been handed over to me by my Father, and no one knows the Son except the Father, and no one knows the Father except the Son and anyone to whom the Son chooses to reveal him" (Matt. 11:27).

Jesus identifies himself as a gentle and humble Messiah, inviting those who are weary and heavy laden—most likely because of the unreasonable religious burdens put on them by the religious leaders—to come to him so that he can give them rest for their souls.

Authority over the Sabbath (12:1–14)

Some of the opposition Jesus has been talking about rears its ugly head when the Pharisees object to Jesus's disciples plucking and eating heads of grain in the fields. To us, this may seem like a small issue, but the problem is that this happens on the Sabbath and violates some of the Pharisees' numerous regulations as to what a person could or couldn't do on this Jewish day of rest.

The Old Testament tells us that God rested on the seventh day of creation (Gen. 2:2–3). Later on, keeping the Sabbath day holy is one of the Ten Commandments. Over time, zealous Jews developed Sabbath observance into an art form by amassing a plethora of stipulations. Thus, while Jesus's disciples may violate some of the Pharisees' added regulations, they don't actually violate the Old Testament Sabbath commandment.

Compared to the religious authorities, Jesus takes a more compassionate approach. His disciples are hungry, and no harm is done if they help themselves to some heads of grain. In support, Jesus adduces an event in David's day as well as a prophetic passage: "I desire mercy, and not sacrifice" (Matt. 12:3–4, 7; cf. 1 Sam. 21:1–6; Hos. 6:6). The Pharisees' scrupulous law-keeping is empty, lacking mercy. "Something greater than the temple is here"; Jesus is greater than the Sabbath (Matt. 12:6, 8; for the connection between the temple and the Sabbath, see v. 5).

At this, Jesus enters a synagogue and heals a paralyzed man, declaring, "So it is lawful to do good on the Sabbath" (v. 12). Further hardened, the Pharisees begin to plot to take Jesus's life. Jesus withdraws, yet he heals all who follow him. The event teaches a powerful lesson on grace and Christian freedom. Tragically, while the Messiah has appeared, the Pharisees reject him because of their traditions, which have in effect replaced the Word of God.

Healing Ministry and Blasphemy Against the Spirit (12:15–37)

At this point, Matthew interjects a lengthy quotation from the prophet Isaiah that sums up Jesus's healing ministry (vv. 18–21; cf. Isa. 42:1–4). The Messiah is God's chosen Servant on whom God's Spirit rests. Gentle and humble, he champions righteousness and is the hope of Gentiles as well.

The tension between Jesus and the Pharisees continues to mount when he heals a blind and mute man. The common people are inclined to think Jesus is the son of David, triggering the Pharisees' rather outlandish argument that Jesus is able to cast out demons only by the power of Satan. Jesus promptly exposes their flawed logic by retorting that "no city or house divided against itself will stand" (12:25). Why would Satan cast out his own demons? That doesn't make any sense at all.

Going on the counteroffensive, Jesus presses, "But if it is by the *Spirit of God* that I cast out demons, then the kingdom of God has come upon you" (v. 28, emphasis added). What's more, if people accuse Jesus of casting out demons by Satan, they offend the Holy Spirit as well. Just as a tree is known by its fruit, people's hearts are revealed by the words they speak. On Judgment Day, they'll have to give an account to God for every careless word they've spoken.

The Sign of Jonah and Jesus's True Mother and Brothers (12:38–50)

Yet the scribes and Pharisees are not easily silenced. Instead, they demand a sign from Jesus to validate his messianic claims. Calling them "an evil and adulterous generation," Jesus offers only the "sign of the prophet Jonah" (v. 39). Just as Jonah was in the large fish for three days and nights, so Jesus will rise from the dead after three days. In fact, both Nineveh and the queen of Sheba will rise up in the final judgment to testify against the Jewish leaders. But now someone greater than Solomon is here.

The unit closes with the arrival of Jesus's mother and brothers, who ask to speak to him. In another lesson on faith and discipleship, Jesus replies that whoever does the will of his Father is part of his spiritual family. To be a disciple of Jesus is to be a member of a new spiritual family, the family of God. In this way, Matthew's narrative moves from the escalating conflict with the Pharisees to another unit, gathering portions of Jesus's teaching on the nature of God's kingdom.

Book 3: Kingdom Parables, Mostly from the Realm of Agriculture (13:1–53)

Chapter 13 contains the third major discourse in Matthew's gospel, in which Jesus explains the spiritual dynamics of the kingdom of heaven. Jesus's chosen teaching tools here are parables—fictional but realistic stories Jesus makes up to convey a spiritual truth or truths, usually about an aspect of God's kingdom. The parables in the present chapter are mostly from the realm of agriculture.

The Parable of the Sower (13:1–23)

In a series of parables, Jesus explains the variety of responses to his message. In the first parable, a man goes out into a field to sow seeds; some fall along the path and are eaten by birds, some fall on rocky ground and wither away, some fall among thorns and are choked, and some fall on good soil and flourish. The four types of soil are emblematic of a spectrum of spiritual heart conditions. People have rejected Jesus's message for various reasons—Satan's work, external opposition, or a preoccupation with the things of this world. Yet Israel's rejection of Jesus has fulfilled Old Testament prophecy (cf. Isa. 6:9–10): just as people rejected Isaiah's message, they reject Jesus's.

Jesus's parable of the sower is instructive not only for his original disciples but for us today as well. We often wonder why it is that those around us aren't catching on and seem indifferent to the gospel. The lesson is this: Don't let the apathy, resistance, or even hostility to spiritual things of those around you keep you from following Jesus and serving him faithfully. You can't control how others respond; they'll have to make their own decision about Jesus and will have to give an account for rejecting him one day. In the meantime, don't let the lack of response to Jesus and the gospel from others make you insecure or cause you to wane in your enthusiasm for serving him.

More Kingdom Parables (13:24–53)

The remaining parables gathered in this chapter each answer an important question Jesus's followers have at this juncture in his ministry.

In the parable of the *weeds*, Jesus accounts for the continuing presence of evil in the world and reassures his disciples that at the proper time—the final judgment—he will punish the wicked and reward the righteous. All that's required, therefore, is patience. There's no need to worry that evil will go unpunished.

Through the parables of the *mustard seed* and the *leaven*, Jesus portrays the unexpected and remarkable growth of the kingdom. If for the moment Jesus's followers constitute only a "little flock," not to worry—it's God's good pleasure to give them the kingdom (Luke 12:32). And they won't always be this small; Jesus's messianic community will grow gradually yet steadily, until it is large enough to benefit many others.

Through the parables of the *hidden treasure* and the *precious pearl*, Jesus shows that God's kingdom is very precious and worthy of any sacrifice his followers may be called on to make. Those who aren't following Jesus are simply unwilling to pay the price. Conversely, those who do can be sure their sacrifice will ultimately be worth it.

The parable of the *fishing net*, similar to the parable of the weeds, portrays the final judgment, at which point God will separate the righteous from the wicked, and those who reject the King and his kingdom will be judged. While this separation has yet to take place, Jesus's followers need not worry that those who seem to prosper but are not followers of Jesus will end up ahead. It ain't over till the Son of Man comes on Judgment Day!

Finally, the parable of the *scribe* depicts Jesus's disciples (including Matthew) as better qualified to teach God's law than the scribes and Pharisees. In their storeroom of instruction, they hold both old and new treasures (i.e., the Old Testament and the teachings of Jesus, respectively). This simple simile provides a fitting conclusion to the series of parables in this unit.

Farther North: Feeding Thousands, Walking on Water, Transfiguration (13:54–17:27)

The Rejection of Jesus in Nazareth (13:54–58)

Matthew now moves from instruction back to narrative. Not only is Jesus rejected by the Jewish leaders who have grown increasingly antagonistic and adversarial; he is rejected even by the people in his own city of Nazareth. While Jesus's contemporaries recognize his unusual wisdom and mighty works, they aren't truly receptive to his message. As Jesus trenchantly remarks, "A prophet is not without honor except in his hometown and in his own household" (Matt. 13:57). Familiarity breeds contempt. Because of their persistent unbelief, Jesus doesn't perform many miracles in his hometown.

The Tragic End of John the Baptist (14:1–12)

The narrative continues with the heart-wrenching, gruesome story of the execution of John the Baptist. Herod Antipas, the ruler of Galilee, upon hearing about Jesus's growing reputation surmises that Jesus is John the Baptist raised from the dead, which occasions the narrative of John's beheading in the form of a historical flashback.

What started out with John's powerful witness to Jesus at the Jordan River had given way to doubt and now ends in tragic death. Yet John's purpose of "preparing the way for the Lord" has been fulfilled, and the mission of the one John heralded continues unabated.

Feeding the Multitudes, Walking on Water, and Healing the Sick (14:13–36)

In what follows, Matthew presents several miracles of Jesus that further demonstrate Jesus's messianic authority. Jesus doesn't merely talk about the coming of God's kingdom; he provides tangible proof that he is the King and that in encountering his person and work, people can get a foretaste of what the kingdom of God will be like. After John's death, Jesus seeks a place of solitude, but the crowds follow him wherever he goes.

Consistent with his normal practice, Jesus doesn't turn people away but instead proves to be a compassionate messianic healer and leader. The humble manner in which Jesus feeds the five thousand contrasts with Herod Antipas's earlier decadent, lavish feast. Just as God fed the people of Israel during the exodus, so now Jesus takes up the mantle and miraculously feeds God's people, showing himself to be the greater Moses and messianic Shepherd-King (cf. Exod. 16).

Immediately following this public miracle, Jesus also amazes his disciples with the private miracle of walking on the Sea of Galilee. The disciples show their superstition by surmising the figure they see is actually a ghost, and they—grown, rugged men—cry out in fear. But Jesus immediately reassures them that it is him. By walking on the water,

Jesus invokes the Old Testament image of God striding on the surface of the water (Job 9:8).

At this, Peter is emboldened to ask Jesus to tell him to walk on water as well. Jesus simply tells him to come. Peter steps out of the boat and into the water and starts walking toward Jesus. Yet when he takes his eyes off Jesus and looks at the wind, he begins to sink and pleads with Jesus to rescue him. Jesus immediately takes his hand, chiding him for his lack of faith. The whole incident leads the shaken disciples to worship Jesus and declare, "Truly you are the Son of God" (Matt. 14:33).

It seems that, at this point in the narrative, the truth finally begins to sink in for the disciples that Jesus really is the Messiah, the Son of God. On a deeper level, the account also instructs us about the life of faith. The moment we get distracted and look at our circumstances, we'll get shaky. Give Peter a lot of credit, though, for asking Jesus to tell him to walk on water in the first place, as well as for immediately crying out for Jesus to save him when he began to sink!

No sooner do Jesus and the disciples come ashore on the other side of the lake than the people there recognize Jesus. The chapter starts out with a reference to Jesus's fame, which has reached even Herod Antipas; it ends with another reference to Jesus's reputation for his miracle-working power, which has spread through the entire region. As a result, many come to him, believing that if they simply "touch the fringe of his garment," they will be healed (vv. 35–36). And they are!

Tradition, Tradition (15:1–20)

In chapter 12, we saw that the Pharisees gave Jesus grief about his disciples' eating ears of grain on the Sabbath. Now, they come to Jesus—all the way from Jerusalem—with a similar grievance: "Why do your disciples break the tradition of the elders? For they do not wash their hands when they eat" (15:2). Jesus immediately goes on the offensive: "And why do *you* break the commandment of God for the sake of your tradition?" (v. 3, emphasis added). God's commandments take precedence over human traditions. By putting their own traditions first, the Pharisees have set aside the word and will of God.

Jesus immediately provides an example of such travesty related to the commandment to honor one's father and mother (cf. Exod. 20:12; Deut. 5:16). By dedicating certain things to God, the Pharisees had cleverly sidestepped this command. Then, when their parents needed material assistance, they would say, "Sorry! I'd love to help but I can't, because what I would have otherwise given to you I've already committed to God!" Quoting Isaiah, Jesus denounces them for paying mere lip service to God while having greedy, selfish hearts. Their worship is empty, but God isn't fooled!

Jesus isn't done yet. Calling people to himself, he further explains the matter to them. The problem, he insists, is not unwashed hands or what goes *into* a person (potentially "defiled" food), but rather what comes *out of* a person, rooted in their heart condition. The Pharisees—denounced as "blind guides" (Matt. 15:14)—predictably are offended. When Peter asks Jesus to explain "this parable" (i.e., illustration), Jesus declares that what people eat is shortly discarded, but what comes out of their hearts is the source of all kinds of wickedness (vv. 15–20). A corrupt heart is what truly defiles a person.

Healing Many and Feeding the Multitudes Again (15:21–39)

Following his exchange with the Pharisees, Jesus withdraws northward from Galilee to the Gentile district of Tyre and Sidon. There, he encounters a Canaanite woman calling out to him, "Have mercy on me, O Lord, Son of David," and imploring him to heal her demon-possessed daughter (v. 22). In stark contrast to the unbelieving Jewish leaders, this woman approaches Jesus with great faith. In response, Jesus heals her daughter. At this news, crowds come to him with their lame, blind, crippled, mute, and many others. Jesus heals them all, and people glorify "the God of Israel" (v. 31).

Jesus's encounter with the Canaanite woman and his healing ministry among the Gentiles signal that the scope of his mission will ultimately encompass all people. This is further underscored by the feeding of four thousand men (plus women and children), which resembles his earlier feeding of the five thousand, except that this time the event takes place in Gentile territory. While Jesus's messianic mission is directed first to Israel, Jesus's love and compassion extends also to Gentiles—who haven't, up to this point, belonged to the people of God. Following the feeding, Jesus dismisses the crowds, gets into a boat, and departs for the region of Magadan.

Give Me a Sign (16:1–12)

Upon his return to Jewish territory, Jesus is once again confronted by Pharisees and Sadducees who are trying to test him. Despite Jesus's numerous and frequent public miracles, they disingenuously ask him for "a sign from heaven" to legitimate his messianic authority (16:1). In response, Jesus chides this "evil and adulterous generation" for being able to interpret the signs of the weather but being unable to interpret the signs of God's kingdom coming (v. 4).

Jesus's answer is exactly the same as last time (cf. 12:38–42). The only sign those people will receive is "the sign of the prophet Jonah"—Jesus's resurrection after three days. Jesus has given a large number of proofs for his messianic identity already. The only thing that's puzzling is how the Pharisees could have missed them all. What will it take to satisfy them? Never one to pass over a teachable moment, Jesus takes the opportunity to warn his followers against the "leaven" (i.e., the corrosive teaching) of the Pharisees and Sadducees (16:6, 11–12).

"You Are the Christ" (16:13–28)

The narrative proceeds to the climax of Jesus's ministry in Galilee, Peter's confession at Caesarea Philippi (far north in Herod Philip's territory, straight east of Tyre). At the outset, Jesus poses a series of pointed questions to his disciples. Who do *people* say that he is? People can't agree: "Some say John the Baptist, others say Elijah, and others Jeremiah or one of the prophets" (v. 14). Without engaging their answer, Jesus immediately proceeds to ask his follow-up question: Who do *they* say he is?

Speaking for the disciples, Peter replies, "You are the Christ, the Son of the living God" (v. 16). Finally, someone understands who Jesus is! Yet Jesus immediately deflects credit from Peter, declaring that he didn't realize this on his own but by divine revelation. Picking up on Peter's name, *Petros* ("the rock"), Jesus adds that it is on this "rock" (Peter's confession of Jesus as Messiah) that he will build his messianic community and that the "gates of hell" will give up those headed for eternal destruction (v. 18).

Also, Jesus will give Peter the "keys of the kingdom of heaven" (v. 19), which means that Peter will be involved in opening access to the church for Jews, Samaritans, and Gentiles (cf. Acts 2:14–41; 8:14–17; 10:1–48). At this, Jesus sternly warns his disciples not to tell anyone that he is the Messiah. He knows that people will misunderstand what "Messiah" means, as they have commonly looked for a national rather than a spiritual deliverer, much less a *crucified* Messiah.

Now that Peter has acknowledged Jesus as Messiah—the major turning point in the narrative—Jesus begins to talk to his followers candidly about his future destiny. This attests to Jesus's divine foreknowledge and makes the important point that none of Jesus's encounters or experiences catches him by surprise. Rather, the entire script of Jesus's life—including his crucifixion, burial, and resurrection—has been written by the sovereign God for the sake of our salvation.

Peter, however, in a bizarre twist, takes Jesus aside and begins to rebuke him, objecting, in so many words, "No way! This is never going to happen to you!" In effect, he denies the necessity of the cross (and claims to know the future better than Jesus). Jesus at once sharply rebukes Peter: "Get behind me, Satan! You are a hindrance to me" (Matt. 16:23). Jesus's crucifixion, no matter how painful, is necessary for our salvation, and he is determined to carry out God's plan.

A Messiah—but not a crucified one! This is the prototypical misunderstanding against which Matthew wants to warn his readers. The implication for Jesus's followers is that anyone who wants to follow Jesus must likewise "deny himself and take up his cross" (v. 24). Jesus's followers must be prepared to identify publicly with him and to suffer rejection by unbelievers just like he did. A noncrucified disciple is a contradiction in terms.

The Transfiguration (17:1–13)

Only six days later, Jesus's earlier statement that there were "some standing here" who would "not taste death until they see the Son of Man coming in his kingdom" (16:28) comes literally true when his three closest disciples—Peter, James, and John—ascend a high mountain with him and in a vision see Jesus supernaturally transformed before their very eyes. The text says that Jesus's "face shone like the sun, and his clothes became white as light" (17:2)—language later replicated in John's vision of Jesus in the book of Revelation (e.g., Rev. 1:16). As Jesus has predicted, he will be killed but, after this, glorified and exalted. The transfiguration provides Jesus's inner circle with a "sneak preview" of his resurrected glory.

What's more, Moses and Elijah appear, representing the Law and the Prophets, and converse with Jesus. Peter, never a man of inaction, proposes to make tents for each of them, but his proposal is at once overshadowed by God's voice declaring, as earlier at Jesus's baptism, "This is my beloved Son, with whom I am well pleased" (Matt. 17:5; cf. 3:17). The disciples are terrified, but Jesus tells them not to fear, and when they look up, Moses and Elijah are gone! The sight of Elijah triggers in the minds of the disciples the question as to when Elijah would come. Jesus instructs them that he had already come in the form of John the Baptist.

Jesus's transfiguration is another high point in the narrative, in some ways even topping the climax of Peter's confession of Jesus as the Christ, the Son of the living God. The vision of glory left an indelible mark in the mind of Peter, who refers to it more than thirty years later (2 Peter 1:16–18). In language and imagery similar to the account of Moses coming down from Mount Sinai after meeting with God in the book of Exodus, the transfiguration shows Jesus as the greater Moses, the Savior and Deliverer of God's people. Moses couldn't see the glory of God on the mountain and live; Jesus, on the other hand, reflects the very glory of God. He is the promised Messiah, the Son of God, who has come to save and redeem his people so they can enter God's kingdom.

Mountain-Moving Faith and Paying the Temple Tax (17:14–27)

On their way down the mountain, Jesus instructs the three disciples not to tell anyone of the vision they've just seen until after his resurrection. He also reiterates that his path to glory will include rejection and suffering. When they reach the foot of the mountain, they find a crowd waiting for them. A man approaches Jesus, pleading with him to have mercy on his son who is demon-possessed and suffering from epilepsy. Apparently, while Jesus was on the mountain, the disciples had tried to cast out the demon but were unsuccessful because of their lack of faith. At once, Jesus expels the demon and tells his disciples that all they need is faith as small as a mustard seed, which reminds the reader of Jesus's earlier parable (cf. 13:31–32).

At this, Jesus predicts for the second time that he'll be killed and raised on the third day, which again greatly distresses the disciples. The narrative portion concludes with the intriguing account of Jesus having a private conversation with Peter about paying the temple tax (a topic that would have been of special interest to Matthew, a tax collector). Even though, Jesus points out, they should have been exempt from paying it, he tells Peter in a sort of off-handed way to cast his fishing line into the lake to find a shekel in the mouth of the first fish he'd catch. "Take that," Jesus says, "and give it to them for me and for yourself" (17:27). (The tax was a half-shekel per person, so one shekel would have paid the tax for two people.)

Book 4: More Kingdom Parables: On Shepherds and Servants (18:1–35)

Thus far, Matthew has showcased three major discourses of Jesus: the Sermon on the Mount (chaps. 5–7), the commissioning of the Twelve (chap. 10), and kingdom parables (chap. 13). Now, he intersperses into the narrative portion of his gospel yet another discourse of Jesus, containing additional kingdom parables. In these realistic, true-to-life stories, Jesus paints a composite picture of what life and relationships will look like in God's kingdom. While the parables in chapter 13 are mainly agricultural in nature (different kinds of soil, weeds, mustard seed), the parables in chapter 18 deal with other spheres of human existence (from the worlds of shepherds and servants).

Relationships in the Community (18:1–14)

The discourse begins with a question posed by Jesus's disciples: "Who is the greatest in the kingdom of heaven?" (18:1). In response, teaching them an object lesson, Jesus calls a child to himself, places him in their midst, and tells his followers that if they want to enter God's kingdom, they must become like this little child. Most likely, the disciples are at a loss as to what Jesus means. Become like a little child? This hardly is what they have in mind. Of course, this is not lost on Jesus. He deliberately tries to jolt them into the realization that success in his kingdom is achieved by means vastly different from climbing the ladder of success in the world. According to Jesus, his followers must forsake all worldly status and take the stance of a powerless, unpretentious child.

Not only should Jesus's followers be willing to humble themselves and become like little children themselves; they should also be willing to receive other "little ones"—those of little or no worldly status—in his name and avoid leading any of them astray (v. 6). They should treat the grave danger of sin with utmost fervency, as "it is better for [them] to enter life crippled or lame than with two hands or two feet to be thrown into the eternal fire" (v. 8; cf. 5:29–30). Sin kills! It keeps us in bondage, breaks our relationship with God and others, and makes us miserable in the end. Don't believe Satan's lie that sin is fun and has no negative consequences.

Jesus continues to impress the precious value of even a single person—no matter how lowly—on his followers by telling them the parable of the lost sheep. Just like a man who has a hundred sheep goes after his one lost sheep because every sheep is precious to him, so God doesn't want even one precious person of his to perish. This is a moving illustration of the value God places on every human life.

Discipline and Forgiveness (18:15–35)

In the same vein, Jesus proceeds to outline a process of confronting a straying brother with the purpose of restoring him to the fellowship of believers. This shows that sin must be taken seriously not only by individuals but also by the believing community as a whole. This process looks as follows:

- *Step 1: private confrontation.* Go and confront the sinning person by yourself. If he listens, he is restored to fellowship.
- *Step 2: more formal confrontation.* If he doesn't listen, take one or two others along so as to establish a given charge before two or three witnesses. If he listens, he is restored to fellowship (implied).
- *Step 3: public announcement.* If he still doesn't listen, bring the matter to the church as a whole. If he listens, he is restored to fellowship (implied).
- *Step 4: church discipline.* If he still doesn't listen, put him out of the fellowship.

In this way, the community holds fellow believers accountable, helping them face up to their sin and encouraging them to repent, while exposing those who are unbelievers and removing them from the church. Thus, only genuine believers will be members of the community. In this process, Jesus awards genuine authority to the leaders of the church—what they don't forgive on earth will be unforgiven in heaven, and what they forgive on earth will be forgiven in heaven. What's more, Jesus assures them of his spiritual presence throughout the process: "For where two or three are gathered in my name, there am I among them" (18:20).

At the outset of this discourse, the disciples had asked Jesus the question "Who is the greatest in the kingdom of heaven?" Jesus responded by affirming their need for humility and stipulated a process of accountability for those in the community who need to be confronted and who need to repent of their sin. Now, Peter asks a second question: "How often do I need to forgive a person who sins against me? Seven times?" (Matt. 18:21; my paraphrase). Presumably, Peter thinks seven times is generous. Yet Jesus declares the correct answer is "seventy-seven times" or even "seventy times seven" (v. 22)—an infinite number of times! There is no limit to forgiveness.

To illustrate this point, Jesus tells the parable of the unforgiving servant. The main point is that Jesus's followers should extend forgiveness to the same extent to which they themselves have received it from God. Since God's grace has no limits, neither should our forgiveness. By contrast, those who don't forgive others as God has forgiven them will be objects of God's wrath for receiving God's unlimited forgiveness yet putting limits on their own. As C. S. Lewis puts it, "To be a Christian means to forgive the inexcusable because God has forgiven the inexcusable in you."[1]

DISCUSSION QUESTIONS

1. What is the blasphemy of the Holy Spirit, and can people still commit this sin today?

2. What is the sign of Jonah?

3. Jesus said, "A prophet is not without honor except in his hometown and in his own household." Why do you think this is true? How have you experienced this yourself?

4. What is your favorite kingdom parable, and why?

1. C. S. Lewis, "On Forgiveness," in *The Weight of Glory: And Other Addresses* (New York: HarperCollins, 2001), 182.

All things have been committed to me by my Father. No one knows the Son except the Father, and no one knows the Father except the Son and those to whom the Son chooses to reveal him. Come to me, all you who are weary and burdened, and I will give you rest. Take my yoke upon you and learn from me, for I am gentle and humble in heart, and you will find rest for your souls. For my yoke is easy and my burden is light.

—Matthew 11:27–30 NIV

Jesus's call is not to the self-satisfied who sense no need for anyone to help them carry their load in life. No, he calls all those who are "weary and burdened." There are plenty of people who, intentionally or unintentionally, burden us; but Jesus wants to ease our burden. It may appear that following Jesus is hard when in fact it is "easy." All we have to give up is our life of sin and our selfish pride, and in exchange we get to learn from Jesus how to live sacrificially and selflessly. We will find that Jesus is no demanding boss but "gentle and humble in heart." And not once, but twice in this passage does Jesus promise those who follow him "rest" for their souls. Will you come to him and exchange your weariness for his rest?

CHAPTER 4—MATTHEW

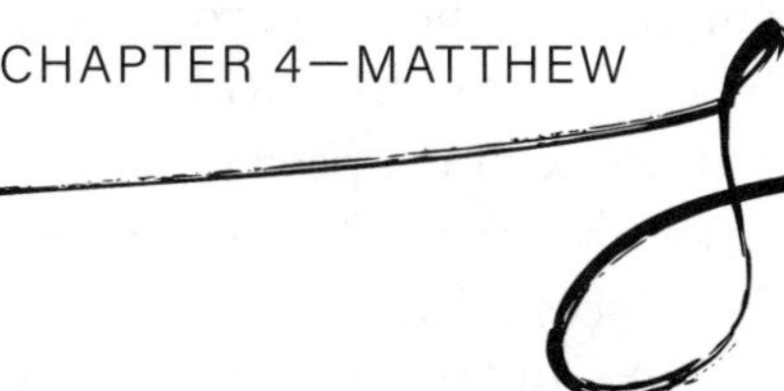

CRUCIFIED AND RISEN

MINISTRY IN JUDEA, DEATH, BURIAL, AND RESURRECTION (19:1–28:20)
Ministry in Judea and Jerusalem: The Humble Entry, Cleansing the Temple (19:1–23:39)
Book 5: The End Times and God's Kingdom (24:1–25:46)
The Plot Against Jesus: Last Supper, Arrest, and Jewish Trial (26:1–75)
The Roman Trial, Crucifixion, and Burial (27:1–66)
Resurrection Appearances and the Great Commission (28:1–20)

MINISTRY IN JUDEA (19:1–25:46)

With chapters 19–28, we enter the final stage of Jesus's ministry and of Matthew's account. This section is often called the "passion narrative," because it is here that Jesus suffers and dies for God's people (the Latin *passio* means "suffering"). In this final unit, Jesus continues his ministry in Judea and Jerusalem, the Jewish capital. He also teaches about the end times in both explicit instruction and creative illustration. After a final meal with the Twelve, Jesus is arrested, tried, crucified, and buried. Once he rises, he commissions his disciples.

Earlier, we saw that Jesus started out his ministry in the Galilean north as an outsider, opposite the Jewish religious establishment based in

Judea's capital, Jerusalem. Now, we see Jesus travel toward Jerusalem, in an ominous sign that his earthly ministry is about to end. In keeping with scriptural prediction, he must be rejected by the Jewish authorities and killed—not for his own sins but for those of the people.

Judea was the province in the south that in Old Testament times was distinct from the ten northern provinces ("Israel") that were taken into Assyrian exile in about 722 BC. Later, Judea (or Judah, as it was called then) was exiled by the Babylonians in three stages starting in 605 BC. Jesus's outsider status is underscored by the fact that when he visited Jerusalem, he typically spent the night outside the city in nearby Bethany. Jerusalem, the capital of Judea, was the site of the temple, the central place of Jewish worship.

Ministry in Judea and Jerusalem: The Humble Entry, Cleansing the Temple (19:1–23:39)

When Is Divorce Legitimate? (19:1–12)

After four cycles of ministry in Galilee, Jesus now leaves Galilee and enters "the region of Judea beyond the Jordan" to embark on his journey to Jerusalem to fulfill his mission to Israel there (Matt. 19:1). Large crowds continue to follow him, and he continues to heal those who come to him. Jesus's popularity with the crowds again stands in marked contrast to the opposition of the Pharisees, who test him with another trick question: "Is it lawful to divorce one's wife for any cause?" (v. 3).

First-century Jews held a range of views on divorce. The conservative school of Shammai interpreted the Mosaic stipulation that a man may divorce a woman only for matters of "some indecency in her" (Deut. 24:1) in terms of sexual immorality—that is, adultery. The liberal school of Hillel interpreted the same stipulation more broadly as referring to "anything displeasing to her husband." When asking "Is it lawful to divorce one's wife *for any cause*," therefore, the Pharisees were asking Jesus to declare whether he aligned himself with the school of Shammai or Hillel. Either way, he was going to antagonize the other side.

Yet Jesus skillfully evades the trap, taking his listeners back to God's original plan for marriage: "Have you not read that he who created them from the beginning made them male and female?" (Matt. 19:4; cf. Gen. 1:27). He also points out that God has said in the Scriptures, "Therefore a man shall leave his father and his mother and hold fast to his wife, and the two shall become one flesh" (Matt. 19:5; cf. Gen. 2:24). The obvious conclusion is: "So they are no longer two but one flesh. What therefore God has joined together, let not man separate" (Matt. 19:6). God's plan has been for marriage to be for life.

Not taking no for an answer, however, the Pharisees query, "Why then did Moses command one to give a certificate of divorce?" (v. 7). Jesus replies that this was merely a concession to human hard-heartedness. At the same time, he stipulates that divorce is permissible in cases of *sexual immorality*. (In Old Testament times, adultery was considered to sever the marriage covenant and was punishable by stoning [cf. Lev. 20:10].)

Jesus's own disciples follow up by saying, "If such is the case of a man with his wife, it is better not to marry," alleging that his standard is too high (Matt. 19:10). But Jesus doesn't back down. All he is willing to say is that there are some who have the gift of celibacy (i.e., of remaining unmarried); if anyone has that gift, he should refrain from marrying in the first place! Again, Jesus leaves both the Pharisees and even his own disciples astonished at the loftiness of his ethical teaching and spiritual vision. Indeed, Jesus is the final and authoritative interpreter of God's law (cf. 5:17–20).

The Kingdom of Heaven and Little Children (19:13–15)

Following this latest interchange, people bring children to Jesus so that he can lay hands on them and pray for them. The disciples, who already have forgotten what Jesus just recently told them about citizens of God's kingdom becoming like children, rebuke those who brought them. In turn, Jesus pointedly rebukes them, reaffirming that the kingdom of heaven belongs to children such as these.

The Wealthy Young Man and Requirements for Discipleship (19:16–30)

Next, a man approaches Jesus, asking, "Teacher, what good deed must I do to have eternal life?" (19:16). In response, Jesus urges him to keep the commandments. The man replies that he has kept them all. What does he still lack? Jesus replies that he should sell his possessions and give to the poor. At this, the young man goes away regretfully, as he cannot part with his wealth.

Ever the opportunist, Peter pipes up: "Look, we've left everything and followed you. What's in it for us, then?" (v. 27, my paraphrase). Jesus replies,

"Truly, I say to you, in the new world, when the Son of Man will sit on his glorious throne, you who have followed me will also sit on twelve thrones, judging the twelve tribes of Israel. And everyone who has left houses or brothers or sisters or father or mother or children or lands, for my name's sake, will receive a hundredfold and will inherit eternal life" (vv. 28–29). He adds the caution, "But many who are first will be last, and the last first" (v. 30).

God's kingdom will bring about a dramatic reversal: those with great power and wealth on earth will be shut out, while the powerless and poor will be put in charge. Taken together, the accounts of the children and of the wealthy young man provide a poignant picture of the kingdom of God.

The Parable of the Workers in the Vineyard (20:1–16)

To illustrate another aspect of God's kingdom, Jesus tells the parable of the workers in the vineyard. In it, a vineyard owner hires various workers at different hours of the day. At the end of the day, he pays everyone the same daily wage regardless of when they were hired. The first ones hired complain that it isn't fair that those who were hired later are paid the same amount, but the vineyard owner insists that it *is* fair—he has paid them the contractual amount. If he chooses to be gracious, that is his prerogative. This is yet another parable by which Jesus makes the point that God is sovereign in extending grace to undeserving sinners—and that none of us is in a position to complain that God is "too gracious" to another person.

Historically, the parable applied uniquely to the Jewish leaders who complained about Jesus fraternizing with tax collectors and Gentile "sinners." They couldn't legitimately complain that God gave the same grace he had given them to these Johnny-come-latelies. Jesus makes a similar point in the parable of the prodigal son (Luke 15:11–32). In the present case, Jesus ends the parable with the statement "So the last will be first, and the first last" (Matt. 20:16), which makes clear that Jesus has told the parable to illustrate the point he had made earlier about the reversal of fortunes in the kingdom (cf. 19:30). Again, the sublime wisdom and inherent truth in Jesus's teaching leave the reader in awe.

The Third Passion Prediction (20:17–19)

As they're headed toward Jerusalem, Jesus takes his disciples aside and predicts his imminent betrayal, crucifixion, and resurrection a third time, specifying that the chief priests and scribes will condemn him (at his Jewish trial) and subsequently hand him over to the Gentiles (at his

Roman trial) to be mocked, flogged, and crucified (cf. 16:21; 17:22–23). This adds drama and suspense, as it heightens the reader's expectation of the events Jesus is predicting with increasing intensity and specificity and serves to focus Matthew's account of Jesus's passion.

An Impudent Request (20:20–28)

Soon thereafter, the mother of James and John approaches Jesus, together with her sons, and asks him to grant them positions of honor in his kingdom. When Jesus asks them if they can "drink the cup" he must drink, they confidently yet foolishly assert that they can (20:22). The other disciples are indignant with James and John—most likely because they didn't think to ask first!

How could they have forgotten so quickly Jesus's response to their question as to who would be greatest in the kingdom (18:1)? What about the object lesson he had taught them by placing a little child in their midst? Similar to the earlier misunderstanding about the "leaven" of the Pharisees and Sadducees (16:5–12), Jesus's earlier teaching has failed to make an impression.

Jesus reiterates that greatness in God's kingdom differs radically from greatness in the world. It is measured not by power or prestige but by service and humility. Even Jesus "came not to be served but to serve, and to give his life as a ransom for many" (20:28). Jesus didn't merely take on a stance of servanthood when dying on the cross; he did so throughout his ministry, modeling one of the hallmarks of God's kingdom: humility.

Two Blind Men (20:29–34)

Still on their way to Jerusalem, passing through Jericho, Jesus is followed by a great throng of people. When two blind men sitting on the side of the road hear that Jesus is passing by, they yell at the top of their lungs, "Lord, have mercy on us, Son of David!" (v. 30). When the people in the crowd tell them to stop bothering Jesus—who, they surmise, has more important things to do than to attend to blind beggars—they cry all the louder, instinctively sensing that this is their once-in-a-lifetime opportunity to be healed. At this, Jesus stops, engages them in conversation, and—full of compassion—touches their eyes. They recover their sight at once and follow him. This is another example of Jesus's mercy toward sinners. He is not the powerful ruler many have expected; he is the gentle, humble, and merciful Servant of the Lord who is touched by human suffering and headed for Jerusalem to take our suffering upon himself in complete identification with our predicament.

The Entry into Jerusalem (21:1–11)

The long journey to Jerusalem has almost come to a climax as Jesus prepares to enter the city—a moment that the readers of Matthew's gospel have anticipated virtually from the very beginning. Jesus arrives at the village of Bethphage by the Mount of Olives, close to the Holy City. He instructs two of his disciples to go into the village where, it seems, divine providence has already orchestrated all circumstances so that they can secure the colt and donkey that are needed for Jesus's entry into Jerusalem. This too takes place in order to fulfill the prophetic word announcing to Zion (i.e., Jerusalem) that her king would be coming to her, humbly mounted on a donkey (cf. Zech. 9:9).

Everything transpires just as Jesus has predicted, foreshadowing the way in which the entire proceedings surrounding his arrest and crucifixion will unfold in keeping with God's sovereign plan. Jesus enters Jerusalem seated on a donkey in humble, royal demeanor (in keeping with scriptural prophecy), and the inhabitants of the city hail him as the long-awaited Son of David, the Jewish Messiah and King. If it weren't for Jesus's threefold prediction that he would be betrayed and killed, the reader would have to assume that the story has a happy ending: the Messiah comes to the Holy City of Jerusalem, and its inhabitants welcome him with open arms! Unfortunately, appearances are deceiving, and events will soon take a sudden turn for the worse.

Cleansing the Temple (21:12–17)

Having entered Jerusalem, Jesus first heads to the temple, where he finds the place a bustling center of commerce. Merchants are making a fast shekel selling sacrificial animals, and money changers are charging steep exchange rates for converting people's money into the proper temple currency. This explains why Jesus drives out all sellers and buyers from the temple area and overturns the money changers' tables and pigeon sellers' chairs. Quoting the Old Testament prophets Isaiah and Jeremiah, Jesus insists that the temple is supposed to be a "house of prayer," but these profiteers have made it into a "den of robbers" (Matt. 21:13; cf. Isa. 56:7; Jer. 7:11).

Following this incident, at which Jesus acts like a prophet cleansing the house of God, the blind and lame come to him to be healed, still in the temple area, and children cry out, "Hosanna to the Son of David!" (Matt. 21:15). The chief priests and scribes are indignant, hinting that Jesus should tell them to be quiet. Yet Jesus doesn't do so but instead quotes an Old Testament psalm: "Have you never read, 'Out of the mouth of infants and nursing babies you have prepared praise'?" (v. 16; cf. Ps. 8:2). You sense that Jesus's relationship with the Jewish leaders is going from bad to worse, and they must be seething at yet another rebuffed request from Jesus.

The Withering Indictment of the Fig Tree (21:18–22)

Jesus spends that night in Bethany, near the city; remarkably, he never stays overnight in Jerusalem. On his return to the city, Jesus engages in another puzzling activity. Hungry, he wants to grab a fig from a nearby tree but finds that the tree has no fruit, only leaves. At once, he curses the barren tree, and it withers instantly. Again, Jesus's action seems strange; it's best to understand the cursing of the fig tree as a form of acted-out parable. The tree gave the appearance of fruit—the very purpose of fig trees—yet there was none. The cursing of the fig tree, therefore, anticipates the destruction of Jerusalem and the temple. Worship in the temple was just as barren as that unfortunate fig tree!

The disciples marvel at Jesus's power to curse a tree by his mere word. There's an almost eerie feeling about Jesus: Who is this guy? Where does he get his powers? There clearly was something supernatural about him that defied mere rational explanation. It must have been quite something to be with Jesus! You'd never know what might happen next. In the present case, Jesus uses the fig tree incident to reinforce to his disciples the importance of faith. If they have faith, they'll be able to move spiritual mountains and will receive whatever they ask for in prayer.

Jesus's Authority Challenged (21:23–27)

Back in the temple area, after having thrown out the merchants and money changers the previous day, Jesus immediately finds himself the center of attention again. With crowds surrounding him, the chief priests and elders confront Jesus pointedly. Does he think he has authority over what happens in the temple area? That is *their* turf! Jesus discerns that their question is insincere. So rather than answering their question straightforwardly and telling them that it is *God* who has authorized him, Jesus responds with a counterquestion: Who was the one who authorized John's baptism?

In this, Jesus is cleverly exploiting the fact that most considered John to be a prophet (like Elijah). So if the chief priests and elders denied that God sent John, they would find themselves contradicting common opinion regarding him. But if they agreed, then on what basis could they deny that Jesus was similarly sent by God—as John, his forerunner, was? Thus, the face-off ends in a stalemate. His interrogators reply, "We do not know." Jesus retorts, "Neither will I tell you by what authority I do these things" (Matt. 21:27). At this, they retreat, humiliated once again. Needless to say, the interchange does nothing to alleviate tensions between Jesus and the religious leaders.

A Trilogy of Parables: Two Sons, Wicked Tenants, and the Wedding Feast (21:28–22:14)

After this latest confrontation with the Jewish authorities, Jesus tells three parables that deal with the leaders' rejection of him. The first, the parable of the *two sons*, draws a contrast between his own disciples and the Jewish leaders. The first son, like those who submitted to John's baptism, rebels at first but later chooses to submit to his father's authority and do what he asks. The second son, like the Jewish leaders, pledge obedience but in the end fail to obey. Which son has carried out his father's instructions? The lesson of the parable is that the tax collectors and prostitutes who have shown genuine contrition will enter the kingdom of God ahead of the Jewish leaders who have failed to truly repent.

In a second parable, the parable of the *wicked tenants*, Jesus tells of tenant farmers who, having been left in charge of a vineyard, mistreat, abuse, and even kill every servant the master sends to collect fruit at harvest time. The parable culminates with the tenants killing the vineyard owner's very own son. When Jesus asks his listeners what punishment the tenants should receive, they reply that they should be killed and that the vineyard be entrusted to others. At this, Jesus declares that, in fact, it is *they* who are the wicked tenants! Jesus tells the parable as a stern warning to the Jewish leaders—namely, that God will punish them by taking the kingdom of God away from them and giving it to "a people producing its fruits" (v. 43). In keeping with Old Testament prediction, Jesus identifies himself as "The stone that the builders rejected," which "has become the cornerstone" (v. 42; cf. Ps. 118:22–23). The chief priests and Pharisees are enraged and renew their resolve to kill Jesus.

In a third parable, the parable of the *wedding feast*, Jesus tells the story of a king giving a joyous wedding celebration for his son. When he sends out his servants to invite people to the wedding, they refuse to attend because they have more important things to do. Some even kill the servants. The king destroys them and burns their city and sends his servants out again to summon as many as will come, and there is a large wedding. At the end, the king comes upon a wedding guest without proper attire; he has him bound and cast out. Often, people think that they can write their own rules and that in the end God will accept them; yet those who are invited must be prepared to play by God's rules. The story closes with Jesus's declaration, "For many are called, but few are chosen" (Matt. 22:14). God has called many, but few have responded; in fact, many have rejected his gracious offer of salvation in his Son. As a result, God will invite others who will be more receptive to God's kind invitation.

Taxes, Marriage in the Resurrection, and the Greatest Commandment (22:15–40)

Following Jesus's three denunciation parables, the Jewish leaders begin to lay a series of traps for him—to justify killing him. These traps pertain to paying taxes, the nature of marriage in the resurrection, and the greatest commandment in the law. In each case, Jesus masterfully deflects their attacks and demonstrates his wisdom and the authoritative nature of his teaching. The first trap is laid with the question, "Is it lawful to pay taxes to Caesar, or not?" (v. 17). If Jesus were to say yes, he would antagonize Jewish zealots who agitated for overthrowing the Roman overlords and engaged in various kinds of civil disobedience. If he were to say no, the Jewish leaders could report Jesus to the Romans as a rebel and zealot, a traitor who must be censored. Jesus, however, masterfully sidesteps this trap by asking for a common Roman coin, a denarius, and querying whose picture is on the coin. "Caesar's" is the answer. Jesus's reply cuts to the chase: "Therefore render to Caesar the things that are Caesar's, and to God the things that are God's" (v. 21). Once again, Jesus's opponents are silenced.

The second trap involves the Sadducees (another Jewish party besides the Pharisees), who denied the future resurrection because they only affirmed the authority of the five books of Moses, which they claimed do not explicitly mention the resurrection. In order to make their case (and to ridicule the whole idea), they concoct the hypothetical scenario of a woman who has been married seven times. "In the resurrection," they ask, "of the seven, whose wife will she be?" (v. 28). Once again, Jesus eludes the trap with ease. Pointedly calling God "the God of Abraham, and the God of Isaac, and the God of Jacob"—all featured in the book of Genesis, whose authority the Sadducees recognized—Jesus affirms that God is a God of the living, not the dead (v. 32). What's more, Jesus reveals that in the resurrection people will no longer marry. The Sadducees, too, have been duly humbled. They have been "silenced" (v. 34), while the crowds are "astonished" (v. 33).

At this, the Pharisees take their turn. One of them asks Jesus about the greatest commandment in the law. Jesus parries the challenge with no problem: it is to love God with all our heart, soul, and mind, and to love one's neighbor as oneself: "On these two commandments depend all the Law and the Prophets" (v. 40).

Whose Son Is the Messiah? (22:41–46)

The chapter ends not with a question by Jesus's opponents but with a query of his own. Jesus asks the Pharisees, "What do you think about the Christ? Whose son is he?" They reply, "The son of David" (v. 42). He follows up: "How is it then that David, in the Spirit, calls him Lord?" (v. 43). At this, he quotes Psalm 110: "The Lord said to my Lord, 'Sit at my right hand, until I put your enemies under your feet'" (v. 44). "If then David calls him Lord," Jesus asks, "how is he his son?" (v. 45). Good question! No one is able to give an answer. The answer, it appears, is that there is a plurality in the Godhead, encompassing both God the Father and God the Son, and that it is God the Father who tells God the Son to sit at his right hand. But admitting this would have required the Pharisees to depart from their rigid monotheism, according to which there is only one God. That is of course true, but it is also true that this God exists in three persons—what in subsequent theology has been called the Trinity.

We've seen that Jesus has been able to answer all his opponents' questions with incredible acuity and wisdom, while they have been completely dumbfounded by both his answers and his counterquestions. In all these ways, Jesus emerges not only as the rightful Messiah but also as the authoritative Teacher who can speak of his "Father in heaven" and of "the kingdom of God" because he knows both God the Father and his kingdom from firsthand experience. This unique identity as Son of God gives Jesus the authority to teach what God's kingdom is like and what God requires from those who would follow him. It also gives him authority to interpret the Scriptures in a way that is far superior to the way the Jewish experts interpret the law. As a result, Jesus's responses leave the Jewish leaders at a complete loss, so that "from that day [no one dared] to ask him any more questions" (v. 46).

Scribes and Pharisees, Hypocrites! (23:1–36)

Following the aforementioned series of challenges from the religious establishment, Jesus warns the crowds and the disciples against the Jewish leaders. They sit in Moses's seat, Jesus says, so they're in rightful positions of authority; so do what they tell you, but realize that they themselves aren't practicing what they're preaching. They lay heavy spiritual burdens on others but themselves don't lift a finger. They "do all their deeds to be seen by others" and "love the place of honor at feasts and the best seats in the synagogues" (23:5–6). They enjoy the perks that come with their jobs and are infatuated with their own power—but they've forgotten that they have been given their position to serve others' interests, not merely their own! By contrast, Jesus's followers shouldn't elevate anyone to the exalted position of "Teacher" or "Father"—the only Father they have is God—but should live a lifestyle of humility. This again bears a chilling resemblance to the mentality of some Christian leaders today, who are detached from church members and live a comfortable life themselves while doing little to alleviate the suffering of those they're charged to shepherd.

Next, in a withering series of seven "woes" reminiscent of prophetic Old Testament language, Jesus scathingly condemns the hypocrisy of the Jewish scribes and Pharisees (cf. Isa. 5:8–24; Amos 5:18–20; Mic. 2:1–4; Hab. 2:6–20):

1. They shut heaven's door in people's faces, so that not only will they not enter God's kingdom, but others won't be able to do so either.
2. They spare no efforts to convert people to their sect, so they can make them "twice as much a child of hell" (!) as they are (Matt. 23:15).
3. They're blind guides who pervert biblical teaching on the taking of oaths, using it to their own advantage.
4. They tithe scrupulously, even minor spices, while neglecting the "weightier matters of the law": justice, mercy, and faithfulness (v. 23).

5. They thinly veil their greed and self-indulgence; they're in dire need of repentance but won't repent.
6. They're masters at projecting a certain public image: everything looks great on the outside but terrible on the inside.
7. They're guilty of righteous blood and are destined straight for hell; but they'll be held accountable.

Lament over Jerusalem (23:37–39)

Finally, Jesus laments the coming desolation of Jerusalem: "O Jerusalem, Jerusalem, the city that kills the prophets and stones those who are sent to it!" (v. 37). For now it's goodbye, as the city won't see Jesus again until he comes as the triumphant King, and people will welcome him, saying, "Blessed is he who comes in the name of the Lord" (v. 39). While reminiscent of his triumphal entry into the city at his first coming, the accolades will soon turn into accusations, and the city will turn its back on Jesus. Only at his return will Jesus be welcomed by the city and its inhabitants who previously rejected him. In this way, Jesus casts an end-time vision that transcends his immediate circumstances and encompasses future events at the end of time.

Book 5: The End Times and God's Kingdom (24:1–25:46)

At this, Matthew presents the fifth and final extended teaching portion of his gospel, which consists of the Olivet Discourse (delivered on the Mount of Olives in Jerusalem) and a final series of kingdom parables.

The Olivet Discourse (24:1–51)

Jesus's Prophecy and the Disciples' Questions (24:1–3). The discourse is occasioned by a stroll Jesus and his followers take on the temple grounds and the disciples' excited remarks about the splendor of the sanctuary. Putting a damper on their enthusiasm, Jesus wastes no time predicting the destruction of the temple, affirming that "there will not be left here one stone upon another that will not be thrown down" (24:2). As they later sit down on the Mount of Olives, halfway back to where they would stay for the night, still processing his earlier remark about the temple's destruction, Jesus's followers ask him a two-pronged question: "Tell us, *when* will these things be, and *what* will be the sign of your coming and of the close of the age?" (v. 3, emphasis added). It is in response to this question that Jesus provides his teaching on the end times, found with some variation in all three Synoptic Gospels.

Possible Signs of the End (24:4–14). Tackling his disciples' two-part question in reverse order, Jesus first addresses the part dealing with signs preceding "these things"—the destruction of the temple. He starts with a warning against messianic pretenders who will appear and deceive many. There'll be man-made conflicts—both wars and rumors of wars—as well as natural disasters such as famines and earthquakes. Also, God's people will experience great tribulation and even martyrdom, so that many will fall away. They'll also witness an increase of lawlessness, violence, and crime, and the commitment of many will wane and falter. Yet none of this is the actual sign; all is part of the proclamation of the good news of God's kingdom to all the nations of the world.

Jesus cautions his disciples against being too quick to assume they know when the temple's destruction is at hand. Even when speaking of various portents of its demise, such as great wars, natural disasters, or major waves of persecution, he makes clear these are not yet the actual signs. Jesus's words call for faithfulness to persevere in view of increasing persecution and wisdom in discerning the signs preceding the end.

The Abomination of Desolation and Destruction of the City (24:15–22). The previous section has indicated what would happen prior to the signs of the temple's destruction. Now, Jesus reveals the actual sign: the "abomination of desolation spoken of by the prophet Daniel, standing in the holy place" (i.e., the temple; cf. Dan. 8:13; 9:27; 11:31; 12:11). Matthew adds the parenthetical comment, "let the reader understand" (Matt. 24:15). The initial fulfillment of Daniel's prophecy was the erection of a "desolating sacrilege on the altar of whole burnt offering" by the Greek ruler Antiochus Epiphanes IV in 167 BC, who sacrificed a pig on the altar in blatant disregard of Jewish sensibilities regarding eating pork (1 Macc. 1:54; cf. v. 59). The Maccabean revolt ensued, and the small band of Judean rebels miraculously defeated the enemy forces and ushered in a century of Jewish self-rule (164–63 BC).

The temple was rededicated in 164 BC, which marked the beginning of the Jewish festival of Hanukkah (cf. John 10:22). Jesus's renewed reference to the "abomination of desolation" indicates that Daniel's prophecy wasn't exhausted by Antiochus's offense but awaited further fulfillment. Luke makes clear that this fulfillment would take place, at least in part, at the temple's destruction by the Romans in AD 70: "When you see Jerusalem surrounded by armies, then know that its desolation has come near"

(Luke 21:20). At that time, Jesus's followers should flee Judea and head for the mountains. This would be a time of great tribulation, but for the sake of the elect God would put a limit on the time of the Roman siege of Jerusalem. Later reports indicate the incredible amount of suffering inflicted on the city's inhabitants by the Romans.

Imposters, Cosmic Upheaval, and the Coming of the Son of Man (24:23–31). The word "then" in Matthew 24:23 marks a transition in the discourse. Most likely, Jesus is here moving from the time leading up to the destruction of the temple to the more distant coming of Jesus, the Son of Man. There will be various imposters, both false messiahs and false prophets. Performing "great signs and wonders," their intention will be "to lead astray, if possible, even the elect" (v. 24).

But God's people must not be deceived. No one will be able to miss the second coming, because it'll be a highly visible, public event. The return of Jesus, the Son of Man, will be accompanied by cosmic upheaval. Then the "sign of the Son of Man" will appear in heaven, and "all the tribes of the earth will mourn," as they will see Jesus "coming on the clouds of heaven with power and great glory" (v. 30). And the angels will come with great fanfare and gather the elect.

The Timing of the Temple's Destruction and of Jesus's Return (24:32–36). Concluding the discourse, Jesus compares the sign of his return to a fig tree. When summer approaches, its branches become tender and it puts out its leaves. With this, at least in part, Jesus answers the disciples' question as to "*when* these things will happen": "Truly, I say to you, this generation will not pass away until all these things take place" (v. 34). Jesus's words will come true within one generation: some of those disciples who heard Jesus say these things would be alive when the temple would be destroyed.

While several of the apostles were martyred prior to the year 70, we know that at least one apostle, John the son of Zebedee, lived to a ripe old age until the end of the first century, so he would certainly have been alive during the temple's destruction. Jesus adds that while heaven and earth—the world as we know it—will come to an end, his words will certainly come to pass (cf. 5:18); and no one—not the angels, nor even Jesus himself—knows the exact time of his return, only God the Father.

Conclusion (24:37–51). Jesus explains that the time of his coming will be like the universal flood in Noah's day. When it arrives, it'll be too late to prepare. "Therefore," Jesus counsels, "stay awake, for you do not know on what day your Lord is coming" (24:42). Also, his return will be like the arrival of a thief. No thief in his right mind announces when he'll break into a house! "Therefore you also must be ready, for the Son of Man is coming at an hour you do not expect" (v. 44).

Jesus gives yet another illustration of his future return in the parable of the *faithful and wicked slaves*. The faithful slave is ready for his master's return, no matter when it happens. The wicked slave, in view of his master's delay, mistreats others and indulges in various kinds of pleasures. Again, Jesus's point remains the same: believers need to be in a constant state of readiness for Jesus's return, no matter when it happens. In essence, we should live each day as if Jesus were coming back that same day

Jesus's coming will be good news for believers, especially those suffering persecution who eagerly await his return. It'll be terrible news for unbelievers, however, because God's patience will have run out and there will no longer be any opportunity to repent and be saved. Thus, Jesus uses the nearing destruction of the temple to point to the more distant time of his return. In both cases, tribulation will precede the arrival of these events, but God will protect all faithful believers.

The Parables of the Ten Virgins and Talents, and the Final Judgment (25:1–46)

The Parable of the Ten Virgins (25:1–13). Seamlessly, the gospel continues with additional parables related to the topic of Jesus's return at the end of time. Jesus has just spoken of the faithful and wise servant who is ready for his master's return, even if it should be delayed. He now tells the parable of the *ten virgins*, five of whom are foolish and five of whom are wise. Again, the scenario involves a delay, this time on the part of the bridegroom. The wise virgins are prepared and ready, while the foolish ones are not and end up being caught off guard by the bridegroom's eventual return. The foolish virgins ask the wise ones to share their oil with them, but the wise ones refuse, saying there wouldn't be enough for all of them. Then the wise virgins join in the wedding celebrations, while the foolish virgins are shut out. Again, this is a picture of Christ's return and the final judgment. Jesus's followers should make every effort to stay in a constant state of readiness, even if there is an apparent delay in his return.

In Jesus's words, "Watch therefore, for you know neither the day nor the hour," a statement that ties in directly with Jesus's closing statement in the Olivet Discourse (25:13; cf. 24:36).

The Parable of the Talents (25:14–30). Jesus continues by telling the parable of the *talents*, which features a man leaving for a trip and entrusting his servants with various amounts of "talents" (i.e., units of currency, not "special aptitudes or natural endorsements" as we would use the word today). One servant receives five talents, another two, and yet another one talent. Then the man leaves on his journey. Upon his return "after a long time," the man settles accounts with his servants (25:19). The first has made five more talents, the second an additional two. Both are thus commended for their faithfulness: "Well done, good and faithful servant" (vv. 21, 23). But when the master comes to the third and final servant, the servant says he was afraid and had buried the talent in the ground. Then he simply gives the money back to the master. At this, the master chastises the servant and tells him he should have invested the money, and he orders the talent to be given to the first servant, who already has ten talents. The lesson is this: "For to everyone who has will more be given, and he will have an abundance. But from the one who has not, even what he has will be taken away" (v. 29). Jesus tells this parable to impress on his followers the importance of faithful and wise stewardship of all that the Lord has given them, a stewardship that is not limited to money but includes all our earthly possessions.

The Final Judgment (25:31–46). At this, Jesus projects the breathtaking vision of his return and the final judgment that will ensue at that time. Jesus will come back in all his glory, with myriads of angels, and he will sit on his throne and gather all nations as a shepherd separating sheep from goats. At the final judgment, Jesus will focus on actions rather than mere words. What's more, he will identify with the hungry and thirsty, those who lack clothing and suffer in prison.

One theme that several of Jesus's end-time parables have in common is that those who are being judged or who are caught unprepared make various kinds of excuses. The servant who had received the one talent blames his inaction on the perceived harshness of his master. Likewise, the "goats" on Jesus's left in the present parable excuse their inaction by saying they never saw Jesus hungry, thirsty, naked, or in prison, so they did nothing to help the poor. Again, however, their excuses avail to nothing.

As in the conclusion to the Sermon on the Mount, Jesus is adamant that our faith be translated into concrete action. In this way, proclaiming and believing the gospel and doing good works are inextricably wedded together. Jesus's half-brother James makes this point in his letter, most likely written only about a decade after Jesus's earthly ministry (James 1:22–27).

DEATH, BURIAL, RESURRECTION, AND THE GREAT COMMISSION (26:1–28:20)

The last of Jesus's five discourses featured in Matthew's gospel transitions to the concluding passion narrative with the customary phrase "When Jesus had finished all these sayings" (Matt. 26:1).

The Plot Against Jesus: Last Supper, Arrest, and Jewish Trial (26:1–75)

The Hideous Plot (26:1–5)

It's now only two days until Passover. Again, Jesus reminds his disciples that he is about to be delivered into the hands of the Jewish authorities in order to be crucified. No one can legitimately say that Jesus is caught unaware. To the contrary, he is utterly determined to accomplish God's purpose for his life. The Jewish leaders, likewise, have their minds made up and merely wait for an opportune moment to arrest Jesus. But they're afraid that Passover may not be the right time, as Jerusalem will be flooded with pilgrims from everywhere.

Anointed for Burial (26:6–13)

At this, the narrative shifts to the house of Simon the leper (not mentioned elsewhere) in the village of Bethany (cf. 21:17). While Jesus and the others are eating, a woman approaches him with a bottle of very expensive perfume and pours it over Jesus's head. That's definitely an event that onlookers would remember for some time! While Jesus's disciples denounce the expensive waste (John tells us the principal spokesman is Judas), Jesus tells them that the woman (no doubt without realizing it) has anointed him for burial. This strikes an ominous note at the outset of the proceedings against Jesus.

On parallel tracks, we witness the unfolding of the plot of the Jewish leaders on the one hand, and the plan of God on the other. In fact, God's plan is sovereignly accomplished *through* the evil designs of Jesus's opponents. As in the case of Joseph the patriarch, what Jesus's enemies have meant for evil, God is working out for good (Gen. 50:20). Jesus affirms that the woman's act of devotion will be proclaimed "in the whole world" in her memory (Matt. 26:13). This prediction too has come true, as the event is included in three of the four Gospels.

Treason (26:14–16)

In a dramatic escalation, Judas Iscariot, one of the Twelve, approaches the Jewish leaders and offers to betray Jesus for thirty pieces of silver. The price harks back to a reference in Zechariah, where the prophet receives that same amount and throws it to the potter (Zech. 11:12–13). According to the book of Exodus, thirty pieces of silver was the price of a slave (Exod. 21:32). It may be an insult that the price for betraying Jesus is nothing more than that paid for a slave. Judas's willingness to betray Jesus will give the authorities a foothold within Jesus's inner circle, so they can arrest Jesus quietly during Passover week.

The Last Supper (26:17–29)

With Passover approaching, Jesus again instructs his disciples to make the necessary preparations, similar to when they fetched the donkey at his triumphal entry. Again, everything works out exactly as Jesus has predicted. That evening, Jesus celebrates Passover with his disciples. While they're eating he announces, doubtless with a heavy heart, that one of them—Judas Iscariot—will betray him. After this, he institutes the Lord's Supper by taking a piece of bread and then a cup, saying, "Take, eat; this is my body"; "Drink of it, all of you, for this is my blood of the covenant, which is poured out for many for the forgiveness of sins" (Matt. 26:26, 27–28). Jesus will not drink wine again until the marriage supper of the Lamb in God's kingdom (Rev. 19:6–9).

To this day, we celebrate the Lord's Supper regularly as part of our worship gatherings. We see here how the Jewish Passover has served as the foundation on which the Lord's Supper is built. In fact, the last Passover—at least for Jesus and his apostles—was also the first Lord's Supper. The underlying symbolism is highly significant. Passover commemorates the blood of a sacrificial animal that became the means of salvation for believing Israelites on the eve of the exodus; the Lord's Supper is instituted to commemorate the blood of Jesus's sacrifice, which has become the means of salvation for all who believe, on the eve of the crucifixion. This shows the deep Jewish roots of Christianity. It also shows that Jesus, in keeping with Old Testament prophecy, has established a new covenant with a believing Jewish remnant—the twelve apostles—that has rendered the old covenant obsolete.

The Prediction of Peter's Denials (26:30–35)

At the end of the meal, Jesus and his disciples sing a hymn and head to the Mount of Olives, east of the city. There, Jesus invokes Old Testament prophecy, predicting that his disciples will all abandon him following his arrest (cf. Zech. 13:7). Peter vehemently protests Jesus's prediction, declaring, "Though they all fall away because of you, I will never fall away" (Matt. 26:33). In response, Jesus predicts that not only will Peter fall away but he'll deny Jesus three times before the rooster crows at sunrise the next day.

Praying at Gethsemane (26:36–46)

After this, Jesus takes his disciples to the garden of Gethsemane. The tension is palpable, and the sense of drama and suspense almost unbearable. Fully aware of what is about to happen, Jesus gathers his inner circle who had been with him at the transfiguration—Peter, James, and John—and asks them to watch and pray with him. Just imagine what it would have been like to be with Jesus during his final hours prior to the crucifixion! Leaving them at a distance, Jesus cries out to the Father, asking if there could be any way for him to escape the cross, yet ultimately pledging submission to the Father's will. Three times he returns to his disciples only to find them sleeping. Sadly, they're unable to stand with him in his darkest hour. Jesus, on the other hand, is victorious in prayer. Just as so many other times when Jesus prayed before important occasions, his victory at Gethsemane would pave the way for his victory at Golgotha.

Betrayed, Arrested, and Abandoned (26:47–56)

At last, Judas arrives with an armed mob assembled by the Jewish leaders, at which Jesus declares, "See, the hour is at hand, and the Son of Man is betrayed into the hands of sinners" (v. 45). Approaching Jesus, Judas gives him a kiss of friendship—the infamous "Judas kiss"—identifying him to the mob as the one they should take into custody. The mystery of one among Jesus's inner circle betraying him to the authorities makes one shudder. Judas has been with Jesus for more than three years and saw countless proofs of his messianic authority. Yet in keeping with God's plan, his heart has remained hard and unmoved.

At that very moment, one of Jesus's disciples (Peter) draws his sword and cuts off the ear of the high priest's servant. Jesus rebukes the disciple, explaining that his Father could dispatch an entire host of angels to rescue him if he so desired. Yet it is God's will that he be arrested and killed in order to fulfill the Scriptures. At this, the disciples take flight, and the mob takes Jesus to Caiaphas the high priest, and an assembly of Jewish leaders, to stand trial. With these dark spiritual storm clouds gathering on the horizon, the reader wonders: How will it all end? Will Jesus's repeated predictions of his own crucifixion and subsequent resurrection come true?

Jewish Trial (26:57–68)

In what follows, Jesus faces two separate yet related sets of interrogation, the first before the Jewish ruling council called the Sanhedrin and the second before Pontius Pilate, the Roman governor. The Jewish trial is a travesty of justice, in which numerous legal principles are set aside in order to hasten the "guilty" verdict against Jesus. The Jewish leaders strenuously look for false witnesses to trump up charges. Two individuals come forward, claiming that Jesus has promised to destroy the temple and rebuild it in three days (cf. John 2:19). Though their charges are false, Jesus remains silent until the high priest demands that he tell them "if [he is] the Christ, the Son of God" (Matt. 26:63). Quoting two messianic Old Testament passages—Psalm 110:1 and Daniel 7:13—Jesus answers: "You have said so" (v. 64). The high priest promptly charges Jesus with blasphemy; now, they have the evidence they need to put Jesus on the cross. The council sentences Jesus to death, and they spit in his face and beat him.

Peter's Threefold Denial (26:69–75)

Adding to the drama, the scene now shifts to Peter sitting in the courtyard, awaiting the results of Jesus's Jewish trial. Others there recognize Peter as one of Jesus's followers. On three separate occasions, with increasing exasperation, Peter denies even knowing Jesus. Immediately after the third denial, the rooster crows, signaling the fulfillment of Jesus's prophecy. Peter breaks down and dissolves into tears.

The Roman Trial, Crucifixion, and Burial (27:1–66)

The Roman Trial and Judas's Demise (27:1–26)

The next morning, the Jewish leaders take Jesus to Pilate to have him sanction their death sentence. Judas, full of remorse for betraying Jesus, returns the blood money, proclaims Jesus's innocence, and hangs himself. In fulfillment of Old Testament prophecy, the Jewish leaders use the money to purchase a burial plot for foreigners.

When Jesus appears before Pilate, he again remains silent. The governor, seeing no legitimate reason to put Jesus to death, tries to defuse the situation by appealing to a custom according to which the Roman governor could release a prisoner to the people at Passover. The crowd is presented with a fateful choice: "Whom do you want me to release for you: Barabbas [a convicted thief and murderer], or Jesus who is called Christ?" (27:17). Incited by the Jewish leaders, the people ask for Barabbas, sealing Jesus's fate. Pilate hypocritically washes his hands in innocence while the Jewish authorities accept full responsibility for Jesus's death, declaring, "His blood be on us and on our children!" (v. 25). Pilate releases Barabbas, has Jesus scourged, and delivers him to be crucified.

Crucifixion (27:27–56)

Soldiers from Pilate's Roman cohort strip Jesus and ridicule his messianic claims. They put a mock robe on him, place a thorny "crown" on his head, and hand him a reed "scepter." Bowing in fake homage, the soldiers exclaim, "Hail, King of the Jews!" (v. 29). After the series of scourgings and beatings, Jesus is weakened to the point of being unable to carry his own cross to the execution site. The soldiers compel a passerby, Simon from the town of Cyrene, to carry Jesus's cross to Golgotha. Upon arrival, the soldiers offer Jesus a mixture of wine and gall to dull his senses, but Jesus refuses. They crucify him on a cross between two robbers—depicting Jesus's identification with sinners—and put a sign over his head that reads, "This is Jesus, the King of the Jews" (v. 37). Some even mock Jesus—the "Son of God"—for being unable to save himself (vv. 40, 43).

Several unusual signs accompany Jesus's death, underscoring its momentous significance. While he hangs on the cross, the sky, as if in solar eclipse, turns black—depicting the darkness of evil—even though it is midday. When Jesus utters a loud cry and gives up his spirit, the heavy curtain separating the Holy of Holies from the rest of the temple—picturing the insurmountable separation between sinful human beings and a holy God—is torn from top to bottom while an earthquake splits rocks and opens tombs in the city. These (figuratively and literally!) earthshaking miracles convey the vital supernatural reality that, with the substitutionary sacrifice of Jesus, the separation between God and sinners has been removed, the wrath of God has been appeased, and God and sinners have been reconciled. Now, believers in Christ can enjoy a restored relationship with God and fellow human beings, as well as numerous other blessings.

If any doubt remains for the reader, the declaration of the Roman centurion and the soldiers overseeing Jesus's crucifixion brings the narrative to a climax: "Truly this was the Son of God!" (v. 54). This shows that, following Jesus's death, those closest to the scene—even unbelievers—recognized that this was no ordinary man. They also recognized that he didn't die an ordinary death. He was none other than God's very own Son, suffering not for his own sins but for those of others.

Jesus's Burial and the Posting of the Guard (27:57–66)

Following Jesus's death, his body is buried in a tomb owned by Joseph of Arimathea, a Sanhedrin member and secret disciple of Jesus. The tomb is sealed with a large stone, and Mary Magdalene, along with several other women, observes the burial. The next day, at the Jewish leaders' request, Pilate orders a cohort of Roman soldiers to guard the tomb in order to prevent Jesus's disciples from stealing his body and alleging that he has risen from the dead.

Resurrection Appearances and the Great Commission (28:1–20)

The Empty Tomb and Appearances of the Risen Jesus (28:1–15)

At dawn on the first day of the week—Sunday—the women return to the tomb. By the inclusive reckoning common in Jesus's day (counting both the first and the last day, Friday as well as Sunday), it has now been three days since Jesus was crucified. As the women arrive, a large earthquake shakes the ground, and an angel appears and rolls the stone away from the tomb. Fear grips the guards as they stand in motionless terror before the angel, who is dazzling in appearance.

The angel declares to the women, "Do not be afraid, for I know that you seek Jesus who was crucified. He is not here, for he has risen" (28:5–6).

He sends them to tell the disciples what has happened and to go to Galilee, where Jesus will meet them. As they run to do so, they encounter the risen Jesus. They fall to the ground and worship him.

Meanwhile, some of the soldiers assigned to guard Jesus's tomb report back to the chief priests what has happened. The Jewish leaders gather and decide to bribe the guards, urging them to give the false report that Jesus's disciples stole his body while they were sleeping. Matthew tells his readers that this fabricated story has spread among the Jews "to this day" (the time when he wrote his gospel; v. 15).

The Great Commission (28:16–20)

The final scene describes Jesus's promised appearance to his disciples in Galilee. Seeing the risen Jesus, many worship, though some doubt. At this, Jesus instructs his disciples to "go and make disciples of all nations," commissioning them to baptize these new disciples and teach them everything that he had commanded them (vv. 19–20). In so doing, his disciples are to rely on Jesus's continued presence to empower them.

The gospel ends on a high note—yet another mountain, on which the risen Jesus gives the believing Jewish remnant, his new messianic community, their mission: extend his rule to all the nations. Jesus had previously commissioned the Twelve to go, but "only to the lost sheep of the house of Israel" (15:24). Now, he tells his followers to go and make disciples of *all* the nations—including, but no longer limited to, Israel.

The good news of salvation and forgiveness in our crucified and risen Lord and Savior Jesus Christ has now become the gospel we preach around the globe. The new covenant Jesus has established with his new community has been ratified in his body and blood, given for *all* who believe that he is the savior who has come in fulfillment of countless scriptural predictions.

The conclusion of Matthew's gospel reminds us that neither the cross nor even the resurrection is the end of the story. The narrative ends with Jesus's commission to the believing community to extend the reach of God's kingdom to the farthest corners of the earth. This is the precious privilege granted to believers in the risen Messiah, a mandate that continues to be in effect until this very day.

DISCUSSION QUESTIONS

1. What do you think about Jesus's prohibition of divorce except for adultery in light of no-fault divorce in our culture?

2. As in the parable of the workers in the vineyard, have you experienced situations that were patently unfair? What was your response?

3. Why did Jesus cleanse the temple? Can you think of current examples of commercialism in the church?

4. Why was Jesus so hard on the Jewish religious leaders in his day? Is there still hypocrisy in the church today?

Hearing that Jesus had silenced the Sadducees, the Pharisees got together. One of them, an expert in the law, tested him with this question: "Teacher, which is the greatest commandment in the Law?"

Jesus replied: "'Love the Lord your God with all your heart and with all your soul and with all your mind.' This is the first and greatest commandment. And the second is like it: 'Love your neighbor as yourself.' All the Law and the Prophets hang on these two commandments."

—Matthew 22:34–40 NIV

So here is "an expert in the law" giving Jesus a test. Will Jesus pass the test? The exam question is this: "What is the greatest commandment in the Law?" Without a moment's hesitation, Jesus replies by quoting Deuteronomy 6:5: "Love the Lord your God with all your heart . . .". As a bonus, he adds a second passage, Leviticus 19:18: "Love your neighbor as yourself." Test passed with flying colors! These two commands, Jesus says, provide the foundation for "all the Law and the Prophets," that is, the entire Old Testament Scriptures. That's quite a statement! So, do we pass the test? Do we love God with all our hearts, and do we love our neighbor as ourselves?

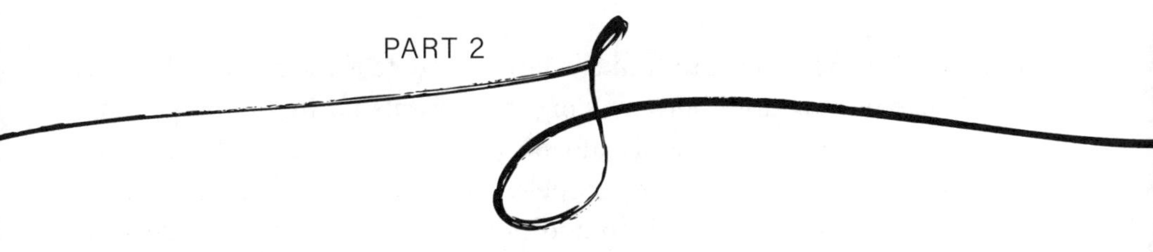

PART 2

THE GOSPEL ACCORDING TO MARK: JESUS, THE MIGHTY SON OF GOD

WHO WAS MARK?

Mark is the John Mark mentioned in the book of Acts, who accompanies Paul and Barnabas on their first missionary journey but deserts them for some unknown reason in order to return home (Acts 12:25; 13:13). He later becomes a bone of contention when Barnabas, his cousin, wants to give him another chance and take him on their second missionary journey but Paul refuses, choosing Timothy and Silas instead (15:37–40). Years later, however, Mark's name resurfaces in the company of the apostle Peter (1 Peter 5:13). Paul too had use for Mark's services again toward the end of his ministry (Col. 4:10; 2 Tim. 4:11; Philem. 24). Thus, Mark, like Peter, was well acquainted with discipleship failure, which may explain why this is a pronounced emphasis in his gospel. On a personal level, Mark had a devout mother (Acts 12:12) and a cousin, Barnabas, who was committed to him, which would have been vital in times of failure and discouragement. Mark may make a cameo appearance in his own gospel as the young man who flees naked (or in his underwear) at Jesus's arrest (Mark 14:51–52).

WHAT IS DISTINCTIVE ABOUT MARK'S GOSPEL?

The gospel of Mark is the shortest of the four gospels, and most of his material is also found in the other Synoptic Gospels, Matthew and Luke. Mark's gospel begins with a remarkable swiftness of movement and a tremendous sense of urgency, highlighted by the frequent use of the word "immediately." Unlike Matthew and Luke, Mark omits any mention of Jesus's birth and infancy, immediately diving into an account of his public ministry. Like Matthew and Luke, Mark largely tells the story of Jesus by depicting the geographic progression of his ministry. In so doing, Mark emphasizes Jesus's actions, especially his miracles, over some of the longer discourses we find in the other gospels. He expresses Jesus's character in vivid style and graphic detail. In addition, Mark occasionally orders the events of Jesus's life and ministry topically to highlight important themes. He also utilizes several other literary techniques, such as irony, patterns of three, and "sandwiching," which refers to placing one event in between another to provide a framework for interpretation.

In terms of literary structure, Mark's blueprint is similar to Matthew's. The first half of the gospel chronicles Jesus's ministry in Galilee and focuses on his authority as the miracle-working Son of God. Following Peter's confession of Jesus, Mark, similar to Matthew, turns to Jesus's journey to Jerusalem and his impending sacrificial death on the cross (Mark 8:29). In the remainder of the gospel, the meaning of Jesus's suffering and death becomes the focal point of the narrative and shapes the account. Bearing Mark's focus on the cross in mind, he was likely writing to believers in Rome who needed assurance and encouragement in view of their own suffering. In many ways, Mark's gospel can therefore be viewed as a defense of the necessity of the cross, answering the question "Why was Jesus crucified?"

WHAT ARE SOME OF MARK'S MAJOR EMPHASES?

First and foremost, Mark demonstrates that Jesus Christ is the authoritative, miracle-working Son of God. Throughout the gospel, he refers to Jesus as the Son of God in strategic places, structuring each section of the narrative around this theme. Correspondingly, Mark introduces his gospel with "Jesus Christ, the Son of God" (1:1), and he concludes with the Roman centurion's climactic confession, "Truly this man was the Son of God!" (15:39). And yet Jesus's identity is not clear to all throughout the course of his earthly mission, which leads to another distinctive of Mark's gospel.

Upon reading Mark's gospel, you'll notice how Jesus repeatedly commands people to keep silent about his identity. In fact, Mark records Jesus's commands to silence more frequently than any other evangelist. At first, the secrecy surrounding Jesus's identity may seem odd: Why would Jesus not want people to know that he's the Messiah? As the narrative unfolds, however, Jesus's purpose emerges with greater clarity. He is refining, even correcting, Israel's expectations of the Messiah, their long-awaited king. He isn't going to be a powerful national deliverer but a suffering savior.

As the narrative works its way closer to the cross, therefore, Mark zooms in on Jesus's identity as the Old Testament Servant of the Lord (Isa. 52:13–53:12). In line with Isaiah's prediction, Jesus has come as God's Servant "to give his life as a ransom for many" (Mark 10:45). "Ransom" means that Jesus won't die for his own sins but for those of others. However, no one will take his life by force; he will give it willingly, knowing that according to God's plan there is no other way for us to be saved. The price of redemption must be paid, and Jesus must give his life as a sacrifice and shed his blood for others.

Finally, in view of Jesus's vicarious suffering, Mark also paints a portrait of discipleship. As the narrative progresses, Mark distinctively highlights the frequent failures and misunderstandings of Jesus's earthly followers. Specifically, they fail to understand that the very purpose of Jesus's mission is for him to suffer and die for sinners. In light of this, contrary to what they think, the nature of true discipleship involves following Jesus in the way of the cross (8:34). The path to glory inexorably leads through suffering—not only for Jesus but for his followers as well.

CHAPTER 5—MARK

THE MESSIAH AND SON OF GOD

JESUS, THE MESSIAH AND SON OF GOD (1:1–8:26)
The Beginning of the Gospel of Jesus Christ (1:1–13)
Initial Ministry in Galilee: Calling the First Disciples, Healing Many (1:14–3:6)
Later Ministry in Galilee: Calling the Twelve, Rejected in Nazareth (3:7–6:6a)
Ministry Beyond Galilee: More Healings, Denouncing the Pharisees (6:6b–8:26)

JESUS, THE MESSIAH AND SON OF GOD (1:1–8:26)

What would you think of a doctor who never took on any patients? You would likely question whether that person was actually a doctor, or at least think they were very bad at their job. *Being* something implies *doing* something. You can't be a doctor and not do what a doctor does. In the same way, Jesus's being the Son of God, the Messiah, implies that he did the things the Messiah does. Mark's gospel brings this out very well. Even though Mark's introduction of Jesus is very brief, Mark goes on to highlight the actions of Jesus, and it is in these actions that we see who Jesus is—not so much by being told who he is but by being shown who he is by what he does. So who does Mark say Jesus is?

The answer, in short, is twofold. First, Jesus is the miracle-working Messiah and Son of God. Second, Jesus is the suffering Servant featured in the Old Testament book of Isaiah, who gives his life as a sacrificial offering—a ransom, as Mark calls it (Mark 10:45)—for God's people. Accordingly, Mark's gospel divides neatly and symmetrically into two halves of roughly equal length. In the first half, we see Jesus launch his ministry in the Galilean north and move gradually further north in three ministry cycles. Jesus's message of the coming of God's kingdom is ever-expanding. The pivotal event, as we'll see, is Peter's confession of Jesus as "the Christ" (8:29). After this, Jesus talks freely about his impending suffering on behalf of his people.

The Beginning of the Gospel of Jesus Christ (1:1–13)

Mark deftly covers all preliminaries in a short thirteen verses. He starts his gospel with the headline "The beginning of the gospel of Jesus Christ, the Son of God" (1:1). Unlike the other Synoptic Gospels, Mark doesn't include a genealogy or infancy narrative of Jesus. Rather, he starts at "the beginning," which Mark identifies as the appearance and baptizing ministry of Jesus's forerunner, John the Baptist, whose role is to make formal announcement of the Messiah's imminent arrival. In characterizing the role of John the Baptist, Mark ties together three interrelated Old Testament passages:

- Exodus 23:20a ("I send an angel before you")
- Isaiah 40:3 ("A voice cries: 'In the wilderness'")
- Malachi 3:1 ("Behold, I send my messenger, and he will prepare the way before me")

As Mark makes clear, John the Baptist is both a "voice" and God's "messenger," who appears in the wilderness to herald the Messiah's launch of a new exodus. John is depicted as a new Elijah, a powerful prophet proclaiming God's mighty work of deliverance, whose mission is to prepare people's hearts by calling them to repentance. John's success is evident in that "all the country of Judea and all Jerusalem" are coming to hear and be baptized by him (Mark 1:5). At this, Jesus, too, comes and is baptized by John. The Spirit descends on Jesus, and a heavenly voice attests to him as God's beloved Son. After this, Jesus is tempted by the devil in the wilderness.

Initial Ministry in Galilee: Calling the First Disciples, Healing Many (1:14–3:6)

The Beginning of Jesus's Ministry (1:14–20)

Jesus launches his public ministry by "proclaiming the gospel of God" (v. 14). The expression "gospel *of God*" is striking; the gospel isn't merely a human message—it's the message of God! Mark sums up Jesus's message about God's kingdom as follows: "The time is fulfilled, and the kingdom of God is at hand; repent and believe in the gospel" (v. 15). Since Jesus has come to usher in God's kingdom, people must respond by searching their hearts and coming clean of their sins. They must repent and believe in his message, which implies they must also believe in him—the Messiah and Son of God.

The opening two verses of this section thus perfectly encapsulate Jesus's ministry and message by bringing the reader back to the way Mark's gospel started: "The beginning of the gospel of Jesus Christ." This gospel—the gospel of God—we're now told Jesus has come to proclaim by making formal, public announcement that in him God's kingdom is near, in keeping with God's promises in the past. This good news demands a response; those who hear Jesus's message are called to repent and believe.

From here on out, Mark narrates the launch of Jesus's public ministry in rapid motion. First, Jesus calls his initial disciples—Simon and Andrew, then James and John, all fishermen. Jesus's call is this: "Follow me, and I will make you become fishers of men" (v. 17). The background of this phrase is found in the Old Testament, where it is used in the context of judgment (cf. Jer. 16:16; Ezek. 29:4–5; 38:4; Amos 4:2; Hab. 1:14–17). Jesus, however, uses this image as one of salvation; to "fish" for people is to rescue them from sin and to call them into God's kingdom.

Power over Demons and Sickness (1:21–34)

Jesus's first act after calling his first disciples is a demon exorcism. They're still on the shores of the Sea of Galilee where Jesus had called his first disciples. There, they enter the synagogue in Capernaum, where Jesus is teaching on the Sabbath as Jews are gathered for worship and instruction in the Scriptures. Mark notes that people there "were astonished at his teaching, for he taught them as one who had authority, and not as the scribes" (Mark 1:22). The difference between Jesus's teaching and that of the other Jewish teachers or scribes was that the scribes merely handed down traditions, while Jesus taught with true spiritual authority.

With the phrase "and immediately" (v. 23), Mark swiftly moves on from Jesus's authoritative teaching to his miracle-working activity. Amazingly, there is a demon-possessed man right there in the Jewish synagogue in Capernaum! It's still the Sabbath, though; unlike at other occasions, Jesus is not given grief by his opponents for breaking the Sabbath. When the man addresses Jesus, it's not actually the man who is speaking but an unclean spirit inside of him, using a plural self-reference. Remarkably, the demons know Jesus's human name and origin ("Jesus of Nazareth") and his divine calling ("the Holy One of God"). They also indicate that they and Jesus have vastly conflicting interests ("What have you to do with us?") and that they are afraid Jesus has come to destroy them (v. 24). In response, Jesus tersely tells them to be quiet and commands them to leave the man—and they comply, with a loud shriek! Mark's summary is to the point: not only does Jesus convey "a new teaching with authority"; he also exerts authority over unclean spirits (v. 27). Thus, Jesus's deeds back up and validate his teaching. He is the messianic Son of God in both word and deed. His reputation immediately spreads like wildfire in the surrounding regions of Galilee.

Immediately again, Jesus leaves the synagogue at Capernaum, apparently still on the Sabbath, and together with James and John enters the home of Simon and Andrew. Simon's mother-in-law is lying in bed with a fever, and immediately they tell Jesus. Jesus promptly heals her, and she begins serving them. This shows that Jesus isn't merely performing miracles to get public attention; here, he heals a disciple's mother in a more private setting.

Later, at sundown—meaning that it is no longer the Sabbath—people bring to him numerous sick or demon-possessed individuals. Mark notes that "the whole city" is gathered outside Peter's house (v. 33). Jesus heals "many" more who are sick and casts out "many" more demons, though again he tells the demons not to divulge his messianic identity (v. 34). Jesus steadfastly insists that the demons not reveal his identity; he doesn't need citizens of the evil supernatural realm to proclaim he's the Messiah.

Prayer, Preaching, and the Healing of a Leper (1:35–45)

The next vignette tells us of a day in Jesus's ministry when he gets up early in the morning "while it was still dark" and goes to a remote place to pray (v. 35). Simon "and those who were with him" track him down and tell him that "everyone" is looking for him (vv. 36–37). He says that he must go "to the next towns" to preach there as well (v. 38). His purpose is to make large-scale proclamation of God's kingdom all over, rather than to proclaim it to a single people group in one location. And so he goes "throughout all Galilee," engaging in his customary twofold activity of preaching and casting out demons (v. 39).

Next, Jesus is approached by a leper who kneels down in front of him and begs him to make him clean. Jesus is moved with compassion and grants the man's request. Immediately, the leprosy leaves the man. Jesus sternly charges him not to divulge the healing to anyone but to go through the proper cleansing rituals with the local priest, "for a proof to them" (v. 44). The man, however, ignores Jesus's stern charge. He's just been healed of leprosy and wants everyone to know about it! As a result, Jesus has to withdraw to remote places, but people still track him down from everywhere.

Five Controversial Encounters (2:1–3:6)

In the next chapter, Jesus continues his healing ministry, which sparks a series of five controversial encounters with the Jewish leaders.

Healing a Paralytic (2:1–12). First, he performs an amazing healing upon his return to Capernaum, where he had cast out a demon in the synagogue on a Sabbath. Word quickly spreads that Jesus is "at home," and there is standing room only as Jesus speaks "the word" to the people there (2:2). Four men, carrying a paralyzed man on his mat (a primitive bed), can't get to Jesus because of the large crowd. Undeterred, they remove the roof above him and lower their friend through the opening right above Jesus. Seeing their faith, Jesus declares to the paralytic, "Your sins are forgiven" (v. 5).

The scribes who are policing Jesus, carefully watching his every move, rightly infer that by claiming to be able to forgive sins, Jesus stakes an implicit claim to deity. They think to themselves, "He is blaspheming! Who can forgive sins but God alone?" (v. 7). At once, Jesus perceives what they're thinking and proceeds to engage them. Ironically, even as the scribes question Jesus's claim to divine authority, he knows what's on their minds, displaying supernatural knowledge. In rabbinic style, Jesus responds to the scribes by arguing from the lesser to the greater: "Which is easier, to say. . . 'Your sins are forgiven,' or to say, 'Rise, take up your bed and walk?'" (v. 9). The implied answer, of course, is the former. Anyone can say, "Your sins are forgiven." But not everyone can actually heal a paralyzed man! So Jesus commands the man, "Rise, pick up your bed, and go home" (v. 11).

Immediately, the man gets up, picks up his bed, and walks off, so that all are "amazed and glorif[y] God" (v. 12). Jesus has performed this amazing healing so that people "may know that the Son of Man has authority on earth to forgive sins" (v. 10)—an astonishing claim to deity—and Jesus backs it up with action! This is only chapter 2 in the gospel, and Jesus has already staked a strong claim to deity, backed up with action. What will he do next? The reader can't help but agree with the crowd: "We never saw anything like this!" (v. 12).

The Calling of Levi (2:13–17). In the next scene, Jesus continues to generate controversy through his choice of disciples. He has already called four fishermen to follow him (1:16–20). Now, he approaches Levi, a tax collector (also called Matthew), and calls him to follow, and he does. At this, Jesus dines with him in his home, which provokes the indignation of the scribes, who ask his disciples, "Why does he eat with tax collectors and sinners?" (2:16). (Tax collectors were Jews who collected taxes for the hated Romans, which made them extremely unpopular.) Jesus's response to the scribes is pointed: "I came not to call the righteous, but sinners" (v. 17). Jesus continues to amaze by his choice of followers: first he calls simple fishermen, and now a hated tax collector. The Pharisees respond with scathing disapproval. Yet Jesus insists that only those who humbly receive his message are fit to enter God's kingdom.

To Fast or Not to Fast? (2:18–22). The third controversy surrounds the issue of fasting. People observe that both the disciples of John the Baptist and the Pharisees fast, but Jesus's disciples do not. Why don't they? Do they lack piety? Jesus responds with three sets of analogies. First, do wedding guests fast while the bridegroom is with them? Second, do people put a patch of new cloth on an old garment? Third and finally, do people put new wine into old wineskins? In each case, the answer is no.

Jesus's point is that he is inaugurating a new stage of salvation history. The messianic bridegroom has arrived, people need a new garment, and new wine must be put into fresh containers. Jesus hasn't come merely to reform the Pharisaic system. His mission is to establish God's kingdom on earth. Even today, we often don't sufficiently appreciate the revolutionary character of Jesus's mission and the radical nature of his call to follow him.

Eating Grain on the Sabbath (2:23–28). The last two controversies center on the interpretation of Jewish law, specifically regarding the Sabbath. In the first instance, the Pharisees accuse Jesus's disciples of working on the

Sabbath when plucking heads of grain. In fact, the way the Pharisees see it, Jesus's disciples' disregard for what is "lawful" on the Sabbath makes Jesus himself a Sabbath-breaker. Why doesn't he properly instruct his followers? In response, Jesus pointedly questions the Pharisees' understanding by citing an example from the life of King David (cf. 1 Sam. 21:1–6). While it could be said that David and his men technically broke the law by eating the sacred bread, they didn't violate the *spirit* of the law. As Jesus puts it, "The Sabbath was made for man, not man for the Sabbath" (Mark 2:27). What's more, "the Son of Man is lord even of the Sabbath" (v. 28).

Healing on the Sabbath (3:1–6). On another occasion, Jesus enters the synagogue on the Sabbath and encounters a man with a withered hand. Again, the Pharisees closely watch to see if Jesus will heal the man on the Sabbath. Jesus probingly asks, "Is it lawful on the Sabbath to do good or to do harm, to save life or to kill?" (3:4). Grieved by the hardness of their hearts, but not deterred, he heals the man.

The Pharisees promptly start plotting "with the Herodians against him, how to destroy him" (v. 6). You might legitimately wonder who it is who truly breaks the Sabbath. These two episodes strike a climactic note in Jesus's early ministry in Galilee. He has proven his divine authority and messianic identity through his powerful deeds and masterful exposition of the law, even as the religious leaders scoff at his claims.

Later Ministry in Galilee: Calling the Twelve, Rejected in Nazareth (3:7–6:6a)

Choosing the Twelve and Opposition from Family (3:7–35)

Mass Appeal and the Messianic Secret (3:7–12). After a series of controversies with the increasingly hostile Jewish leaders, Jesus begins a new phase of ministry in Galilee. Mark begins this section by summarizing Jesus's powerful activity and highlighting his growing popularity. Jesus even has to instruct his disciples to have a boat ready for him because of the large size of the crowd, "lest they crush him" (v. 9). All who need healing press around him to touch him, and all the demons cry out, "You are the Son of God" (v. 11). Once again, he strongly rebukes those spirits and tells them not to reveal who he is.

This stage of Jesus's ministry is characterized by a mounting degree of polarization. Increasingly, what emerges is a sharp spiritual division between "insiders" and "outsiders." On the one hand, Jesus appoints the Twelve and sends them out on mission; they are the chosen remnant, who are given the inside scoop of his messianic mission and message. On the other side are the Jewish leaders who intensify their efforts to oppose him and make his life difficult at every turn. In addition, even some in Jesus's own family and hometown reject his authority.

The key questions Mark wants his readers to ponder, therefore, are "Who is Jesus?" and "Where do you stand in relation to Jesus—are you for him or against him?" This is one case where choosing sides is absolutely essential.

Calling the Twelve Apostles (3:13–19). At this strategic juncture in his ministry, Jesus ascends a mountain and appoints twelve apostles (or "messengers") for the purpose of being with him, of being sent out to preach, and of being given authority to exorcise demons. The number twelve is designed to establish a connection with the twelve tribes of Israel, designating the twelve apostles as the new messianic community. While many of the individual apostles play a limited role in the rest of the gospel, corporately the Twelve represent a believing remnant of Israel. Thus, their appointment signals a critical development in Mark's narrative, as they will constantly be with Jesus, learning from him and participating in his mission. While plagued by persistent failure and misunderstanding and struggling to fully comprehend his identity and mission, they're given special insight into Jesus's teaching and are apprenticed to continue his mission. With the Twelve in place, Mark draws the lines of division more sharply in the controversies that ensue.

Opposition from Jesus's Own Family and Blasphemy Against the Holy Spirit (3:20–35). Upon hearing of his growing ministry, Jesus's family tries to "seize him," having concluded, "He is out of his mind" (v. 21). Presumably, they were in Nazareth when they heard the news of Jesus's growing ministry and the increasing scrutiny and opposition he faced. In response, they set out to seize or restrain him. Jesus is now facing opposition from multiple sides. To compound the situation, a group of scribes from Jerusalem arrive and accuse Jesus of being demon-possessed. This is a serious charge meant to undercut his authority. Ironically, both Jesus's family and the scribes allege that Jesus has gone off the rails.

In response, Jesus no longer speaks to people in plain language but only in parables (i.e., stories invented by Jesus to drive home important spiritual truths). In this way, he draws a sharp line between insiders and outsiders in God's kingdom. The point of the ensuing parables is that through his exorcisms, Jesus has begun to invade Satan's domain. For Jesus to cast out demons, he first needs to overcome Satan. There's no way he can cast out demons by the power of Satan, for "if a kingdom is divided against itself, that kingdom cannot stand" (v. 24). Thus, all other sins people commit can be forgiven, but blasphemy against the Holy Spirit—attributing the power of Jesus to Satan—constitutes an unforgiveable "eternal sin" (v. 29).

The scene closes with another reference to Jesus's mother and brothers calling for him. Again, Jesus's response is pointed and powerful: "For whoever does the will of God, he is my brother and sister and mother" (v. 35).

Parables of the Kingdom (4:1–34)

The Parable of the Sower (4:1–20). Chapter 4 consists largely of Jesus's teaching in the form of parables. The parable of the sower, which takes up the lion's share of this unit, is of strategic importance, as it illustrates the various responses to Jesus's message about God's kingdom. By now, Jesus's disciples are probably wondering why—if Jesus is in fact the Messiah, as they've come to believe—some receive him, while many (if not most) others reject him. Jesus tells the parable of the sower to answer this question. There are several reasons why people might not be open to Jesus and his message, despite the fact that he is the Messiah and his message is true. All of these reasons are rooted in people's sinful hearts, in conjunction with the world in which they live, which is full of distractions, temptations, and persecutions.

Jesus proceeds to explain the parable:

- The sower is God (or Jesus).
- The seed is God's word—Jesus's message about the kingdom—sown generously.
- The first type of soil, the area along the *path*, resembles the hardened heart, while the birds represent Satan, who immediately snatches away the truth conveyed by Jesus's teaching.
- The second type of soil, the *rocky ground*, symbolizes a heart that immediately receives the message about the kingdom with joy but, when persecution comes, immediately falls away. This heart immediately receives the word but then immediately rejects it. There is only a surface response that is, sadly, short lived.

- The third type of soil is the *thorny patch*, symbolizing hearts in which a preoccupation with material possessions suffocates the word so that it proves unfruitful. While there may be a variety of reasons why God's word fails to take permanent root in a person's heart, the first three types of soil all represent hearts that are unregenerate.
- The fourth type of soil, *good soil*, represents the receptive human heart that bears various multiples of fruit—thirty, sixty, or even a hundredfold.

Two Sayings and Two More Parables (4:21–34). Jesus continues his teaching with two sayings and two additional parables. The two sayings extend Jesus's teaching in the parable of the sower. First, Jesus asks, "Is a lamp brought in to be put under a basket, or under a bed, and not on a stand?" (v. 21). The light of God's truth has been revealed, and its recipients must respond accordingly; a lamp's purpose is to shine and give light to others. Second, he says, "Pay attention to what you hear: with the measure you use, it will be measured to you" (v. 24). We must generously share with others what God has given to us, as the measure by which we give will be the measure God uses to give to us. Thus, those who already have will receive even more, while those who don't have will lose even the little they have. This too is a spiritual law revealed by Jesus that may not seem fair to us but reflects the way things work in God's kingdom.

The two ensuing parables describe the nature of the kingdom. In the parable of the *seed growing* (unique to Mark's gospel), a man scatters seed onto the ground. He goes to sleep while the ground produces grain, until it is ripe for harvest. In the parable of the *mustard seed*, a tiny mustard seed is sown, resulting in a plant so large that birds can nest in the shade of its large foliage. The parables illustrate two other facets of God's kingdom. While starting out small, the kingdom will grow gradually but steadily (as depicted in the parable of the mustard seed), not by human effort but by the mysterious inner dynamics of God's spiritual truth doing its work and bearing fruit (as portrayed in the parable of the seed growing).

Both the sayings and the parables highlight the spiritual hiddenness of God's kingdom. The kingdom has been inaugurated in unexpected ways. Many Jews expected God to establish his rule by overthrowing the Romans. But Jesus has come preaching the good news, healing the sick, and casting out demons. God's work is like a tiny mustard seed that will eventually grow to exceed all the other plants in size. How different from the way a mere human would go about launching a new movement! The section concludes by reiterating the clear line of demarcation between kingdom insiders and outsiders. To outsiders, Jesus "did not speak . . . without a parable"; to insiders, he "explained everything" (v. 34).

The Fourfold Scope of Jesus's Authority (4:35–5:43)

After his account of Jesus's teaching, Mark returns to the theme of Jesus's authority. In a series of miracles, Jesus demonstrates the vast range of his messianic authority over

- the forces of nature (4:35–41),
- demonic spirits (5:1–20),
- chronic disease (5:25–34), and
- even death (5:21–24, 35–43).

Calming the Storm (4:35–41). The calming of the storm is one of the most famous miracles Jesus performs. While he and the disciples are crossing the Sea of Galilee in a boat, a violent storm arises and waves break into the boat. Jesus, exhausted from a long day of ministry, is in the stern of the boat, asleep on a cushion. The disciples wake him up, chiding him, "Teacher, do you not care that we are perishing?" (4:38). At this, Jesus wakes up, "rebukes" the wind as one might an unruly child, and tells the sea to be quiet—and the storm obliges! Instead of the fear-inspiring torrent, "there [is] a great calm" (v. 39). Jesus looks at the dumbfounded disciples and says, "Why are you so afraid? Have you still no faith?" (v. 40). By now, they should know who he is—they don't need to be afraid when a storm arises because he, the Son of God, is with them.

Healing the Gerasene Demoniac (5:1–20). Crossing over to "the other side" of the Sea of Galilee with his disciples, Jesus has barely stepped out of the boat when he is met by a man with an unclean spirit who emerges, forebodingly, "out of the tombs" (5:2). The man clearly is demon-possessed, displays self-destructive tendencies, and can't be subdued by anyone. Like a magnet, Jesus seems to attract demonic attention wherever he goes. The account bears testimony to the incredible power Jesus wields over the spirit world; even an entire horde of demons is no match for him.

The fact that the man is possessed by multiple demons poses no problem for Jesus. He casts them out and sends them into a herd of pigs feeding on a nearby hillside. When the herdsmen see them drowned in the Sea of Galilee, they "beg Jesus to depart from their region" (v. 17). The healed man, for his part, begs Jesus to take him along, but Jesus tells him instead to go home and spread the news among his friends. The man promptly proclaims all over the Decapolis—the area southeast of the Sea of Galilee and east of the Jordan River—what Jesus has done for him.

Raising Jairus's Daughter and Healing a Woman with Blood Flow (5:21–43). What can top calming a violent storm on the Sea of Galilee, followed by exorcisms of an entire horde of demons from a violent man in Gentile territory? How about raising a twelve-year-old girl from the dead? And if that weren't enough, sandwiched in between is Jesus's encounter with a woman with blood flow, whom he heals on his way to the girl's parents' house.

The raising of the synagogue ruler Jairus's daughter is one of only three raisings from the dead recorded in the Gospels, and shows Jesus's tender compassion for a father who has lost his beloved child. Still, Jesus is cautious about revealing his identity; he simply tells people to give the raised girl something to eat. This understated response shows that Jesus's focus is not on the miracle itself but on God's kindness.

Rejected in Nazareth (6:1–6a)

Jesus is back in his hometown synagogue in Capernaum, where he teaches on the Sabbath. People marvel at the depth of his understanding and his "mighty works" (6:2). They wonder, "Is not this the carpenter, the son of Mary and brother of James and Joses and Judas and Simon? And are not his sisters here with us?" They also take "offense" at him (v. 3). How could the Jesus they know be the messianic Son of God?

At this, Jesus coins the well-known saying "A prophet is not without honor, except in his hometown and among his relatives and in his own household" (v. 4). Thus, he stands in the tradition of the prophets, who were rejected throughout Israel's history (cf. 1 Kings 19:10; 2 Chron. 36:16; Jer. 11:2; 12:6). For this reason, Jesus "could do no mighty work there," except for healing a few sick people (Mark 6:5).

Now it is Jesus's turn to "marvel"—at people's unbelief. He couldn't see why people wouldn't believe in him! The primary purpose of Jesus's miracles is not to wow people with his amazing powers but to lead them to faith in him. Yet here we see the opposite dynamic: no faith, no miracles. And so Jesus goes off to teach in the adjacent villages.

Ministry Beyond Galilee: More Healings, Denouncing the Pharisees (6:6b–8:26)

Sending Out the Twelve (6:6b–13)

Jesus now expands his ministry beyond Galilee, drawing crowds from all over the region. First, he summons the Twelve. He commissions them in pairs and delegates to them authority over unclean spirits, instructing his followers to take only minimal supplies and to accept the hospitality of receptive individuals, while pronouncing God's judgment on those who reject them. The disciples go on their way, casting out many demons and healing many sick people.

As Mark makes clear, the missions of Jesus and his disciples are both linked to John the Baptist. Jesus's mission began after John's imprisonment, while that of his followers commences as John is executed. This ominously forecasts that Jesus's disciples, following in Jesus's footsteps, will preach the gospel and engage in ministry in a hostile world, where many will reject them and where the message won't be welcomed.

Flashback: Execution of John the Baptist (6:14–29)

The account of John's execution—a flashback—foreshadows Jesus's journey to Jerusalem. Even Herod Antipas, a Gentile ruler, knows John to be a "righteous and holy man" (v. 20), yet he executes him in deference to his wife, who has held a grudge against John because he has courageously denounced her illegitimate marriage to Herod, as she had previously been the wife of his brother Philip.

The story of John's beheading is placed between the commissioning of the Twelve (vv. 7–13) and their return (v. 30). The disciples have gone out, preaching the good news, driving out demons, and healing the sick. But the news of John's fate is a sober lesson on the cost of true discipleship. John had suffered a gruesome death—not because he had done anything wrong, but because he had completed his mission from God.

Feeding the Five Thousand (6:30–44)

After the disciples return from their mission, Jesus takes them away to get some rest. But even as they depart in a boat to a "desolate place" (v. 32), many see where they're headed, and a great crowd forms on the shore. Rather than sending people away, Jesus has "compassion on them, because they were like sheep without a shepherd" (v. 34; cf. Num. 27:16–17). The allusion to the leadership transition from Moses to Joshua indicates Mark's understanding that Jesus is the new Joshua who would bring about a new exodus by leading God's people into the Promised Land.

Jesus's care for the people is also reminiscent of Psalm 23:1, which says, "The LORD is my shepherd." Jesus is the Good Shepherd who cares for God's flock. Five thousand men, plus women and children, are fed that day, as Jesus multiplies five loaves of bread and two fish, and twelve baskets are left over. And yet the disciples, who had just recently been told to take no bread on their journey, struggle to grasp the true significance of Jesus's actions, initially telling Jesus to send the people away to buy food.

Walking on Water and Expansive Work (6:45–56)

In the next scene, Jesus dismisses the crowd and sends his disciples by boat to Bethsaida while he prays on a mountain. The scene recalls Jesus's earlier calming of a storm. Once again, the disciples face a strong wind on the lake, though this time Jesus has stayed behind on the shore, praying well into the night. Very early in morning, Jesus comes to them, "walking on the sea" (Mark 6:48). By treading the waves, he performs an act that God alone can perform. What's more, walking on water, "he meant to pass by them" (v. 48)—the language of Old Testament epiphanies (e.g., Exod. 33:22). However, the disciples fail to grasp this and react in fear; yet Jesus identifies himself in divine terms: "It is I" (i.e., "I am"; v. 50; cf. Exod. 3:14). Their failure compounds as they also "did not understand about the loaves" because their hearts were "hardened" (Mark 6:52). The disciples and Mark's readers are left with a deep sense of awe-filled mystery.

What Truly Defiles a Person (7:1–23)

The unit opens with a controversy between Jesus and the Jewish leaders, including Pharisees and some of the scribes, who resurface after a prolonged absence from the Markan narrative. The dispute revolves around what appears to be a rather petty issue of ritual purity. As guardians of their tradition, the Pharisees and scribes scrutinize Jesus's disciples who, they allege, "[eat] with hands that [are] defiled, that is, unwashed" (7:2). In a lengthy aside, Mark informs the reader that this is part of what might be described as the scribes' obsession with washings and purification rituals, extending even to objects such as cups, pots, copper vessels, and dining couches. These myopic concerns stand in marked contrast to

Jesus's amazing miracles, such as his healings, demon exorcisms, and feeding of the multitudes.

When approached with these allegations against his disciples, Jesus denounces his opponents for their hypocrisy and for elevating their tradition above God's word: "Well did Isaiah prophesy of you hypocrites . . . 'This people honors me with their lips, but their heart is far from me; in vain do they worship me, teaching as doctrines the commandments of men'" (vv. 6–7; cf. Isa. 29:13). With biting irony, Jesus goes on the counteroffensive: "You have a fine way of rejecting the commandment of God in order to establish your tradition!" (Mark 7:9). He proceeds to cite the policy of *corban*, in which the Pharisees declare a given item "dedicated to God" in order to circumvent the command to honor their father and mother. Jesus adds that they have done many similar things.

In this way, Jesus rejects the Pharisees' entire approach to God's law, which involves focusing on minor details while neglecting "the weightier matters of the law" (Matt. 23:23). In a follow-up session with the common people and his disciples, when asked by the latter about the meaning of the illustration, Jesus notes, "What comes out of a person is what defiles him" (v. 20). God's law deals with matters of the heart. Jesus, Mark notes in an important aside, therefore declares all foods clean. This prepares the reader for what comes next.

Faith of a Gentile Woman (7:24–30)

Up to this point, the primary context of Jesus's ministry has been Jewish. However, following Jesus's indictment of the Pharisees, Jesus will engage in frequent withdrawals from Galilee. In the next episode, he travels to the region of Tyre. There, Jesus encounters a Syrophoenician or Canaanite woman—a Gentile—who pleads with Jesus to cast out a demon from her daughter. Jesus's response is shocking at first glance, as he refers to Israel as "children" while calling Gentiles "dogs" (v. 27). A closer look at the context, however, reveals that Jesus is speaking about the order of God's plan of salvation.

The priority of Jesus's mission is to the Jews first, who are called to be a light of revelation to the Gentiles (cf. Isa. 42:6; 49:6). What's more, Jesus seems to use provocative language to arouse the woman's persistence. Without challenging Jesus's statement, she responds with remarkable humility and faith. Impressed by her reply, Jesus grants her request and casts out the demon, even from a distance. Having already declared all foods clean, Jesus now breaks through the Jewish-Gentile barrier. In fact, this Gentile woman is the first character to recognize the universal scope of God's salvation of Jesus's work in Mark's gospel, serving as a model disciple.

Healing a Deaf Man (7:31–37)

Following this important episode, Mark records the second of three miracles performed in Gentile territory. Jesus continues his journey and reaches the city of Decapolis. There, he encounters a deaf man (who also has a speech impediment) and heals him. Mark here reproduces the very words of Jesus in Aramaic: *Ephphatha*, "Be opened" (v. 34). The reaction to this latest of Jesus's miracles is similar to previous responses. The more Jesus tells people to be quiet, the more they spread the news of his miracle-working powers. Everyone is astonished and recognizes that Jesus is doing the things that Old Testament prophets predicted the Messiah would do (cf. Isa. 35:5).

Feeding the Four Thousand (8:1–10)

The next miracle in this section is the feeding of the four thousand. Again, Jesus, the messianic Shepherd, is moved with compassion for the people who have been with him for three days. He even expresses concern that if he were to send them away hungry, some may faint on their way home, as many have come from quite a distance. Undeterred by his disciples, who point out the impracticality of procuring bread for all these people in a remote location, Jesus feeds the crowd by multiplying seven loaves and a few fish. Even after all have eaten, seven basketfuls are left over.

While this miracle resembles the first miracle of feeding the five thousand, some of the details differ; also, this second miraculous feeding takes place in Gentile territory. The openness of Gentiles stands in marked contrast to the intransigence of the Jews, at times including even the disciples.

Pharisees' Demand of a Sign (8:11–13)

This contrast emerges even more clearly in the next scene, which takes place in the district of Dalmanutha, on the west side of the Sea of Galilee near Magdala. There, in the final conflict episode during Jesus's Galilean ministry, the Pharisees approach him and demand "a sign from heaven" to test him (Mark 8:11). Jesus sighs at their unbelief and refuses to comply.

Warning Against the "Leaven" of the Pharisees and Herod (8:14–21)

What follows is the third and final boat episode in this unit. The scene quickly turns to the disciples, whom Jesus warns to "beware of the leaven of the Pharisees and the leaven of Herod" (v. 15). In another instance of misunderstanding, the disciples think Jesus is chiding them for their failure to bring bread, when in fact he is referring to the corrupting influence of Pharisaic teaching.

Healing a Blind Man (8:22–26)

At the end of their journey, Jesus and his disciples encounter a blind man in Bethsaida, located on the north side of the Sea of Galilee. Jesus proceeds to heal the man, fulfilling Isaiah's prophecy that at the coming of the Messiah, "the eyes of the blind shall be opened" (Isa. 35:5). What's most intriguing about this episode is the gradual nature of the healing. At first, the man sees only faintly. Then, when Jesus lays hands on him again, "his sight [is] restored, and he [sees] everything clearly" (Mark 8:25). This two-stage healing may function as an "acted parable" for the disciples' spiritual understanding, which similarly emerges in stages and over time.

DISCUSSION QUESTIONS

1. Can you relate to Mark's life story of failure and restoration? Why or why not?

2. How is Mark's gospel different from Matthew's, and what are the benefits of having both?

3. If you are a believer, have you faced opposition in your family about your faith? If you're still exploring Christianity, how would your family respond if you were to become a Christian?

4. Looking at your own heart, which type of soil in the parable of the sower and the soils do you identify with the most?

Then Jesus entered a house, and again a crowd gathered, so that he and his disciples were not even able to eat. When his family heard about this, they went to take charge of him, for they said, "He is out of his mind." . . . Then Jesus' mother and brothers arrived. Standing outside, they sent someone in to call him. A crowd was sitting around him, and they told him, "Your mother and brothers are outside looking for you." "Who are my mother and my brothers?" he asked. Then he looked at those seated in a circle around him and said, "Here are my mother and my brothers! Whoever does God's will is my brother and sister and mother."

—Mark 3:20–21, 31–35 NIV

Jesus was certainly not anti-family, but he taught that family loyalty is not the ultimate priority for a Christian believer. Rather, by trusting Christ, a person becomes part of the family of God, which is united not by flesh and blood but by spiritual values. Specifically, Jesus says that obedience to God binds together his "family members" in spiritual kinship. Our natural family, like Jesus's, may not understand why we sacrifice to serve; they may even think we are out of our minds! If so, we are in good company; Jesus's family didn't understand his priorities either. While they should honor their parents, followers of Jesus should be prepared to put membership in God's family over being part of their natural family.

CHAPTER 6—MARK

RIGHTEOUS SUFFERER

JESUS, THE MESSIAH AND SUFFERING SERVANT (8:27–16:8)
The Journey to Jerusalem: Peter's Confession, Jesus's Passion Predictions (8:27–10:52)
In Jerusalem: The Humble Entry, the Wicked Tenants, and the Olivet Discourse (11:1–13:37)
The Passion Narrative: Jesus's Death, Burial, and Resurrection (14:1–16:8)

JESUS, THE MESSIAH AND SUFFERING SERVANT (8:27–16:8)

In the first half of his gospel, Mark has explored what it means for Jesus to be the Messiah and Son of God. Following Peter's pivotal confession of Jesus as the Christ, Mark transitions in the second half of the gospel to presenting Jesus as the Messiah and suffering Servant. In the heart of his gospel, Mark narrates Jesus's journey to Jerusalem—during which Jesus predicts, as many as three times, that he must be killed and rise on the third day. The following three chapters portray Jesus's final ministry in Jerusalem, followed by Mark's passion narrative, also in three chapters. The gospel concludes on an ominous and somewhat surprising note, as we'll see below.

The Journey to Jerusalem: Peter's Confession, Jesus's Passion Predictions (8:27–10:52)

Peter's Confession of Jesus (8:27–9:1)

While departing for Caesarea Philippi, Jesus continues to develop his disciples' understanding of his true identity. As they walk along the road, he first asks them, "Who do people say that I am?" (Mark 8:27). When they respond, "John the Baptist; and others say, Elijah; and others, one of the prophets," he follows up, "But who do *you* say that I am?" (vv. 28–29, emphasis added). Having witnessed Jesus's powerful words and deeds for some time now, Peter has come to a settled conviction regarding who Jesus is. Answering for the disciples, he bluntly replies, "You are the Christ" (v. 29). After repeated instances of failing to grasp the meaning of Jesus's teachings and miracles, the disciples (or at least Peter) have finally arrived at a greater level of understanding of Jesus's true identity. Nevertheless, Jesus "strictly charge[s] them to tell no one about him" (v. 30); while the Twelve understand at last, for "kingdom outsiders," such as the crowds or the Jewish leaders, the "messianic secret" is still in effect.

From now on, Jesus will increasingly reveal that he, the Son of Man, must suffer, be rejected by the Jewish leaders, be killed, and rise again after three days. In a surprising twist, however, Peter "rebukes" Jesus, apparently for suggesting that he must be killed. Jesus, in turn, "rebukes" Peter, calling him "Satan" and telling him he is looking at matters from a merely human perspective (v. 33). This pointed exchange serves to clarify what kind of Messiah Jesus is going to be—not, as widely expected, a national deliverer who would lead Israel to overthrow its foes, but one who would be rejected and crucified and rise again. This has important implications for Jesus's followers. They too must deny themselves, take up their cross, and follow him, unashamed and unafraid.

This episode serves as a watershed in Mark's gospel. In the first half, Jesus's *messianic authority* took center stage. In the second half, Jesus's *vicarious suffering* becomes the central focus. The first half narrated Jesus's ministry in and around *Galilee*, while the latter half focuses on *Jerusalem*. Peter's acknowledgment of Jesus's messianic identity, followed by the first of three passion predictions and instructions regarding what it means to follow Jesus, thus serves as a segue into the second half of the gospel. Readers already know who Jesus is, as do the Twelve. The Jewish leaders, on the other hand, will further harden in their opposition to Jesus until they reach a point of no return. This, in turn, will set the stage for the concluding passion narrative.

The Transfiguration and Aftermath (9:2–29)

Six days after his first passion prediction, Jesus gathers his inner circle of disciples—Peter, James, and John—and leads them up a high mountain to be alone. The scene recalls the exodus account, where Moses was given special revelation from God (Exod. 24:15–16). On the mountain, Jesus is transfigured to reveal his divine glory to his disciples. In a surreal moment, Moses and Elijah appear, corroborating Jesus's fulfillment of Old Testament prophecy. A heavenly voice confirms that Jesus is God's beloved Son. The account of Jesus's transfiguration follows immediately after Jesus's first passion prediction. The Jesus who will suffer at the hands of those who reject him is the same Jesus they see in his radiant splendor. Jesus is the Son of God in both his humble and exalted state.

As Jesus and the three disciples come down the mountain, Jesus charges them to "tell no one what they had seen, until the Son of Man had risen from the dead" (Mark 9:9). At this, the disciples wonder what "risen from the dead" means. Having just seen Elijah, they also wonder why the scribes say Elijah must come first. Jesus explains that Elijah has already come, by implication, in the form of John the Baptist, though "they did to him whatever they pleased, as it is written" (v. 13).

As Jesus returns to the rest of the disciples, he finds a large crowd and some scribes engaged in a major dispute. Apparently, Jesus's disciples had been asked to cast out a demon from a boy but were unable to do so. Was it due to their lack of power? That's what the consensus seems to be. Jesus, however, makes clear that the issue is rather a lack of faith: "All things are possible for one who believes" (v. 23). At once, the boy's father exclaims, "I believe; help my unbelief!" (v. 24). At this, Jesus casts out the demon, who comes out of the boy, but not without throwing him into convulsions and leaving him lying on the ground as if dead. But Jesus takes him by the hand, and he gets up.

Later, the disciples ask Jesus why they couldn't exorcise the demon from the boy, and he tells them it was because this kind of demon comes out only with prayer. Not only does this reveal the disciples' prayerlessness and lack of dependence on God; it also shows that Jesus's miracles are undergirded by his relationship with God and his dependence on him, rather than being manifestations of sheer power. It also shows that people often lack faith and fail to pray, which renders them powerless in the spiritual struggle in which they are engaged. If we want spiritual power, we must grow in faith and prioritize prevailing, persistent prayer.

The Second Passion Prediction and Discipleship Struggles (9:30–50)

After this, Jesus and his disciples pass through Galilee, though Jesus keeps a low profile. For the second time, he predicts his passion, while his followers fail to grasp the meaning of his words. Upon their arrival in Capernaum, as if to underscore their intransigence, the disciples argue about who is the greatest among them. This display of selfish ambition on their part doesn't bode well for what lies ahead. By placing a child in their midst, Jesus instructs them that true greatness manifests itself in servanthood. This is the intriguing paradox Mark tries to get across in the second half of his gospel. The first will be last, and the last first.

At this, John (the son of Zebedee) tells Jesus, in well-intentioned but misguided zeal, that someone outside the apostolic circle has been performing miracles. Does Jesus want John to stop him? Jesus replies, "Do not stop him. . . . For the one who is not against us is for us" (vv. 39–40). This cautions us against drawing the boundaries of the faith too narrowly.

At the same time, Jesus tells his followers that those who cause little children to stumble would be better off if a millstone were hung around their neck. Their judgment will be severe. But the disciples should root out anything that might cause them to sin, so they might not come into judgment, for it is better to enter heaven with only one hand or eye than to enter hell with two! At this stage of the narrative, we no longer see Jesus engage in major miracles or even confrontations; rather, he instructs his followers about various lessons in ministry.

The Question of Divorce (10:1–12)

Jesus now travels to Judea and the region on the other side of the Jordan, where he addresses marriage and divorce, the status of children in the kingdom, and people's possessions. First, Mark includes an episode in which Jesus disputes a matter of the interpretation of the law with the Pharisees. The topic is divorce: "Is it lawful for a man to divorce his wife?" (10:2). In response, Jesus cites both Genesis 1:27 and 2:24 and affirms that marriage is a divinely instituted, lifelong union. Following up with his disciples, Jesus elaborates, "Whoever divorces his wife and marries another commits adultery against her, and if she divorces her husband and marries another, she commits adultery" (vv. 11–12). Neither men nor women have a right to divorce.

Welcoming Children (10:13–16)

In the next scene, Jesus, despite his disciples' resistance (even rebuke!), receives little children to bless them. He declares, "whoever does not receive the kingdom of God like a child shall not enter it" (v. 15). By this, he means, among other things, that people need to be open to God's rule in their lives without preconditions. In both episodes, Jesus affirms and protects those who are among the most vulnerable—women and children. Neither group should be the victim of discrimination or disregard but should be valued, as God made and cherishes them.

The Rich Young Ruler (10:17–31)

The following scene shows Jesus's encounter with someone quite different—a rich young ruler. Though a righteous man, he lacks one thing: he can't turn away from his great wealth to follow Jesus. How hard it is for the wealthy to enter God's kingdom! As Jesus has just affirmed, one must receive the kingdom with childlike faith. The disciples, on the other hand, as Peter points out, "have left everything and followed" Jesus (v. 28). In response, Jesus solemnly assures Peter and the other disciples that they'll be amply rewarded both in this life, in which they are made part of a new spiritual family; and in the age to come, in which they'll receive eternal life. In addition, following Jesus also entails the prospect of persecution. In this way, Jesus encourages his disciples but also prepares them for what lies ahead.

Third Passion Prediction (10:32–34)

In the final cycle of prediction, failure, and teaching, Mark identifies Jesus's destination as Jerusalem. The third cycle parallels the second one closely and functions as the climax of the three. It also prepares the way for Jesus's entry into Jerusalem. The third passion prediction is the most detailed, including information about to whom Jesus will be handed over ("the Gentiles"; v. 33) and about the way he will be treated ("they will mock him and spit on him, and flog him"; v. 34).

James and John's Request (10:35–45)

Despite the disciples' astonishment and fear, James and John ask Jesus to be seated at his right and left in glory. They envision an earthly kingdom in which they will share in Jesus's reign, yet their request reveals that they've completely misunderstood Jesus's passion predictions. The same is true of the other disciples, who respond with indignation toward the two brothers. Jesus responds by speaking of the nature of his mission. He will drink the "cup" of suffering. Despite the disciples' repeated failure to comprehend the nature of his mission, Jesus uses the occasion to further explain the nature of true discipleship by contrasting the world's leaders, who "lord it over" their subjects, with his followers, who "must be slave[s] of all" (vv. 42, 44).

Up to this point, Jesus has predicted his death three times, but he has yet to reveal *why* he must die. Here, at the end of his warnings to his disciples, we discover the reason: "For even the Son of Man came not to be served but to serve, and to give his life as a ransom for many" (v. 45). The concept of ransom in the Old Testament is linked with the notion of substitution and atonement. Jesus's words also recall Isaiah's prophecy of the suffering Servant who would be slain as an "offering for guilt" in order to bring forgiveness to many (Isa. 53:10). Jesus, the Messiah, is the suffering Servant who died for our salvation and the forgiveness of our sins.

Healing Blind Bartimaeus (10:46–52)

Jesus's journey to Jerusalem closes with the healing of a blind man named Bartimaeus in the city of Jericho. While James and John have asked for positions of prestige and power, Bartimaeus cries out, "Son of David, have mercy on me!" (Mark 10:47). Jesus tells people to call the man. The man throws off his cloak, jumps up, and runs to Jesus, who engages him in conversation and heals him. Immediately, the formerly blind man follows Jesus on the way to Jerusalem. With this, the road is prepared for the Son of David to enter Jerusalem to fulfill his messianic mission.

Three times, Jesus predicts in increasing detail to his followers that he will be betrayed and killed and will rise on the third day. The passion narrative shows that Jesus's predictions are accurate. Not only does this fulfillment confirm Jesus's credibility; it also confirms the kind of Messiah Jesus is—not a political, national deliverer, as most Jews have expected, but a suffering servant-type Messiah, as Isaiah has predicted. In contrast, the Jewish leaders who oppose Jesus all the way to the cross are part of an obstinate trajectory of Jews who have resisted God for centuries—both during the time of Moses (the wilderness generation) and the time of Isaiah (the exile generation).

What's more, Mark—writing to a Gentile, Roman audience—has increasingly hinted that Jesus's coming ultimately benefits not only believing Israelites but Gentiles as well. During Jesus's earthly ministry, Gentiles have benefited from his healing powers only at their initiative and only as a few representative individuals—Jesus's primary focus has been to come as the Jewish Messiah, the Son of David inaugurating God's kingdom. But following the resurrection, the scope of the benefits of Jesus's ransom-payment death will encompass Gentiles as well.

In Jerusalem: The Humble Entry, the Wicked Tenants, and the Olivet Discourse (11:1–13:37)

The Humble Entry (11:1–11)

Thus far, Mark's narrative has been moving slowly but surely from Galilee to Jerusalem. Upon depicting Jesus's arrival in the Jewish capital, Mark zeroes in on the events leading up to Jesus's death and resurrection. Jesus's arrival in Jerusalem also witnesses a marked shift in his approach. No longer does Jesus perform healing miracles or exorcisms; rather, he focuses on teaching in the temple area. In fact, all of the events in 11:1–13:37 occur on the way to, in, or on the way out of the temple precincts.

The narrative presents three successive journeys by Jesus to the temple, which get longer each day (11:1–11; 11:12–19; 11:20–13:37). Jesus's denunciation of the Jewish leaders and his prediction of the temple's destruction cut to the very heart of Jewish religious and political life. The conflict between Jesus and the authorities escalates until Jesus is betrayed and sentenced to death. At the heart of this gargantuan spiritual battle is the Jewish leaders' rejection of their Messiah.

Traditionally (though perhaps somewhat inaccurately) called the "triumphal entry," Jesus's approach to Jerusalem, while exceedingly humble, is brimming with messianic overtones. After making proper preparations that reveal God's providence in every detail, Jesus enters the city riding on a colt, while people shout, "Hosanna! Blessed is he who comes in the name of the Lord! Blessed is the coming kingdom of our father David! Hosanna in the highest!" (11:9–10; cf. Ps. 118:26). Jesus's riding on a colt is reminiscent not only of King Solomon's entrance into the Holy City but also of the words of the prophet Zechariah (Zech. 9:9).

Notice that the emphasis is not merely on the fact that Jesus enters the city of Jerusalem as King but more specifically on *what kind of king* Jesus has proven to be: "righteous and victorious," yet "lowly and riding on a donkey" (Zech. 9:9 NIV). Jesus doesn't come on a war horse but on a lowly beast of burden, showing that the purpose of his coming is not military conquest but humble service—giving his life as a ransom for sinners. In this sense, Jesus is the Son of David, Israel's long-awaited King.

Cursing the Fig Tree and Cleansing the Temple (11:12–25)

On the next day, Jesus returns from Bethany, a village less than two miles outside Jerusalem, and engages in a rather curious action that constitutes the last-recorded miracle in Mark's gospel: he curses a barren, fruitless fig tree—an action rendered even more curious because, as Mark mentions, "it was not the season for figs" (Mark 11:13). Apparently, Jesus expected that the leaves might conceal at least some indication that the tree would bear fruit in season, but he discovers no sign of life. Thus, he declares, "May no one ever eat fruit from you again" (v. 14).

This is more than the frustrated reaction of a hungry, disappointed fig lover! A closer look reveals that the next scene—the temple cleansing—is followed by a second reference to the withering fig tree. This "Markan sandwich," where Mark encloses a story within another story on either end, points to the mutually interpreting nature of the cursing of the fig tree and the temple cleansing. The barren fig tree symbolizes unfaithful Israel and its failure to keep its covenant with God, while Jesus's condemnation of the tree symbolizes God's judgment on Israel (cf. Isa. 28:3–4; Jer. 8:13; Hos. 9:10, 16; Joel 1:7, 12; Mic. 7:1).

Later, when Jesus enters the temple, he similarly condemns the profiteering taking place there as he drives out the merchants and overturns the money changers' tables and the dove sellers' seats. In so doing, he cites Isaiah's prophecy, "My house shall be called a house of prayer for all the nations" (Mark 11:17; cf. Isa. 56:7). The temple is meant to be a place where everyone, including Gentiles, can pray to God. Clearly, the presence of these merchants in the Court of the Gentiles makes worship there all but impossible.

What's more, in keeping with Jeremiah's prophecy, Jesus calls the temple in its current condition a "den of robbers" (Mark 11:17; cf. Jer. 7:11). This stands in marked contrast to God's intended purpose for the temple—namely, that it is to be a "house of prayer" not merely for Israel but, in keeping with Isaiah's prophecy, "for all the nations." Thus, Jesus's denunciation pertains not only to profit-hungry merchants but also to the priestly authorities, under whose leadership the temple has become a corrupt place.

As Jesus enters Jerusalem, therefore, he acts with compelling messianic authority, calling the Jewish leaders to account for their corruption of the temple. God has intended for the sanctuary to be holy ground devoted to spiritual worship, yet Israel has profaned and defiled it, which makes a mockery of the worship of God and shows any religious activities to be nothing but a charade. Like the barren fig tree, Israel looks good from a distance but at closer scrutiny proves to be spiritually barren and devoid of genuine fruit.

The temple cleansing marks a pivotal moment in salvation history. Yahweh, in the person of the Messiah, visits his temple and confronts the travesty of worship perpetrated there. After this, Jesus and his followers make the short trek back to Bethany, where they stay for the night. Upon returning to the fig tree the next morning, the disciples notice that it has "withered away to its roots" (Mark 11:20). Jesus seizes the teachable moment by impressing on them the importance of believing, "mountain-moving" prayer. Jesus adds that, as his followers pray, they should forgive others so that they too will be forgiven by their heavenly Father.

Six Controversies (11:27–12:37)

Who Gave You Authority to Do These Things? (11:27–33). Jesus returns to the temple and is confronted by the chief priests, scribes, and elders. This episode is the first of six controversy stories, each of which depicts the escalating conflict between Jesus and the Jewish leaders. Jesus had just asserted his authority by cleansing the temple. But who had given him the authority to do this? Jesus cleverly turns the tables on them—figuratively, this time—and asks, "Was the baptism of John from heaven or from man?" (v. 30) The leaders are at a loss as to how to answer Jesus's question, so Jesus declines to answer theirs as well.

What Will the Vineyard Owner Do with the Wicked Tenants? (12:1–12). Jesus speaks to them again in parables. The parable of the tenants, a masterful salvation-historical allegory alluding to Isaiah's Song of the Vineyard, depicts Israel's leaders as wicked tenant farmers (cf. Isa. 5:1–7). In the parable, God, the owner of the vineyard, sends a series of servants—symbolizing the Old Testament prophets—who are mistreated or even killed. At last, he sends his own son, thinking the tenants will respect him. Yet shockingly, they kill him, thinking that if they kill the heir, the vineyard will be theirs.

At the conclusion of the parable, Jesus asks the provocative question, "What will the owner of the vineyard do?" Answering his own question, he replies, "He will come and destroy the tenants and give the vineyard to others," quoting a well-known Old Testament passage that predicted that "the stone that the builders rejected [would] become the cornerstone" (Mark 12:9–10; cf. Ps. 118:22). The Jewish leaders continue to be conflicted. They have enough spiritual perception to realize that the parable is directed against them. Yet their hearts are hardened, so rather than repenting they are bent on arresting Jesus and putting him to death. For the moment, though, they delay out of fear of the ordinary people, with whom Jesus is very popular.

Is It Lawful to Pay Taxes to Caesar? (12:13–17). In the next several confrontations, Jesus answers his questioners' challenge to reveal his authority to interpret the law. In each case, Jesus silences his detractors and amazes the people. First, some Pharisees and Herodians (sympathizers with the Herodian dynasty) approach Jesus and seek to trap him by asking, "Is it lawful to pay taxes to Caesar, or not?" (Mark 12:14). They think Jesus is caught, because either way he answers he will incriminate himself. If he says people should pay taxes to Caesar, he is un-Jewish and cannot be the national deliverer people are expecting. If he says people shouldn't pay taxes, they can report him to the Romans as a rebel.

How will Jesus wriggle out of this no-win situation? In response, he asks for a denarius (a silver coin minted by the Romans that represented the typical wage for a day's work), queries whose image is on the coin (i.e., Caesar's—in Jesus's day, Tiberius's [reigned AD 14–37]), and distinguishes between different realms of authority: "Render to Caesar the things that are Caesar's, and to God the things that are God's" (v. 17). People should honor the Romans as God-given civil authorities by paying taxes to them, and at the same time, they should honor God in the spiritual realm by worshiping him. By answering the trick question in this way, Jesus not only sidesteps an apparent dilemma; he also confronts the Pharisees once again for failing to worship God the way he deserves.

Whose Wife Will a Remarried Widow Be in Heaven? (12:18–27). Now, the Sadducees take their turn. As Mark informs his readers, the Sadducees "say that there is no resurrection" (v. 18). On this point, they and the Pharisees disagree. Historical records show that the Sadducees only held to the authority of the five books of Moses, claiming that there was no clear reference to resurrection there and therefore denying it. This explains why Jesus pointedly refers to "the book of Moses" in his response, noting that, in the account of Moses and the burning bush, God identified himself as being "the God of Abraham, and the God of Isaac, and the God of Jacob" (v. 26; cf. Exod. 3:6).

In the narrative, Mark tells his readers how Jesus's opponents concoct a hypothetical and highly implausible scenario designed to put Jesus on the spot. A woman has had seven husbands: Whose wife will she be at the final resurrection (the reality of which, of course, the Sadducees didn't acknowledge in the first place)? Again, the trick question poses no problem for Jesus, who replies that in heaven people won't marry at all! What's more, God is not the God of the dead but of the living, so the Sadducees' denial of the final resurrection is quite wrong. Another "gotcha moment" has failed to materialize. In fact, it is Jesus's challengers who stand exposed as engaging in an erroneous interpretation of Scripture.

What Is the Greatest Commandment? (12:28–34). The Pharisees, the Herodians, and the Sadducees have all taken turns in challenging Jesus. Who's next in line to trip him up with an "unanswerable" question? Up steps one of the scribes. He seems less bent on exposing Jesus as a fraud, having overheard some of the previous challenges and witnessed Jesus's apt responses. Rather, he simply asks Jesus, "Which commandment is the most important of all?" (Mark 12:28).

Without hesitation, Jesus says that the greatest commandment is to love God and that the second, related commandment is to love other people (cf. Lev. 19:18; Deut. 6:4–5). The scribe concurs, to which Jesus replies that he is "not far from the kingdom of God" (Mark 12:34). Sadly, however, this particular scribe is the exception; Jesus's verdict on the scribes in general is not as kind. At this point, "no one dare[s] to ask [Jesus] any more questions" (v. 34). Where have all the challengers gone? They've all disappeared.

Whose Son Is the Christ? And the Widow's Offering? (12:35–44). With Jesus's adversaries having run out of questions, he raises a question of his own: "How can the scribes say that the Christ is the son of David" when David himself, "in the Holy Spirit," said that "the Lord said to my Lord, 'Sit at my right hand, until I put your enemies under your feet'" (vv. 35–36; cf. Ps. 110:1)? How can the Messiah be both David's *Lord* and *son*? And how can two persons be called "Lord"? The first person is the God of Israel, but who is the second? The scribes have no answer. Here, the reader sees that Jesus makes the point that David's calling the Messiah both his Lord and his son meant that the Messiah would be both his descendant and his superior. But since "Lord" in the Old Testament regularly refers to God, this meant David believed the Messiah would also be divine! The Messiah would be both human in his human ancestry of David and divine as the Son of God—a point Jesus's opponents fail to appreciate.

At this, the evangelist again notes the contrast between the common people who hear Jesus "gladly" and the scribes who hold positions of privilege in society, and who "for a pretense" utter "long prayers" but "devour widows' houses" (Mark 12:37, 40). They are long on prayers but short on actual piety expressed in active concern for those who are poor, lowly, and in need of help. As one such example, Jesus notes a poor widow who humbly puts two small coins in the offering box in the temple area. In terms of proportionate giving, Jesus points out, this widow has given infinitely more than those who have "contributed out of their abundance": she, out of her poverty, has given "everything she had" (v. 44). Similar to the Canaanite woman before her, this poor widow emerges as an unlikely example of true devotion to God. The lesson is that it's not what you *know* about God that matters; it's what you *do* with what you *know* that makes you either a hypocrite or a true worshiper.

The Olivet Discourse (13:1–37)

Jesus's Prophecy and the Disciples' Question (13:1–4). As Jesus leaves the temple for the last time, his followers draw his attention to the beauty of the temple building. In response, Jesus predicts that the temple will soon be destroyed—a prediction that came true in the year 70, when the Romans laid siege to Jerusalem and razed the temple. At this, Jesus sits down on the Mount of Olives overlooking the temple and is asked by Peter, James, John, and Andrew to elaborate on the prophesied destruction of the Jewish sanctuary: "Tell us, when will these things be, and what will be the sign when all these things are about to be accomplished?"

(13:4). In response, Jesus delivers the Olivet Discourse, which serves as a transition from the temple controversies to the passion narrative.

Throughout the discourse, Jesus repeatedly exhorts his disciples to watch out in light of the staggering events to come (vv. 5, 9, 23, 33). The discourse deals with events leading up to the destruction of Jerusalem in the year 70 as well as the more distant future return of Christ. When interpreting the Olivet Discourse, it's important to keep two audiences in mind: (1) Jesus's original listeners, and (2) believers at the time of the writing of Mark's gospel. First, Jesus is addressing his disciples, who must be vigilant in view of the destruction of Jerusalem, which will occur in their lifetime ("this generation"; v. 30). Second, Mark is addressing believers in his day who have been confronting (potential or real) persecution, if not actual martyrdom. (Mark wrote about twenty to thirty years after the events of Jesus's ministry originally took place.)

Possible Signs Preceding the End (13:5–13). Dealing initially with the second part of the disciples' question (the part dealing with the sign preceding the temple's destruction), Jesus says that both audiences need to be aware that messianic pretenders will appear; there'll be wars and rumors of wars; and earthquakes and famines will occur, as well as persecution—yet none of these will constitute the actual sign about which Jesus's disciples are inquiring.

The "Abomination of Desolation" and the Destruction of Jerusalem (13:14–20). Jesus continues, "But when you see the abomination of desolation standing where he ought not to be . . . then let those who are in Judea flee to the mountains" (v. 14). The sign, therefore, is "the abomination of desolation," the desecration of the temple predicted in the book of Daniel. Initially, this prophecy was fulfilled at the inception of the Maccabean period in the second century BC; but as Jesus explains here, there will be a second fulfillment of Daniel's prophecy in the near future, at which the temple will once again be desecrated. This will be a time of great distress and tribulation for the inhabitants of Jerusalem and Judea. In addition, the events surrounding the year 70 will foreshadow the events accompanying the second coming of Christ at the end of human history.

Imposters, Cosmic Upheaval, and the Coming of the "Son of Man" (13:21–27). Finally, there are warnings and exhortations that apply to later generations of believers. The crucial transition from the more immediate to the more distant future is found in verse 24, with the phrase "But in those days, after that tribulation," where the scene shifts from the destruction of Jerusalem and the temple in the year 70 to the second coming of Jesus. Amid cosmic upheaval, "they will see the Son of Man coming in clouds with great power and glory. And then he will send out the angels and gather his elect" (vv. 26–27).

This Generation and the Timing of Jesus's Return (13:28–37). Having discussed the second part of the disciples' question regarding the sign preceding the temple's destruction, which would serve as a portent of Jesus's eventual return, Jesus now turns to the first part of their question regarding the timing of these events. In this regard, he urges his disciples to learn the lesson of the fig tree—namely, that when the branch becomes tender and the tree puts out its leaves, the summer (and thus the tree's bearing of ripe fruit) is near. While they should look for these signs, he tells them that no one knows the exact time of his return: "not even the angels in heaven, nor the Son, but only the Father" (v. 32).

In a mini-parable, Jesus explains that his coming will be like the return of a master whose servants are left in charge of the estate. They don't know when their master will come back, but they must be ready whenever he finally returns. The bottom line, therefore, is this: Be on guard. You don't know when the time will come. This admonition applies to all believers: we must be vigilant, because none of us knows the exact time when Jesus will return.

The Passion Narrative: Jesus's Death, Burial, and Resurrection (14:1–16:8)

It's now only two days before Passover. The Jewish leaders are plotting to arrest Jesus by stealth, but not during the festival, in order to avoid any undue commotion. The Romans would have been very sensitive to that, as they wanted to avoid any public unrest that could spiral out of control. This is why the Roman governor, who otherwise spent his time in the posh Caesarea Maritima on the coast, came to the capital during feast times—just to make sure everything stayed calm and under control. The Jews had a certain measure of political and religious autonomy, but were on a short enough leash that they couldn't exact capital punishment. Nor did they want to stir up the crowds so as to attract undue attention from the Romans, lest they crack down violently to quell any popular uprising.

Throughout the passion narrative, Mark makes clear that it is God's sovereign purpose to accomplish the work of salvation through Jesus's vicarious suffering and substitutionary sacrifice on the cross. Jesus is betrayed, rejected, abandoned, condemned, and executed according to God's sovereign purpose. One of the primary ways in which Mark expresses this is by demonstrating that the final events of Jesus's life occur in fulfillment of Scripture. Everything happens according to God's preordained plan—just as the Old Testament writers envisioned and predicted it would. This is at the heart of Mark's apologetic for the cross—his explanation that, even though both Jews and non-Jews couldn't see how a crucified "criminal" could be the Messiah and Savior of the world, the cross was a central plank in God's plan, because it was there that Jesus would give his life as a ransom for sinners.

The Plot Against Jesus, and His Anointing and Betrayal (14:1–11)

The narrative begins with yet another reference to the plot to arrest Jesus. The three opening scenes in the passion narrative form another Markan sandwich, in which the anointing of Jesus at Bethany—the place outside Jerusalem where Jesus and his followers typically lodge for the night—is framed by the Jewish leaders' plot and Judas's betrayal. The sandwich contrasts the treacherous character of Judas and the religious leaders with the pure devotion of the woman who anoints Jesus. (John tells us it is Mary of Bethany, sister of Martha and Lazarus, whom Jesus had by this time raised from the dead.)

When Jesus dines at the house of a man named Simon the leper (presumably a leper healed by Jesus), a woman appears with a bottle of very expensive perfume and proceeds to pour its contents over Jesus's head. Some of those present object to the extravagant "waste" (John tells us it is principally Judas), but Jesus rises to the woman's defense and says she has done a "beautiful thing" to him (v. 6). In fact, she has acted prophetically by anointing his body for burial, even prior to the crucifixion. In addition, Jesus says her story will be told wherever the gospel is preached.

With this pronouncement, Jesus is implicitly predicting his death once again. While the woman is likely unaware that Jesus must soon die, there's no doubt that Jesus's mind is firmly fixed on the cross. Like the poor widow, the woman serves as a model of true discipleship and devotion, in contrast to the greedy, self-seeking religious leaders (not to mention Judas the traitor). The disciples have a choice to make as to whom they will emulate—the woman's devotion or the leaders' devious scheming. Tragically, Judas will cast his lot with the latter. The text tells us that from this point forward, "he sought an opportunity to betray [Jesus]" (v. 11).

The Last Supper (14:12–25)

In the next episode, Jesus celebrates the final Passover with his disciples. This is a poignant moment, as Jesus commemorates the Passover that originated on the eve of Israel's exodus from Egypt and that institutes the new covenant with a believing Jewish remnant, the Twelve. In each scene, Jesus demonstrates his foreknowledge of what is about to happen; he foreknows

- the details for the meal's preparations,
- Judas's betrayal,
- Peter's denials,
- the disciples' falling away, and
- his imminent death.

Jesus proceeds "as it is written of him," in fulfillment of God's foreordained plan (v. 21). During the supper, he takes the bread and wine that represent his body and blood. By this symbolic gesture, Jesus illustrates the purpose of his vicarious sacrifice, as both elements jointly point to his atoning death on the cross. He prays, breaks the bread, and says, "Take; this is my body" (v. 22). After this, he takes the cup, again gives thanks, and gives it to the disciples, saying, "This is my blood of the covenant, which is poured out for many" (v. 24). Jesus's words here echo Moses's sealing of God's covenant with Israel through the atoning blood of animal sacrifices (Exod. 24:8).

The phrase "for many" echoes Isaiah's prophecy, according to which the suffering Servant "[bears] the sin of many" (Isa. 53:12). In the context of Mark's gospel, Jesus's words build on the previous reference to Jesus giving his life as a ransom "for many" (Mark 10:45). Just like these animal sacrifices in the old covenant, only with infinitely greater effectiveness, Jesus's blood will be poured out "for many" as he dies on the cross as God's suffering Servant. In this way, Jesus will effectively die for others, paying the penalty for their sins by dying in their place.

The Prediction of Peter's Denials, and Praying in Gethsemane (14:26–42)

After eating, Jesus and the disciples sing a hymn, leave the upper room, and head toward the Mount of Olives. No doubt with a heavy heart, Jesus tells his followers that they will all fall away, in fulfillment of Scripture (cf. Zech. 13:7). Nevertheless, after the resurrection, he will go before them to Galilee. This is an important forward-looking reference, as the Markan narrative ends with the angel's words to the women at the empty tomb following the resurrection: "He has risen; he is not here. . . . But go, tell his disciples and Peter that he is going before you to Galilee. There you will see him, just as he told you" (Mark 16:6–7). In this way, the present reference constitutes the opening bookend that frames the account of Jesus's arrest, trials, crucifixion, burial, and resurrection, which are about to follow.

Jesus's submission to the Father's will is contrasted with the disciples' ignorance. They boldly claim that they'll never deny Jesus. Peter tells Jesus, "Even though they all fall away, I will not" (14:29). Yet while his love for Jesus and his resolve to remain loyal to him are moving and commendable, Peter's best intentions will carry him only so far. Instead, Jesus predicts that Peter will deny him three times.

Nevertheless he takes Peter, along with James and John, with him as he prays in the garden of Gethsemane (an olive grove in the outskirts of Jerusalem). There, he agonizes over the imminent prospect of his death. Prior to his threefold denial, Peter, together with the other two, is caught napping three times by Jesus upon his return from praying. While the disciples fall asleep, Jesus remains alert and trusts in the Father even in the face of suffering and death. Jesus urges them on: "[T]he hour has come. The Son of Man is betrayed into the hands of sinners" (v. 41).

Jesus's Betrayal and Arrest (14:43–52)

Immediately, while Jesus is still declaring that he will be betrayed into the hands of sinners, Judas the traitor arrives on the scene with an unruly crowd from the Jewish leaders. Completely unnecessarily, they carry swords and clubs, as if they've come to arrest a common criminal who is likely to resist arrest. Judas the betrayer steps up to Jesus and gives the crowd the agreed-upon sign. With deep irony, as he had likely done many times before, he greets Jesus with "Rabbi!" and a kiss. At this, they arrest Jesus. Yet "one of those who [stand] by" (from the other gospels, we know it is Peter) draws his sword and cuts off the ear of the high priest's servant (v. 47).

The other gospels tell us that Jesus intervenes and heals the ear, but Mark only records that Jesus says, "Have you come out as against a robber, with swords and clubs to capture me? Day after day I was with you in the temple teaching, and you did not seize me. But let the Scriptures be fulfilled" (vv. 48–49). In this way, Jesus exposes the cowardly covert operation Judas and the Jewish leaders are performing. Then, in keeping with Jesus's prediction, the text tells us that "they all left him and fled" (v. 50; cf. v. 27; Zech. 13:7). In all this adversity, Jesus is in no way caught off guard but retains his composure, as each event transpires according to God's predetermined purpose that "the Scriptures be fulfilled."

One unique and curious feature of Mark's account of Jesus's arrest is the reference to a young man who follows Jesus—remarkable because Mark has just said that "they all left him and fled"—dressed in "nothing but a linen cloth" (Mark 14:51). Those who have arrested Jesus take the man into custody as well, but leaving the linen garment behind, he apparently breaks free and runs away naked. It's possible that here the author of the gospel—Mark himself—makes a cameo appearance.

The Jewish Trial and Peter's Denial (14:53–72)

With his disciples scattered, Jesus is first led to a hearing before the Sanhedrin—the Jewish highest court—and subsequently to Pilate, the Roman governor, who alone can pronounce the death sentence. Throughout the latter half of Mark's gospel, the Jewish leaders have sought "a way to destroy," "arrest," and "kill" Jesus (11:18; 12:12; 14:1). The mischievous plan they have hatched is at last moving forward. Nevertheless, while Jesus is crucified according to God's will and in fulfillment of Scripture, the Jewish leaders, as well as Judas and the Roman governor, are clearly the human agents responsible for Jesus's suffering and death.

In the unfolding narrative, Mark records what happens to Jesus, the titles ascribed to Jesus (prophet, King of the Jews, Christ, King of Israel, and Son of God), and the response of the witnesses.

The trial scene opens with a reference to Peter following Jesus "at a distance, right into the courtyard of the high priest" (v. 54). Peter's timid presence at the scene is juxtaposed with Jesus's bold testimony. From a safe distance outside, Peter warms himself by the fire, while Jesus is "under fire" from the Jewish leaders inside. Though falsely accused, Jesus chooses to remain silent, just as Isaiah's suffering Servant "open[s] not his mouth" (Isa. 53:7). Jesus's only words are uttered in response to the high priest's question as to whether he is "the Christ, the Son of the Blessed" (Mark 14:61; cf. Ps. 110:1; Dan. 7:13–14). Strikingly, in a gospel that up to now has been pervaded by the messianic secret, Jesus boldly acknowledges, yes, "I am." He adds—in an affirmation that he surely knows will prove to be exceedingly provocative—"and you will see the Son of Man seated at the right hand of Power, and coming with the clouds of heaven" (Mark 14:62). This was clearly beyond the humanly possible and amounted to a claim of deity.

Sure enough, the high priest at once tears his robes (a cultural expression of outrage) and exclaims, "What further witnesses do we need? You have heard his blasphemy" (v. 63). The entire scene is dripping with irony. By sentencing Jesus to death, the Jewish leaders are advancing his mission of dying for people's sins as God's suffering Servant-Messiah. What's also ironic is that some of the Jewish leaders mock and spit on Jesus, calling on him to prophesy. As Mark's readers know, Jesus has predicted repeatedly that he would be delivered into their hands in order to be killed. He even predicted that Judas would betray him, that all his disciples would be scattered, and that Peter would deny him three times on that very night! In the very next scene, Peter fulfills Jesus's words and breaks down and weeps. In all these ways, Jesus proves to be a true prophet whose words will never pass away (cf. 13:31). The mockery and travesty of justice that unfolds is hard to fathom.

The Ratification of the Sanhedrin's Verdict, and the Roman Trial (15:1–15)

The nighttime meeting of the Sanhedrin has resulted in a "guilty" verdict on account of blasphemy. In the early morning hours, the entire council meets to ratify the verdict and sends Jesus on to Pilate, the Roman governor, who alone can legally approve the death sentence. While Jesus's Jewish trial has been marked by false testimony and a rejection of his deity, his Roman trial is crippled by the governor's cowardly indecision. While the Sanhedrin has leveled the *religious* charge of blasphemy against Jesus, Pilate frames his identity in *political* terms: "Are you the King of the Jews?" (15:2). The term *King* appears repeatedly in the remaining passion narrative; the irony, of course, is that while Pilate conceives of kingship in political terms, Jesus is King in a broader sense that transcends mere human politics. For this reason, Jesus has consistently proclaimed the coming of the "kingdom of God"—God's reign in repentant, believing human hearts.

Jesus's response to Pilate's question resembles his conduct at the Jewish trial. He simply says, "You have said so," refusing to incriminate himself by his words (v. 2). The Jewish leaders (who are apparently right there with Jesus and Pilate) keep accusing Jesus "of many things" (v. 3). When Pilate asks Jesus to respond, he says nothing. One reason why all of the proceedings against Jesus are a travesty of justice is that he is refused proper legal representation. This unmasks any pretense at fairness and makes Jesus's "trial" nothing but a charade. Yet Jesus remains composed and stays above the fray, dignifying neither Pilate's nor the Jewish leaders' charges with a response. If they want to condemn him unjustly, he is not going to supply them with further ammunition.

Rather than take control of the proceedings, Pilate, in a weak move of shirking and shifting responsibility, puts the matter into the hands of the Jewish crowd, presumably thinking they will exonerate Jesus, whom he considers not guilty. He invokes a custom according to which the Roman governor releases a prisoner at the festival. Yet when faced with the fateful decision as to whether to release Jesus or Barabbas, a murderous rebel, the people inexplicably choose the latter, having been incited by the chief priests. The irony is palpable: the people choose Barabbas, whose name means "son of the father" (cf. 10:46; 14:36), rather than Jesus, the Son of (God) the Father (15:6–15). When Pilate asks the crowd what he should do with Jesus, they cruelly shout, "Crucify him" (v. 13). Believing Jesus to be innocent, Pilate asks the crowd, "Why? What evil has he done?" (v. 14). But they merely repeat their call for Jesus's crucifixion. Lacking the moral fortitude to stand up to the Jewish leaders and the raucous mob, and "wishing to satisfy the crowd," Pilate accedes to their demand, releasing Barabbas and sentencing Jesus to be scourged and crucified (v. 15).

The Crucifixion (15:16–41)

When Jesus arrives at the governor's headquarters—the Praetorium—the soldiers call together their entire battalion. As was common, those rough characters don't miss the opportunity to amuse themselves at Jesus's expense. They drape a purple coat around him, mocking his royal claim, and put a crown made of thornbush branches on his head. After this, they prostrate themselves in mock homage and salute him: "Hail, King of the

Jews!" (v. 18). While doing so, they strike his head with a reed, spit on him, and keep prostrating themselves. After a while, they get bored, take off the robe, and put Jesus's own clothes back on. Then they lead him away to be crucified.

Mark's depiction of Jesus's crucifixion is succinct and presents the salient facts in rapid succession. Unable to carry his own cross, Jesus is helped by a man identified as Simon of Cyrene, who is pressed into service. When they arrive at Golgotha (Aramaic for "Place of a Skull"), they crucify Jesus. An inscription states the charge: "The King of the Jews" (v. 26). Jesus is crucified at about nine o'clock in the morning between two robbers, "one on his right and one on his left" (v. 28). This expression recalls James and John's ungranted request to sit at Jesus's right and left in glory. Certainly, dying on crosses at Jesus's side—being crucified with Christ—is not what they had in mind.

While dying on the cross, Jesus is mocked as the "King of Israel" (v. 32). Passersby wag their heads and say, with deep irony, "Aha! You who would destroy the temple and rebuild it in three days, save yourself, and come down from the cross!" (v. 30). The Jewish leaders too join in the mockery, saying to one another, "He saved others; he cannot save himself. Let the Christ, the King of Israel, come down now from the cross that we may see and believe" (vv. 31–32). Even the robbers who are crucified at Jesus's side hurl abuse at him.

Then, around noon, darkness falls over the land until about three o'clock in the afternoon. Having hung on the cross for an excruciating six hours, Jesus cries out, citing the opening line of Psalm 22, "My God, my God, why have you forsaken me?" (Mark 15:34). Psalm 22 is a well-known Davidic psalm, presenting David as a prototypical righteous sufferer. Throughout, Jesus has been identified as the "King of Israel"—albeit in ironic, even mocking, ignorance. By citing Psalm 22, Jesus further identifies himself as Israel's Davidic king and God's righteous sufferer. While Jesus is not actually separated from God, he identifies with our sin and bears the full weight of God's wrath.

Time	Event	Reference
Nine in the morning	Jesus's crucifixion	15:25
Around noon	Darkness over the land	15:33
Three in the afternoon	Jesus's death	15:34

Some of the bystanders think that when Jesus speaks the opening words of Psalm 22, *Eloi, Eloi* ("My God, my God"), he is actually calling for Elijah—yet another instance of misunderstanding. Mark's entire account of the crucifixion is an almost incessant string of grotesque, tragic, and ironic misunderstandings reflecting people's spiritual incomprehension, obduracy, and dullness. So people say, mockingly, "Wait, let us see whether Elijah will come to take him down" (Mark 15:36). That's the last mockery Jesus has to endure. With a loud cry, the Son of God dies.

Mark records two remarkable things that happen as soon as Jesus breathes his last. First, the curtain of the temple is torn in two, marking the end of temple sacrifices as well as new, open access for all to God. By Jesus's death, the sin barrier between God and humanity is forever removed for those who recognize Jesus as Messiah and trust in his sacrifice on their behalf. No more offerings are needed, because Jesus brought the once-for-all sacrifice. In fact, Jesus is the substitute for the temple, because people can now enter God's presence through the body and blood of Christ.

Second, upon witnessing Jesus's death, a Roman centurion confesses at the climax of Mark's gospel, "Truly this man was the Son of God!" (v. 39). At Jesus's baptism, the voice from heaven declared, "You are my beloved Son" (1:11). Then, halfway through the gospel, Peter, speaking for the Twelve, confessed Jesus as "the Christ" (8:29). Now, a Roman soldier, a Gentile, comes to the identical conclusion: Jesus is the Son of God. The Jewish leaders have been blind to this truth, but outsiders such as the Gentile centurion perceive it by faith. The messianic secret has now been lifted, even for the Gentiles: Jesus is the Son of God! The gospel is ready to be proclaimed to all nations.

In some ways, the remainder of the gospel is almost anticlimactic: How does one follow the Roman centurion's confession of Jesus as the Son of God? Mark briefly mentions the presence of several women at the cross who look on from a distance, including Mary Magdalene, Mary the mother of James, and Salome. These are the same women who "followed him and ministered to him" in Galilee (15:41). In addition, "there were also many other women who came up with him to Jerusalem" (v. 41). Thus, we see that Jesus had a large contingent of committed, devoted female followers. And while Jesus's male disciples all fled at Jesus's arrest, these women faithfully followed Jesus amid his adversity and gruesome death.

Jesus's Burial (15:42–47)

In between sections on the women at the cross and at the tomb, Mark records the burial of Jesus's body by Joseph of Arimathea, a respected member of the Sanhedrin, "who was also himself looking for the kingdom of God" (v. 43). This shows that the Sanhedrin was not unanimous in its rejection of Jesus. This Joseph goes to Pilate and asks for Jesus's body.

After verifying with a centurion that Jesus is dead, Pilate releases the body. Joseph has it taken down from the cross, wrapped in a linen shroud, and laid in a new tomb, and a rock is rolled against the entrance, sealing the tomb. Mary Magdalene and the other Mary see where Jesus is put, which ensures that both women know where to go to finish the burial on Sunday morning.

The Women at the Tomb (16:1–8)

When Sabbath is over, Mary Magdalene and the other women set out for the tomb to finish what had been left undone at Jesus's burial. On their way, they worry how they'll be able to roll away the large stone at the entrance, but their concerns are allayed when they arrive and the stone has already been rolled back. As if this is not startling enough, as they enter the tomb, they're alarmed at the sight of an angel dressed in a white robe, who announces to them that Jesus has risen. "See the place where they laid him," the angel says (16:6); the reader knows that Jesus is no longer there.

What's more, the angel commissions the women, "But go, tell his disciples and Peter that he is going before you to Galilee. There you will see him, just as he told you" (v. 7). This harks back to Jesus's earlier prediction that after the resurrection, he would go ahead of the disciples to Galilee and meet them there. The gospel closes with the women trembling in fear and astonishment. And while the angel had told them to "go, tell his disciples," Mark tells his readers that the women "said nothing to anyone, for they were afraid" (v. 8).

THE ENDING OF MARK'S GOSPEL

Most likely, this is how Mark's story about Jesus ends. The ending may seem abrupt, but apparently the evangelist believes he has conveyed the essential facts of Jesus's story in his characteristically succinct style. Some later scribes tried to "finish" Mark's story by adding longer endings, as is attested in later manuscripts, but the earliest versions of Mark's gospel that we have close with the so-called short ending (v. 8). If this is indeed how Mark wraps up his story, what are we to conclude?

Mark leaves the reader with a massive cliffhanger. From the angel's report, we know that Jesus has risen (v. 6). We also know that the Roman centurion has confessed Jesus as the Son of God (15:39). Like the women at the empty tomb, we're left to ponder what it all means. Jesus has risen from the dead just like he said. If so, everything else he said in the gospel is true, and his miracles prove he is the Messiah and Son of God. It also means his disciples will see him again, and their decision to follow him was the right one.

Beyond the brutal cross and the ignominious grave is the glorious resurrection.

Mark leaves us with a lot to think about. But one thing is clear: Jesus has risen, and we must follow him.

DISCUSSION QUESTIONS

1. What is so pivotal in Jesus's ministry about Peter's confession of Jesus as the Christ?

2. Are you ready for Jesus's return? Why or why not?

3. In what ways is the Roman centurion's confession of Jesus at the cross the climax of the gospel?

4. Assuming Mark's gospel ends with chapter 16, verse 8, why would Mark end his gospel this way?

Then he called the crowd to him along with his disciples and said: "Whoever wants to be my disciple must deny themselves and take up their cross and follow me. For whoever wants to save their life will lose it, but whoever loses their life for me and for the gospel will save it. What good is it for someone to gain the whole world, yet forfeit their soul? Or what can anyone give in exchange for their soul? If anyone is ashamed of me and my words in this adulterous and sinful generation, the Son of Man will be ashamed of them when he comes in his Father's glory with the holy angels."

—Mark 8:34–38 NIV

Missionary martyr Jim Elliot once said, "He is no fool who gives what he cannot keep to gain what he cannot lose." C. T. Studd, who served as a missionary in China, India, and Africa, stated, "Only one life, 't will soon be past. Only what's done for Christ will last." And Helen Roseveare, missionary to the Congo, said, "The privilege [Jesus] offers you is greater than the price you have to pay." These voices bear eloquent testimony to the truth of Jesus's words. When I trusted Christ, I shuddered at the thought of him being ashamed of me at his return and decided to follow him in baptism. Not everyone is called to be a missionary, but every disciple of Christ must deny himself, take up his cross, and follow him.

PART 3

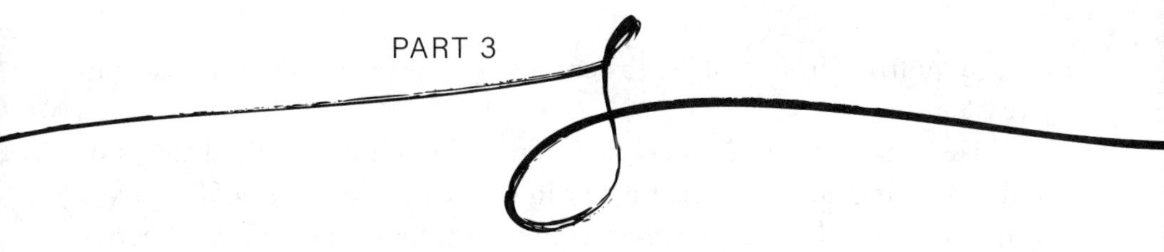

THE GOSPEL ACCORDING TO LUKE:

JESUS, THE SAVIOR OF THE WORLD

WHO WAS LUKE?

Luke was a medical doctor; the apostle Paul calls him "the beloved physician" (Col. 4:14). He was highly educated, as his elegant Greek and the careful research underlying his gospel and the book of Acts attest. As he candidly admits, he was not an eyewitness of Jesus's earthly ministry (Luke 1:1–3). At the same time, he was an eyewitness of portions of Paul's missionary exploits and a participant in the early church's mission (cf. Acts 16:10–17; 20:5–15; 21:1–18; 27:1–28:16).

Luke is not only an evangelist and a theologian; he is also a careful historian. As such, he presents the origins of Christianity and the early Christian mission within the compass of world history—in particular, Roman history (e.g., Luke 2:1; 3:1). Luke was with Paul in Caesarea during the apostle's two-year imprisonment there (ca. AD 55–57). He also was with Paul during his first Roman imprisonment (Col. 4:14). Thus, he could have completed his gospel in Caesarea, Rome, or anywhere in between.

WHAT IS DISTINCTIVE ABOUT LUKE'S GOSPEL?

Luke is unique among the Gospels in having a sequel—the book of Acts—which continues the story of Jesus with an account of the early Christian movement. Luke's is also the longest of the four gospels, beginning earlier (with the announcement of John's birth) and ending later (with the ascension of Jesus into heaven) than the other Synoptic Gospels. By and large, Luke follows a geographical pattern, presenting an account of Jesus's ministry in three parts: (1) his initial ministry in Galilee, (2) his lengthy journey from Galilee to Jerusalem, and (3) his final ministry in Jerusalem.

Like Matthew and Mark, Luke starts by tracing the initial stages of Jesus's teaching and healing ministry in Galilee (Luke 4:14–9:50). Luke's distinctive contribution, however, comes with his extensive "travel narrative," where he narrates Jesus's journey to Jerusalem (9:51–19:27). This section also includes many parables unique to Luke. At last, Jesus arrives in Jerusalem, culminating in Luke's passion narrative (22:39–24:51). Jesus suffers and rises from the dead to fulfill the Scriptures so that forgiveness of sins "should be proclaimed in his name to all nations" (24:44–47).

WHAT ARE SOME OF LUKE'S MAJOR EMPHASES?

The most prominent theme in Luke's gospel is salvation. Luke highlights this theme in several ways. First, he uses the language of salvation more than any other gospel writer. Jesus's mission is summarized by the programmatic declaration: "For the Son of Man came to seek and to *save* the lost" (19:10, emphasis added). Luke includes many unique parables that highlight this theme, such as the parables of the lost sheep, the lost coin, and the prodigal son (15:3–32).

Luke also portrays the life of Jesus as fulfilling God's promises to Israel as recorded in the Old Testament and as the culmination of God's purposes in salvation history (22:44–49). Everything that takes place in the life of Jesus—including his death on the cross, his burial, and his resurrection—is necessary and happens according to God's plan. God's plan entails that, in addition to believing Jews, the Gentiles will be recipients of salvation as well (2:32; 3:6; 24:47).

Last but not least, Luke highlights Jesus's concern for those of low status in society, such as women, children, the poor, the sick, and other outsiders. Contrary to the expectations of the Jewish leaders, Jesus is a "friend of sinners" who has come to call them to repentance and faith in him for the purpose of salvation (5:32; 7:34). As you read the gospel, keep an eye on how this idea of a "great reversal" of expectations plays out through the characters highlighted by Luke (e.g., Zacchaeus).

CHAPTER 7—LUKE

PREPARATION

JESUS'S BIRTH AND PREPARATION FOR MINISTRY (1:1–4:13)
Luke's Purpose (1:1–4)
Two Special Births (1:5–80)
The Birth and Childhood of the Messiah (2:1–52)
The Beginning of John's Ministry and Jesus's Preparation for Ministry (3:1–4:13)

JESUS'S BIRTH AND PREPARATION FOR MINISTRY (1:1–4:13)

Luke's Purpose (1:1–4)

Luke validates Jesus's identity in three key ways. The first thing Luke does is present Jesus as a real historical person in world history. He mentions King Herod, the Roman emperors Augustus and Tiberius, the governors Quirinius and Pontius Pilate, and a host of other officials. Second, Luke speaks of "the things that have been accomplished among us" (Luke 1:1), by which he means Jesus's fulfillment of Old Testament prophecy. Third, Luke presents Jesus as divine, in terms evocative of the God of Israel, in events such as the transfiguration. The genius of writing like this is that it creates a threefold strand to Jesus's identity: "A threefold cord is not quickly broken" (Eccl. 4:12).

Luke's is the only gospel that begins with a preface that sets out the purpose of writing—namely, that his readers might have "certainty" concerning the truth of the gospel (Luke 1:4). Luke seeks to achieve this through his presentation of an "orderly account" of the life of Jesus, from his birth to his ascension (v. 3). (The word "orderly" doesn't refer so much to chronological sequence as to a coherent arrangement of the material.) Both Luke's gospel and the book of Acts are dedicated to a man named Theophilus, most likely a Roman government official, who may have served as the patron sponsoring the publication of Luke's work. Beyond this, Luke clearly had a broader audience in mind, including in his scope Gentile Christians who required solid information regarding the things they had been taught.

In the first major portion of Luke's gospel, we read about Jesus's origins and preparation for ministry. There are three parts to Luke's presentation, each of which begins with reference to a ruler. As mentioned, Luke refers to Herod, king of Judea, in 1:5, Caesar Augustus in 2:1, and Tiberius Caesar in 3:1. In this way, Luke frames his narrative in the context of Roman history for the benefit of Theophilus who, as mentioned, most likely was a Roman government official.

Two Special Births (1:5–80)

Luke begins his account of Jesus by imitating Old Testament language. He intends for the reader to draw parallels between the characters in the story of Jesus's birth and prominent figures in the Old Testament who are righteous and faithful to God. The central theme of the birth narrative is the arrival of God's salvation, which fulfills his promise of redemption for Israel. Highlighting this theme are two noteworthy features in Luke's literary presentation.

First, Luke records the birth accounts of John the Baptist and Jesus in parallel fashion. The two accounts are artfully interwoven as both births are foretold by the angel Gabriel and elicit songs of praise by one of their parents. This is part of Luke's continual focus on the witness theme in Luke's two-volume work, which in turn may hark back to the requirement of two or three witnesses in the book of Deuteronomy (17:6; 19:15).

The Background to John the Baptist's Birth (1:5–25)

When sketching the background of the account of John the Baptist's birth, Luke notes that his parents are childless—Elizabeth is barren, and both Zechariah and Elizabeth are well advanced in years (reminiscent of Abraham and Sarah). Humanly speaking, there is no chance they would conceive in their old age. This underscores the miraculous nature of John's birth. What's more, when Zechariah ministers in the temple, an angel of the Lord suddenly appears and delivers the news that Zechariah and Elizabeth will have a son, whom they are to name John. He will be filled with the Holy Spirit, turn many Israelites to the Lord, and minister in the spirit of Elijah, the powerful Old Testament prophet. When Zechariah expresses doubt, the angel identifies himself as Gabriel and says that Zechariah will be unable to speak because of his unbelief. In keeping with Gabriel's words, Elizabeth conceives and is five months along in her pregnancy when the section ends.

The Background to Jesus's Birth (1:26–38)

At this point, Luke skillfully weaves the second birth account into his narrative. Again, God dispatches the angel Gabriel, this time to Nazareth in Galilee. He appears to a young woman named Mary, a virgin engaged to a man named Joseph, a descendant of David. Gabriel tells Mary that she will conceive a son whose name will be Jesus. He will be the Son of God and the Son of David who will inherit God's promise to David of an eternal kingship and royal dynasty. When Mary inquires as to how she, a virgin, will conceive, Gabriel explains that the Holy Spirit will impregnate her. Thus, while John the Baptist's birth was miraculous in that God enabled barren old Elizabeth to conceive, Jesus's birth will be even more miraculous in that his conception will bypass a human father altogether. In exemplary faith and humility, Mary responds, "Behold, I am the servant of the Lord; let it be to me according to your word" (Luke 1:38).

Mothers Meet and Mary's Magnificat (1:39–56)

The births of Jesus and John the Baptist are tied together even further when Mary visits Elizabeth. In a moving recognition scene, Elizabeth greets Mary, her relative, and tells her that she is blessed among women to carry the Messiah and blessed also because she has believed that the angel's words will be fulfilled. In fact, the child in her own womb—John the Baptist—leaps for joy at the sight of Mary. Elizabeth humbly adds, "And why is this granted to me that the mother of my Lord should come to me?" (v. 43). Both birth accounts signal that God is visiting his people once again. Nevertheless, John's role is quite distinct from that of Jesus. John will prepare the way for the

Lord's salvation as the Messiah's herald. Thus Zechariah, his father, quotes the prophet Malachi, which speaks of an Elijah-like forerunner to the Messiah (Mal. 4:5–6). Yet while John is to be a prophet, Jesus is to be both Savior and King. The angel Gabriel tells Mary that Jesus will be called "the Son of the Most High," who will sit on the "throne of his father David" (v. 32).

A second noteworthy feature is the series of hymns or songs of praise offered by Mary, Zechariah, and Simeon. The two birth narratives are structured around the following hymns:

- Mary's song (vv. 46–55) highlights God's exaltation of the lowly and humbling of the proud at the coming of Jesus, the Messiah and descendant of Abraham, in keeping with Luke's emphasis on the reversal Jesus has come to bring.
- Zechariah's song (vv. 68–79) focuses on John the Baptist's role in preparing the way for the Messiah and Son of David, which will include the preaching of forgiveness, in accord with Luke's emphasis on the gospel's social implications.
- Simeon's song (2:29–32) extols God's salvation and the Messiah's coming as a light to the Gentiles, in keeping with Luke's emphasis on the implications of Jesus's coming not only for Jews but also for Gentiles.

These hymns are reminiscent of Old Testament psalms reciting the account of God's coming salvation. Especially pronounced are parallels between Hannah's song when conceiving the prophet Samuel and Mary's song (cf. 1 Sam. 2). The hymns also continue parallels between John and Jesus. Clearly both are key participants in God's plan, but Jesus is the Messiah, whose coming John heralds.

The Birth of John the Baptist and Zechariah's Song (1:57–80)

John's birth narrative is placed between Mary's and Zechariah's hymns. After some back and forth regarding John's name—unusual because none of his relatives is called John—there is amazement and a sense of excited anticipation as to what kind of ministry John will have. The unit closes with John's coming of age and his appearance in the wilderness prior to his public ministry, which is paralleled by a similar later reference to Jesus's growth in wisdom and stature.

The Birth and Childhood of the Messiah (2:1–52)

The Birth of Jesus (2:1–20)

John's arrival sets the stage for the birth of Jesus. On account of a census during the reign of Caesar Augustus when a certain Quirinius is governor of Syria in the north, Joseph returns to his hometown of Bethlehem. Remarkably, Augustus's decree becomes the providential means by which Jesus's parents are induced to travel from Nazareth to Bethlehem, where Jesus will be born in keeping with Old Testament messianic prophecy.

Augustus presided over the golden age of Roman history, which was characterized by political stability and the flourishing of Roman culture, politics, and the arts. Placing the birth of Jesus within Augustus's reign signals that Jesus's birth will eclipse the golden age and the Roman peace. Jesus will be the Prince of Peace and the herald of the eternal kingdom of God. By calling Bethlehem "the city of David" and noting that Joseph is "of the house and lineage of David," Luke draws attention to Jesus's descent from king David (Luke 2:4, 11).

Yet the circumstances surrounding Jesus's birth don't seem fitting for a king. He is born in the humble town of Bethlehem. He is laid in a feeding trough for animals, because there is no room for him in the local inn. An angel announces the news of his birth to a group of lowly shepherds, who become the first messengers of the good news of salvation. Jesus's birth is hailed by a host of angels, saying, "Glory to God in the highest, and on earth peace among those with whom he is pleased!" (v. 14).

Naming and Dual Recognition of the Infant Jesus (2:21–40)

Just like John, Jesus is given his name and circumcised on the eighth day. The offering brought by his parents—"a pair of turtledoves, or two young pigeons"—marks them as poor (v. 24; cf. Lev. 5:11; 12:8). The first ones to recognize God's activity are a devout man named Simeon and an elderly widow named Anna.

As Luke—the only Gentile evangelist—is careful to point out, not only does Jesus come as "the consolation of Israel"; he also appears as "a light for revelation to the Gentiles" (Luke 2:25, 32; cf. Isa. 42:6; 49:6). In keeping with the reversal of popular messianic expectation, Simeon tells Mary ominously that her child will cause "the fall and rising of many in Israel" and that a sword will pierce her own soul, referring to Mary's grief at Jesus's crucifixion (Luke 2:34–35).

At this, Luke records the infant Jesus's return to Nazareth along with his parents. A summary statement notes that "the child grew and became strong"; he was "filled with wisdom," and God's favor rested upon him (v. 40; cf. 1 Sam. 2:26).

Twelve-Year-Old Jesus in the Temple (2:41–52)

Jesus's parents, as was customary, went up to Jerusalem every year at Passover. Luke skips a decade and recounts the twelve-year-old Jesus's visit to Jerusalem. At the end of Passover, Jesus's parents set out on their return trip, presumably as part of a caravan, but after a day's journey they realize that Jesus isn't with them. They hurry back and search for him among their relatives. After three days, they find him in the temple, sitting among the teachers and amazing them with his grasp of Scripture. When Mary addresses him as any concerned mother would have, Jesus responds that she should have known he was going to be "in his Father's house" (i.e., the temple; Luke 2:49). This unique account of the twelve-year-old Jesus serves as a segue to his public ministry.

The Beginning of John's Ministry and Jesus's Preparation for Ministry (3:1–4:13)

The Messiah's Forerunner, John the Baptist (3:1–22)

Picking up where he left off with John the Baptist, Luke returns to John in preparation for narrating Jesus's ministry. As in the case of the Old Testament prophets, "the word of God came to John" (3:2). The fact that God's call comes to John in the wilderness anticipates the words of Isaiah in verse 4—namely, that in the last days a "voice of one crying in the wilderness" will be raised in order to "prepare the way of the Lord" (cf. Isa. 40:3).

Luke highlights three vital features of John's ministry. First, he sets it in historical context by providing the actual names and dates of those in authority: Emperor Tiberius; Pontius Pilate; Herod Antipas; Antipas's brother Philip; Lysanias, tetrarch of Abilene; Caiaphas, the high priest; and Annas, his father-in-law and high-priestly patriarch. In so doing, Luke, an excellent historian, takes great pains to locate the beginning of John the Baptist's ministry in world, Roman, and Jewish history.

Second, similar to Matthew and Mark, Luke cites the opening words of the second half of the book of Isaiah with reference to John's role in preparing the way for the Lord. John would be the herald of a new exodus in which God's Servant leads his people through the wilderness as Moses did with regard to Israel of old. What's more, in a fascinating move, Luke doesn't end the quotation where the other gospel writers do but goes on, which makes clear that this new exodus is not only for Israel but for *all* people, so that "all flesh" will "see the salvation of God" (Luke 3:6). This underscores that Jesus's messianic mission has a vital universal dimension.

Third, Luke is the only evangelist to include special details of John's preaching regarding right relationships. John warns his fellow Jews against presuming on their Abrahamic descent, asserting that God could raise up children for Abraham "from these stones" (v. 8). The Jews' presumption of favorite status as God's chosen people will have dire consequences unless they repent and turn to the Messiah in contrition and faith. What's more, John's baptism of repentance must result not merely in outward expressions of faith but in a radically transformed life characterized by integrity in one's dealings with others.

The impact of John's ministry leads some to wonder whether he is the Messiah. However, John affirms that his baptism is only with water and that the Messiah will baptize with the Holy Spirit. At this, Luke notes that Herod Antipas throws John into prison for publicly chastising him for taking his brother Philip's wife. Almost casually, Luke mentions that Jesus is baptized, along with "all the people" (v. 21). Yet several supernatural manifestations occur that indicate his unique identity: "the heavens [are] opened"; "the Holy Spirit descend[s] on him in bodily form, like a dove"; and a heavenly voice affirms, "You are my beloved Son; with you I am well pleased" (vv. 21–22).

Jesus's Ancestry: The Son of Adam (3:23–38)

Noting that Jesus was "about thirty years of age" when he began his public ministry (v. 23), Luke includes Jesus's genealogy at this point in the gospel. If Jesus was born in 2 or 1 BC and started his ministry in AD 29, he would have been about thirty years old at that time. In tracing Jesus's genealogy, Luke goes all the way back to Adam. Jesus is not just Israel's Messiah but the Savior of all people; also, he is not merely the descendant of David and Abraham but a true human being descended from Adam. This qualifies him, together with his divine credentials made apparent at his baptism, to serve as the Savior of all humanity, Jew as well as Gentile.

The Temptation (4:1–13)

The conclusion of Luke's genealogy, which identifies Adam as "the son of God" (3:38), sets the stage for Jesus's temptation by the devil. Fresh from John's baptism, the descendant of Adam returns from the Jordan River, "full of the Holy Spirit," and is led by that same Spirit into the wilderness to be tempted for forty days (4:1). In response to each of the devil's temptations (and citations of Scripture!), Jesus cites passages from Deuteronomy that recall Israel's failures in the wilderness:

- "It is written, 'Man shall not live by bread alone'" (Luke 4:4; cf. Deut. 8:3).
- "It is written, 'You shall worship the Lord your God, and him only shall you serve'" (Luke 4:8; cf. Deut. 6:13).
- "It is said, 'You shall not put the Lord your God to the test'" (Luke 4:12; cf. Deut. 6:16).

In each case where Adam and Israel failed to believe and obey God, Jesus resists temptation and succeeds. God's son Adam failed his test of obedience at the original temptation; he ate the fruit from the forbidden tree his wife gave him after succumbing to the serpent's deception (Gen. 3:1–19). But Jesus refuses to eat when doing so would transgress God's command. He affirms that God alone must be worshiped and rejects idolatry and Satan worship.

Likewise, God's son Israel failed when tested in the wilderness for forty years, being barred from entering the Promised Land because of persistent unbelief (Ps. 95:8–11). But unlike Israel, which repeatedly put God to the test during the wilderness wanderings, Jesus rebuffs the devil's challenge to treat God presumptuously. Jesus, the true Israelite and sinless Son of God, lives the perfect life in complete obedience to God, so that those who trust in him can enjoy a righteous standing before God.

DISCUSSION QUESTIONS

1. What can we learn from Luke's preface about the way he wrote his gospel?

2. How is the fact that Luke was a medical doctor, and a Gentile (non-Jew), helpful for understanding his gospel?

3. What is unique about Luke's birth narrative of Jesus when compared to Matthew's gospel?

4. Imagine being John the Baptist. What would it be like to be the forerunner of the Messiah?

Many have undertaken to draw up an account of the things that have been fulfilled among us, just as they were handed down to us by those who from the first were eyewitnesses and servants of the word. With this in mind, since I myself have carefully investigated everything from the beginning, I too decided to write an orderly account for you, most excellent Theophilus, so that you may know the certainty of the things you have been taught.

—Luke 1:1–4 NIV

None of us has seen Jesus in the flesh, but our faith rests on the reliable eyewitness of those who have. Luke, who was a medical doctor and thus well educated, writes in his elegant preface that he "carefully investigated everything from the beginning," that is, engaged in scrupulous research, including talking to eyewitnesses. He frankly acknowledges that "many" had already attempted to write similar accounts, and that he himself was not an eyewitness, but he clearly instills confidence in his readers that his research can be trusted. In fact, he writes to his literary patron, a man by the name of Theophilus, that by reading Luke's account, he may know with "certainty" "the things that have been fulfilled among us." Therefore we can have a very high degree of confidence that what we read in the Gospels about Jesus is true.

CHAPTER 8—LUKE

GETTING DOWN TO WORK

MINISTRY IN GALILEE (4:14–9:50)
Introductory Sermon, Calling the Twelve, Healing Many (4:14–7:50)
Parable of the Sower, Calming a Storm, Casting Out a Demon (8:1–39)
Raising the Dead, Training the Twelve, the Transfiguration (8:40–9:50)

MINISTRY IN GALILEE (4:14–9:50)

In the second major portion of his gospel, similar to Matthew and Mark, Luke presents Jesus's Galilean ministry in three parts. After emerging victorious over the devil's temptation, Jesus returns to Galilee in the "power of the Spirit," poised to formally begin his public ministry (Luke 4:14). Luke mentions that word about Jesus has spread throughout the entire region and that he has taught in many synagogues, "being glorified by all" (v. 15).

Introductory Sermon, Calling the Twelve, Healing Many (4:14–7:50)

The Inaugural Address: Jesus Rejected at Nazareth (4:14–30)

On one Sabbath, Jesus preaches in the synagogue at Nazareth, his hometown. In a scene pregnant with meaning, he is given the scroll of Isaiah, unrolls it, and finds the place where it says, "The Spirit of the Lord is upon me, because he has anointed me to proclaim good news to the poor. He has sent me to proclaim liberty to the captives and recovering of sight to the blind, to set at liberty those who are oppressed, to proclaim the year of the Lord's favor" (vv. 18–19; cf. Isa. 61:1–2). At this, he rolls the scroll back up, gives it to the person who handed it to him, and sits down. Everyone's gaze in the synagogue is fixed on him, and he says, "Today this Scripture has been fulfilled in your hearing" (Luke 4:21).

This is truly a remarkable moment in history and a climactic exclamation point in Luke's gospel. Jesus proclaims that Isaiah's prediction has now been fulfilled—in him! *Jesus* is the Spirit-anointed Messiah. Fittingly, Jesus makes this announcement in his hometown of Nazareth which, in keeping with Isaiah's prediction, has served as his base for ministry. This climactic moment in Luke's gospel uniquely presents Jesus as a liberator of the oppressed, a friend of the poor, and a healer of the sick and weak. This is the kind of Messiah Jesus is, according to Luke. Great news! Great news, that is, if you know yourself to be poor, weak, and needy. These are the people for whom Jesus has come, and that's the Jesus Luke portrays in his gospel.

At first, all speak well of Jesus and commend his gracious words. And yet they wonder: "Is not this Joseph's son?" (v. 22). Jesus picks up on their skepticism by saying, "Doubtless you will quote to me this proverb, 'Physician, heal yourself'" (v. 23). And he anticipates their demand that he do in Nazareth what he has done elsewhere. He goes on to point out that in the days of Elijah and Elisha there was great famine and sickness, and many people were in need; yet God sent his prophets only to two Gentiles—the widow of Zarephath and Naaman the Syrian, unlikely recipients of his grace (cf. 1 Kings 17:8–16; 2 Kings 5:1–14).

Upon hearing this, the people of Nazareth are enraged and drive Jesus out of the city. In fact, they bring him to the edge of a cliff so they can throw him down! Yet he passes through their midst and slips away. This episode underscores two important emerging themes in Luke's gospel—God's salvation extending to the Gentiles and the rejection of the Messiah.

Capernaum: Casting Out Demons, Healing Many, and Further Work (4:31–44)

The fulfillment of Isaiah's prophecy is further confirmed by the actions that follow Jesus's rejection in Nazareth. Jesus next goes to his adoptive hometown of Capernaum, where he preaches in the town's synagogue and all are astonished at his authority. He sternly casts out a demon from a man right there in the synagogue: "Be silent and come out of him!" (Luke 4:35). The demon, speaking in the plural, had just addressed him as "Jesus of Nazareth" and stated, "I know who you are—the Holy One of God" (v. 34). Ironically, what the people of Nazareth have failed to realize, demons know full well: Jesus is God's Messiah, the Holy One of God.

After a brief interlude in which Jesus, after leaving the synagogue, enters Peter's house and heals his mother-in-law, who had come down with a "high fever" (noted only by Luke, the physician), people at sunset bring all their sick and even demon-possessed to Jesus, "and he [lays] hands on every one of them and heal[s] them" (vv. 38, 40). These are incredible scenes! Demons come out of many at Jesus's command, crying, "You are the Son of God!" Yet Jesus doesn't need their witness. He orders them to be quiet because "they knew that he was the Christ" (v. 41). At this, Jesus wants to withdraw, but people try to keep him from leaving. He tells them he must preach "the good news of the kingdom of God" in other towns as well and moves on to synagogues in Judea (vv. 43–44).

Calling His First Disciples (5:1–11)

During the first stage of his Galilean ministry, Jesus also calls his first disciples. In Peter's case, he had fished all night and come up empty-handed. When Jesus tells him where to cast his nets, Peter takes him at his word and catches so many fish that the nets break. Peter is deeply struck by Jesus's authority, so much so that he tells him to depart from him, for he is nothing but a sinful man. Yet this is exactly where Jesus wants him. He calls him to follow him and tells him that from now on he will no longer be catching fish but people. You can hardly blame Peter and his friends for leaving everything behind to follow Jesus.

Cleansing a Leper and Healing a Paralytic (5:12–26)

A series of events in Jesus's ministry now incites the growing opposition of the Jewish leaders. First, "in one of the cities" (5:12), Jesus cleanses a leper, telling him to be quiet about the healing, to show himself to the local priest, and to bring the required offering for the cleansing. Yet word about Jesus spreads everywhere; great crowds gather to hear him teach and to be healed. Jesus, for his part, withdraws to pray.

Second, Jesus heals a paralyzed man. The man's friends creatively lower him through the roof, and Jesus promptly pronounces the man's sins forgiven, exercising authority reserved for God alone. The scribes and Pharisees promptly accuse Jesus of blasphemy. Inciting their anger further, Jesus tells the man to get up, take his mat, and go home, which he does. People are amazed, yet Jesus's opponents are seething.

Calling Levi and Answering Questions About Fasting (5:27–39)

At this, Jesus calls another disciple, Levi (Matthew), a tax collector. Tax collectors were despised by all because they collected taxes for the hated Romans (and a little extra for themselves). Yet Jesus is willing to forgive outcasts such as these and, in Levi's case, even call one to join his mission. This is the kind of Messiah Luke portrays—one who calls those the world rejects and who forgives those who repent of their sins, while rebuffing those who are proud of their standing in society.

In fact, Levi has a huge party at his house, celebrating Jesus's call with many of his friends, with Jesus right in their midst. The Pharisees and scribes voice their disdain and disapproval, but Jesus retorts that it is the sick who need a doctor (as Luke was well aware) and that he has come not to call the righteous but sinners to repentance. It's hard to overstate just how revolutionary Jesus's approach was when compared to other Jewish religious teachers of his day.

After criticizing his association with "sinners," Jesus's opponents go on to question his disciples' failure to fast. Jesus says that one can hardly blame the disciples for rejoicing while the bridegroom (Jesus) is with them! Plus, new wine—the gospel about Jesus—must be put into fresh wineskins. Luke doesn't record any rebuttal by the Pharisees. The reader surmises they don't understand the true meaning of Jesus's words.

Authority over the Sabbath (6:1–11)

Finally, the Pharisees object to Jesus's disciples plucking out and eating some heads of grain, rubbing them in their hands on the Sabbath. Apparently, this breaks one of the Pharisees' numerous regulations of what constitutes work on the Sabbath. In response, Jesus pointedly defends his disciples' conduct by citing a scriptural precedent involving David and his men (1 Sam. 21:6). The disciples haven't violated any biblical command but only Jewish tradition. Jesus claims authority to interpret the Sabbath command in Scripture, ultimately on the basis that he is one with the Creator and covenant God of Israel.

On another Sabbath, Jesus teaches in a synagogue in the presence of a man with a limp right hand. Despite the Pharisees' opposition, Jesus heals him in plain view, knowing it would only exacerbate their antagonism toward him. Sure enough, they are "filled with fury" and begin to plot how to take action against Jesus (Luke 6:11). Why are they so strongly opposed to him? As Jesus has repeatedly said, they have built an entire system of regulations on top of Scripture and have increasingly failed to distinguish between what is directly stated in Scripture and their own interpretations and applications.

Calling the Twelve Apostles (6:12–16)

"In these days," when opposition to him gradually mounts, Jesus goes "to the mountain" to pray all night before appointing twelve apostles the next morning (v. 12). In the specific men he selects, Jesus makes some interesting choices that fly in the face of conventional wisdom. Yet he discerns the condition of people's hearts and knows that he can always train them in ministry skills and in the performance of various tasks. He also knows that over time they will grow in understanding their own sinfulness and their need for spiritual enablement. Yet what cannot be learned as easily is the willingness to leave everything behind to follow Jesus and to put him first in all things. The Twelve (except for Judas) are prepared to do that out of true love for and devotion to him and at least an initial understanding of who Jesus is. In due course, they all (except for John—and Judas, of course) will give their lives for him and die a martyr's death. This proves that, while not conforming to the world's criteria of what a good résumé looks like, Jesus chooses well.

The Sermon on the Plain (6:17–49)

After this, Jesus descends to a "level place" to engage in an extended period of teaching. The ensuing sermon begins with a series of blessings highlighting the present condition of the disciples: poor, hungry, weeping, and rejected. Conversely, Jesus pronounces four woes on those who are presently rich, full, laughing, and popular. A great reversal is taking place with the arrival of Jesus. Throughout his gospel, Luke shows how social and economic realities go hand in hand with spiritual ones. The Sermon on the Plain serves as an example of the Messiah's mission to preach good news to the poor. It also summarizes Jesus's ethical message, emphasizing the radical values of God's kingdom, including the call to love one's enemies.

Jesus's teaching is as compelling as it is convicting. "Can a blind man lead a blind man?" he asks. "Will they not both fall into a pit?" We need to make sure we ourselves see clearly if we want to guide others in the truth and confront them with their sin. Just as a tree is known by its fruit—and a bad tree cannot bear good fruit—so our hearts are revealed and reflected in our words and actions. Those who act on truth and fail to do so are likened to two men who respectively build a house on a proper foundation (rock) and on shaky ground. Again, the message is obvious: only those who build their lives on the foundation of Jesus's teaching will withstand the final day of judgment; all others will be swept away.

Healing a Centurion's Servant (7:1–10)

How will people respond to Jesus's radical message? The rest of his early ministry in Galilee meets with various responses. As he returns to Capernaum, his Galilean headquarters, Jesus encounters a Roman centurion who pleads with him to heal his servant. While those who know the centurion tell Jesus "he is worthy," the centurion himself tells Jesus he is "not worthy" to have him come to his house (7:4, 6). Instead, he asks Jesus just to say the word so his servant will be healed. As a military commander, he knows the compelling power of a command spoken by a person in authority.

What incredible faith! Here is someone who believes in the power of Jesus's word. This is one of the rare occasions in Luke's gospel when Jesus marvels at another's faith and promptly does what is requested. Jesus exclaims, "I tell you, not even in Israel have I found such faith" (v. 9). In this way, Luke again highlights that now Gentiles have come under the orbit of Jesus's salvation. In fact, they surpass the Jewish people by their receptivity to Jesus and his word.

Raising a Widow's Son (7:11–17)

Next, Jesus, approaching a town called Nain, learns of a poor widow's only son, who had recently died and was being carried away. Jesus has compassion on her and raises him from the dead: "the dead man sat up and began to speak, and Jesus gave him to his mother" (v. 15). The episode is brimming with Jesus's messianic authority to raise the dead, intermingled with moving compassion for weak and needy people—in this case, a poor widow and her deceased son, who likely was her only means of support. At the sight of this amazing miracle, people are seized by fear and give glory to God, saying, "A great prophet has arisen among us!" and "God has visited his people!" (v. 16). This is nice but still falls short of understanding who Jesus truly is—the Messiah and Son of God. Again, Jesus's amazing miracles provide powerful advertising, and the news about him is broadcast far and wide all over Judea and the vicinity.

Messengers from John the Baptist (7:18–35)

Jesus's identity continues to be a central focus when news of his ministry reaches John the Baptist. The last thing we had heard about John was that he had been thrown in jail by Herod Antipas (3:19–20). Now, Luke tells us that John's disciples report to John the feats Jesus has performed. Upon receiving the news, John sends some of his followers to Jesus to inquire, "Are you the one who is to come, or shall we look for another?" (7:19). This is both sad and surprising, as John was Jesus's forerunner who had heralded him as the Messiah. Now, apparently—languishing in a dark dungeon—John is plagued by doubts. The Baptist's followers relay his question to Jesus who, rather than giving a direct yes or no answer, responds by saying, "the blind receive their sight, the lame walk, lepers are cleansed, and the deaf hear, the dead are raised up, the poor have good news preached to them" (v. 22). Jesus points to the messianic manifestations he has provided and allows John himself to draw the inexorable conclusion: anyone who has done the *works* of the Messiah *is* in fact the Messiah (cf. Isa. 26:19; 29:18–19; 35:5–6; 61:1–2).

Upon sending the messengers back to John, Jesus talks to the crowds about him, affirming that he indeed is the one of whom it is written, "Behold, I send my messenger before your face, who will prepare your way before you" (Luke 7:27; cf. Mal. 3:1). As the forerunner of the Messiah, John is second to none; and yet every citizen of God's kingdom is greater than him. At this, the tax collectors and sinners rejoice, because they had been baptized by John as a sign of their repentance, while the Pharisees and experts in the law cringe, as they had "rejected the purpose of God for themselves" and refused John's baptism (Luke 7:29–30). The stubborn refusal of "this generation" (v. 31) is a sign of the rise and fall of many in Israel. Jesus compares people to children on the playground who can't agree on which game to play. They don't like John's asceticism, and they don't like Jesus's gregariousness either! No matter what Jesus does, they are going to reject him. Yet wisdom will be vindicated by her children, who will listen to her.

Anointed by a "Sinful" Woman (7:36–50)

Jesus's comment on wisdom is further illustrated in the story of the Pharisee and the "sinful" woman. The Pharisee invites Jesus to his home for a meal. As they recline, a woman anoints Jesus's feet with expensive ointment. At this, the Pharisee thinks to himself that Jesus must not be a true prophet or else he would have known that this is a sinful woman.

Jesus, knowing his thoughts, tells him a story about a moneylender with two debtors, one who owes a small amount and the other who owes a large amount. Neither is able to pay, so the moneylender cancels their debts. Which of them will love him more?

The obvious answer: the one with the larger debt! Similarly, Jesus argues, those who are forgiven much will have much greater love for the one who has forgiven them. In this way, he provides a fitting commentary on what had just transpired: the woman had loved Jesus by anointing his feet, while the Pharisee had criticized him. At this, Jesus turns to the woman and tells her that her sins are forgiven. The Pharisee, on the other hand, fails to acknowledge his need for forgiveness. The sinful woman proves herself a true child of wisdom, while those at table pose a poignant question: "Who is this, who even forgives sins?" (v. 49).

Parable of the Sower, Calming a Storm, Casting Out a Demon (8:1–39)

Jesus's Female Followers (8:1–3)

At this juncture, Luke mentions a group of female followers of Jesus who have sacrificially supported him in his ministry. Some of them "had been healed of evil spirits and infirmities"; in Mary Magdalene's case, Jesus had cast out seven demons (8:2). One of them, Joanna, was the wife of Herod Antipas's steward. And many even contributed to Jesus and the Twelve financially so that they could go about their mission. In this way, these women exhibit true gospel partnership with Jesus.

The Parable of the Sower (8:4–15)

Each of the four types of soil portrays a heart condition that yields a certain response to Jesus's message. Yet only the "good soil" is responsive to God's word and produces a rich crop through perseverance and obedience, while the other types of soil prove unfruitful. Jesus explains the meaning of the parable at the request of his disciples.

Truth Brought to Light (8:16–18)

At the end of his explanation of the parable of the sower, Jesus speaks of an "honest and good heart" that produces spiritual fruit upon hearing the word of God (v. 15). He continues by urging his followers to let their light shine, because eventually the truth will come to light. Therefore,

Jesus warns them to "take care then how you hear" (v. 18). According to a spiritual law enunciated by Jesus, those who have will receive even more, while those who don't have will lose even what they think they have.

True Family Relationships (8:19–21)

At this, Jesus's mother and brothers come to see him. When Jesus is told that his family is waiting to see him, he declares, "My mother and my brothers are those who hear the word of God and do it" (v. 21). This may seem harsh, as some may wonder why Jesus doesn't go out to see his mother and brothers, who may have come from a great distance. But Jesus is seeking to drive home the point that those who follow him make up a new spiritual family, which is even closer than natural families.

Calming the Storm (8:22–25)

Jesus's parable and his interaction regarding his mother and brothers are followed by a series of encounters. Each of these demonstrates his divine power and authority. First, while on a boating trip with his disciples, Jesus calms a fierce storm by his mere word. In awe, the disciples ask one another, "Who then is this, that he commands even winds and water, and they obey him?" (v. 25).

The Gerasene Demoniac (8:26–39)

In the final scene of this portion of Luke's narrative, the disciples meet a demon-possessed man from the region of Gadara. The demon-possessed man who charges at Jesus is naked and roams among the tombs. The demons inside the man challenge Jesus: "What have you to do with me, Jesus, Son of the Most High God?" (v. 28). Jesus proceeds to cast the legion of demons out of the man and into a herd of pigs, which rush down a steep bank into the Sea of Galilee and drown. Not only does Jesus wield power over creation; demons submit to his authority as well.

At the conclusion of the account of the Gadarene demoniac, Luke strikingly hints at Jesus's divine nature by referring to him in the same vein as God. When the man begs Jesus to allow him to follow him, Jesus instead tells him to go home and "declare how much *God* has done for you." At this, Luke tells us that the man "went away, proclaiming throughout the whole city how much *Jesus* had done for him" (v. 39, emphasis added). It's not hard to put two and two together: Jesus is God, and God has done amazing things through Jesus!

Raising the Dead, Training the Twelve, the Transfiguration (8:40–9:50)

Raising Jairus's Daughter and Healing a Woman with Blood Flow (8:40–56)

The third part of Jesus's Galilean ministry picks up where the second left off. Jesus previously raised a widow's *son* from the dead; now, he raises a man's *daughter*. Upon Jesus's return from his excursion with his disciples, he is met by a synagogue leader named Jairus, whose twelve-year-old daughter is deathly ill. On his way to Jairus's home, Jesus encounters a woman who has been suffering from bleeding for twelve years. (Doctor Luke adds that this poor woman "had spent all her living on physicians," though no one could heal her [v. 43].) Despite Jairus's urgent need, Jesus attends to the suffering woman and heals her. He then proceeds to the girl despite news of her death, brushing aside a messenger's remark not to "trouble the Teacher any more" (v. 49).

Jesus enters the house, taking only his inner circle (Peter, James, and John) with him. The parents are heartbroken, and everyone is weeping and mourning for the girl who has died. When Jesus tells the bystanders that she isn't dead but only asleep, they laugh at him because they know she is dead. Yet Jesus tenderly takes her by the hand and says, "Child, arise" (v. 54). At this, her spirit returns, she immediately gets up, and Jesus gives instructions to give her something to eat.

The obvious conclusion is that this is no mere human! Jesus has divine authority over sickness and even death. While it makes sense to call a doctor or healer when a person is sick or even close to dying, people intuitively realize that once a person has died, even a doctor is no longer able to help. Yet Jesus is no mere physician. He is the divine physician who can bring people back to life even when they've died. Jesus only did this a few times literally during his time on earth, but he did so as a sign that, as God, he has the power to bring people back to life in the resurrection from the dead. This is our hope as Christians: that when we die, he will raise us up again on the last day, and we will spend eternity with him in the new creation.

Sending Out the Twelve; Herod Is Perplexed (9:1–9)

Having established Jesus's messianic authority, Luke shifts the focus onto the Twelve. Jesus has trained his followers for a considerable amount of time, and he now grants them authority over demons and diseases and commissions them to proclaim the kingdom of God and to heal. By commissioning his followers and putting them to work, Jesus demonstrates that following him involves participating in his mission. News of their mission even reaches Herod Antipas, who asks, "John I beheaded, but who is this about whom I hear such things?" (9:9). Luke tantalizingly mentions that Herod even seeks to see Jesus, though apparently his efforts are unsuccessful, at least at this time. At this, Jesus's followers return and report to Jesus what they have done.

Feeding the Five Thousand (9:10–17)

Next, Jesus takes his followers aside and they go to Bethsaida, a town on the north shore of the Sea of Galilee and hometown of several of Jesus's disciples. Again, Jesus tells them about the kingdom of God and cures those in need of healing. This is followed by the feeding of the five thousand, the final miracle of this section. Again, Jesus's authority is shown to be all-encompassing. Luke shows Jesus to be a gentle healer and a compassionate shepherd, whose heart goes out to the needs, frailties, and weaknesses of people in the variety of struggles they face.

Peter's Confession and Jesus's Passion Prediction (9:18–27)

The stage is set for two climactic moments in Luke's narrative: Peter's confession of Jesus as the Messiah at Caesarea Philippi and Jesus's glorious transformation on the Mount of Transfiguration. Paradoxically, Luke tells us that Jesus was praying "alone," yet the disciples "were with him." Apparently as an outflow of his praying, Jesus asks the Twelve who the crowds say that he is. When they indicate that there is no consensus, Jesus follows up with an even more vital question: "But who do *you* say that I am?" Peter, speaking for the Twelve, replies, "The Christ of God" (v. 20, emphasis added).

This is truly a watershed moment, when Jesus's revelation of himself breaks through and one of his closest followers accurately understands who he is—the long-awaited Messiah. This is what people had intimated when Jesus was born (Jesus's mother, Mary; John's father, Zechariah; and Simeon). This is also what Jesus's entire earthly ministry up to this point has indicated. It's almost as if, after all this pent-up tension, struggle, and hopeful expectation, Peter's confession breaks the ice and erupts as an exclamation point for what the entire gospel has been building toward.

Peter's confession also serves as a significant pivot in Jesus's ministry, at which Jesus shifts his attention to preparing his disciples even more intensely for their future mission by predicting that he must suffer and be rejected, killed, and raised on the third day. Contrary to the prevailing expectation of a powerful national deliverer, Jesus reveals that he is a *suffering* messiah. His mission involves being rejected and even killed, taking up a cross and dying for the forgiveness of sinful humanity. In the same vein, he calls every disciple to "take up his cross daily and follow [him]" (v. 23).

This call to follow Jesus in his sacrifice and suffering is at the very heart of biblical discipleship. Don't gloss over this too quickly! Jesus doesn't identify himself merely as a religious leader or national hero. He's not just another prophet, rabbi, or charismatic figure. Remember, as C. S. Lewis argued, he is either a lunatic, a liar, or Lord! As those who have carefully read Luke's gospel thus far, witnessing Jesus's sane yet strikingly transcendent spiritual authority, we're compelled to conclude that this is no lunatic and certainly no liar.

As the account continues, we witness the second climactic moment in Jesus's earthly ministry narrated in Luke's gospel thus far. Following his convicting, powerful words that "whoever is ashamed of me and of my words, of him will the Son of Man be ashamed when he comes in his glory and the glory of the Father and of the holy angels," Jesus adds, "there are some standing here who will not taste death until they see the kingdom of God" (vv. 26–27). This is indeed a stirring prospect, which no doubt leaves the disciples at a loss as to what Jesus means.

The Transfiguration and the Second Passion Prediction (9:28–45)

We don't have to wait long to find out. Again, Jesus goes off to pray. And again, he takes only Peter, James, and John with him. As he is praying on the mountain, his inner circle is given a tantalizing glimpse of Jesus's glory as the appearance of his face changes and his clothes turn radiant white. All of a sudden, Moses and Elijah appear and speak with Jesus about his "exodus" in Jerusalem. And the disciples hear a heavenly voice reiterating what was said at Jesus's baptism, "This is my Son, my Chosen One," with the additional charge, "listen to him!" (v. 35; cf. Deut. 18:18–19). They witness an unforgettable scene—one that Peter will recall more than thirty years later (2 Peter 1:16–18).

In the meantime, while Jesus and the three disciples are on the mountain, the other disciples are unable to cast out a demon from a young boy. Jesus chastises them for being part of a "faithless and twisted generation"

(Luke 9:41), and he promptly casts out the demon and gives the boy back to his father. All are amazed at the "majesty of God" on display in Jesus (v. 43). It's hard to see how the remarkable displays of Jesus's majesty won't inexorably lead to his messianic victory. Yet Jesus reiterates the prediction of his imminent demise for a second time: "Let these words sink into your ears: The Son of Man is about to be delivered into the hands of men" (v. 44). Yet they don't understand what Jesus is saying and are too afraid to ask him.

True Greatness in the Kingdom (9:46–50)

At this, the disciples proceed to argue with one another as to who among them is the greatest. While Jesus *just* reminded them that he will soon be killed, they continued to presumptuously divide the spoils of Jesus's conquests that, they were sure, would follow in short order. You can only imagine Jesus's exasperation. With astonishing forbearance and patience, Jesus challenges their selfish attitudes and says that "he who is least among you all"—devoid of any formal status, like a little child—"is the one who is great" (v. 48).

Changing the topic, John tells Jesus that the disciples have witnessed someone cast out demons in Jesus's name and have tried to stop him. Again, Jesus rebukes them and tells them that "the one who is not against you is for you" (v. 50). It seems that at this juncture in Jesus's ministry, the disciples can't get anything right! Despite Peter's confession, it's clear that Jesus's followers don't fully grasp what it means to follow him. They still have a long way to go; they indulge in delusions of grandeur, while Jesus is thinking about the cross.

DISCUSSION QUESTIONS

1. In what ways did Jesus's sermon in his hometown synagogue in Nazareth set the tone for his ministry?

2. Reflect on who Jesus chose as his twelve apostles. What does that reveal about Jesus's values and approach to leadership?

3. At one point, John the Baptist doubted whether Jesus was the Messiah. Have you experienced doubts in your spiritual journey? If so, what were they, and how did you overcome these?

4. When Jesus's family came to see him, he said, "My mother and my brothers are those who hear the word of God and do it." How do you navigate your relationship with your natural family and with those in the family of God?

He told them this parable: "No one tears a piece out of a new garment to patch an old one. Otherwise, they will have torn the new garment, and the patch from the new will not match the old. And no one pours new wine into old wineskins. Otherwise, the new wine will burst the skins; the wine will run out and the wineskins will be ruined. No, new wine must be poured into new wineskins."

—Luke 5:36–38 NIV

First-century Jews kept wine not in bottles but in wineskins. Over time, these wineskins got porous and eventually burst. Thus, new wine must be poured into new wineskins. Jesus uses this practice as an analogy for his own messianic mission. He came not merely to reform Judaism, or add another interpretation of the Mosaic law as many of his contemporary Jewish rabbis habitually did. Rather, he came to bring something entirely new: salvation and forgiveness through the once-for-all shed blood of Christ at the cross of Calvary. Thus what his followers are called to do is not merely integrate faith in Jesus into their existing belief system but understand that a paradigm shift was required. Jesus was here to fulfill the law and to usher in the new age of the Spirit.

CHAPTER 9—LUKE

THE LONG JOURNEY

THE JOURNEY TO JERUSALEM (9:51–19:27)
The Cost of Discipleship, the Good Samaritan, and the Lord's Prayer (9:51–11:54)
The Rich Fool and the Importance of Being Ready (12:1–13:9)
The Mustard Seed, the Narrow Gate, and the Trilogy of Lost Things (13:10–15:32)
The Dishonest Steward, the Rich Man and Lazarus, and Unworthy Servants (16:1–17:10)
The Ten Lepers, the Persistent Widow, the Rich Ruler, and Zacchaeus (17:11–19:27)

THE JOURNEY TO JERUSALEM (9:51–19:27)

A little more than a third into his gospel, Luke writes that Jesus, with steely determination and in certain expectation of his rejection by the Jewish leaders, "set his face to go to Jerusalem" (Luke 9:51). Not only this; Luke also refers, at this still relatively early stage in his narrative, to Jesus's future ascension to heaven. This underscores the pivotal nature of this passage in his narrative. The references to Jesus's resolute determination to head toward Jerusalem and to his ascension introduce the remainder of Luke's gospel and form a bookend with the conclusion of the Lukan narrative.

This section is often called the "Lukan travel narrative," as Luke devotes more space to Jesus's journey to Jerusalem than any other gospel writer. You'll notice an equivalent of the phrase "as they were traveling" appear repeatedly as a way of keeping the narrative moving (e.g., v. 57; 10:38). However, the travel narrative doesn't read like a travelogue. Rather, it records a large amount of Jesus's teaching, most notably several unique Lukan parables, such as the parable of the good Samaritan and the parable of the prodigal son.

The travel narrative highlights an intensified focus on the cross and the salvation it will accomplish. Jesus is determined to fulfill his mission as the suffering Messiah. It's impossible to fully grasp who Jesus is without grappling with the purpose of his impending death. So Luke casts the rest of his gospel in the shadow of the cross. This is underscored by the emphasis on Jerusalem, where previous prophets, such as Isaiah and Zechariah, were put to death (e.g., Matt. 23:35, 37; Luke 13:34; cf. 2 Chron. 24:20–22). Yet Jerusalem is also where Jesus will accomplish humanity's salvation.

The Cost of Discipleship, the Good Samaritan, and the Lord's Prayer (9:51–11:54)

Rejected by a Samaritan Village (9:51–56)

Jesus sends an advance team to a Samaritan village, but the people there don't receive him. The reason Luke gives for the Samaritan rejection of Jesus is that "his face was set toward Jerusalem" (Luke 9:53). This ties in the account with the just-mentioned Lukan reference to Jesus "set[ting] his face to go to Jerusalem." On one level, this may simply mean that the Samaritans are engaged in their long-standing feud with the Jews, who have considered them a mixed race and have looked at their rival sanctuary on Mount Gerizim with disdain (John 4:9, 20). At a deeper level, Luke shows that the Samaritans are seeking to obstruct the very purpose for which Jesus came: to die on the cross for the sins of all people.

Nevertheless, when James and John ask him if he wants them to call down fire from heaven and consume the Samaritans, Jesus rebukes them at once. We admire their self-confidence (could they really call down fire from heaven?) and their zeal for Jesus (they're obviously outraged that the Samaritans have rejected him), but their over-the-top reaction shows that they've misunderstood the nature of Jesus's mission. He hasn't come to exact wrath on humanity but, rather, to save it. One thinks of Sodom and Gomorrah, Elijah, or Jonah's stance toward Nineveh (Luke 9:30; 10:12;

11:29–32). While there will be a time for God to judge the world, this is the time of salvation.

Three Would-Be Followers (9:57–62)

"As they were going along the road" reinforces the Lukan travel narrative: Jesus and his followers are on the road to Jerusalem (9:57). As they're on their way, Jesus is approached by three potential disciples. In each case, Jesus reveals the radical cost of following him—a willingness to leave behind the comforts of home, occupation, and loved ones. "Foxes have holes, and birds of the air have nests," Jesus tells the first, "but the Son of Man has nowhere to lay his head" (v. 58).

In the second instance, it is Jesus who calls a man to follow him, but the man asks Jesus for time to go and bury his father. This would seem like a reasonable request if his father had already died; yet the man may be saying he wants to *wait until* his father dies (at which time he would get his inheritance), and *then* he will follow Jesus. Yet while waiting for his inheritance may be appropriate, Jesus tells him to let the dead bury the dead, but he must proclaim God's kingdom. This man too, one assumes, ends up not following Jesus.

Yet a third prospective follower asks Jesus to allow him to say goodbye to his loved ones. Jesus says, "No one who puts his hand to the plow and looks back is fit for the kingdom of God" (v. 62). Here, one thinks of Lot's wife, who looked back toward Sodom and Gomorrah and turned into a pillar of salt (cf. Gen. 19:26; Luke 17:32). Following Jesus requires wholehearted devotion and dedication. Anyone who thinks he can focus simultaneously on both serving Jesus and attending to his family has divided interests.

This is illustrated by the call narratives in the Gospels, which show that Jesus's disciples leave their families and sources of livelihood to follow Jesus. They don't look back; their interests aren't divided. By gathering these three vignettes and joining them together at the outset of Jesus's travel narrative, Luke skillfully highlights what it means to follow Jesus. It requires radical commitment and must be one's top priority. Nothing is more important than one's commitment to follow Jesus.

Sending Out the Seventy(-two) (10:1–20)

In the next scene, Jesus sends out seventy(-two) other disciples to highlight the importance of mission (an event recorded only in Luke;

manuscripts variously list the number as seventy or seventy-two; Jewish tradition used the numbers interchangeably). The fact that Jesus sends out not only the Twelve but now also a larger circle of followers shows that his mission is expanding. Jesus prepares his disciples, instructing them to travel light, heal the sick, announce the arrival of God's kingdom, and expect rejection. The number seventy (or seventy-two) carries symbolic significance and represents all the nations of the earth (cf. Gen. 10:2–31).

The seventy return in amazement, having experienced the same kind of success as the Twelve. In a striking image, Jesus tells his followers, "I saw Satan fall like lightning from heaven" (Luke 10:18). However, Jesus instructs them that their joy should be grounded not in their success in ministry but in the certainty of their eternal destiny. Jesus's disciples are engaged in a cosmic conflict and mortal combat with the forces of evil, yet in the power of Jesus they can and will prevail.

The Privilege of Knowing Jesus (10:21–24)

Jesus rejoices in the Holy Spirit, because God the Father has revealed his true identity to his disciples. He contrasts them with the Galilean cities that have rejected this revelation and praises God that he has chosen to hide these spiritual truths from the proud, while revealing them to the humble.

Then Jesus tells the disciples that they're blessed to see and hear what many Old Testament prophets and kings desired to witness but didn't. The disciples are in a privileged position to catch a glimpse of God's revelation at this extraordinary juncture in human history.

The Parable of the Good Samaritan (10:25–37)

Next, Jesus is tested by an expert in the law who asks, "Teacher, what shall I do to inherit eternal life?" This is not a question by someone who really wants an answer and is open to following Jesus. Rather, this "legal expert" is putting Jesus "to the test" (v. 25). This is both sad and tragic, as Jesus's coming requires a response at a much deeper level than catching him in some contradiction! This scribe has totally missed the point. For him, interpreting Scripture is like playing a game in which you outmaneuver your rabbinic opponent and show how clever you are. One thinks of Jesus's just-uttered prayer, in which he praises his Father in heaven for having "hidden these things from the wise and understanding and revealed them to little children" (v. 21).

In response, Jesus coolly asks the scribe a counterquestion: "What is written in the Law? How do you read it?" (v. 26). The scribe replies by quoting two well-known passages from Deuteronomy and Leviticus: "You shall love the Lord your God with all your heart and with all your soul and with all your strength and with all your mind, and your neighbor as yourself" (v. 27). Jesus responds, "You have answered correctly; do this, and you will live" (v. 28). This is both astute and ironic, because Jesus knows that loving God with all one's heart and loving one's neighbor as oneself are a lot more easily said than done! Sure enough, the scribe tightens up and gets defensive. In fact, Luke tells us that he wants "to justify himself," once again trying to involve Jesus in a rabbinic squabble: "And who is my neighbor?" (v. 29).

Rather than respond with a straight answer or definition, Jesus tells the scribe a parable. As the story goes, a man is robbed on his way from Jerusalem to Jericho. Both a priest and a Levite pass by without helping him; then a despised Samaritan comes along, who movingly cares for the man. At the end of the parable, Jesus asks the scribe, "Which of these three, do you think, proved to be a neighbor to the man who fell among the robbers?" (v. 36). The scribe is forced to admit, "The one who showed him mercy"—though he can't get himself to pronounce the word "Samaritan"! At this, Jesus simply tells him to "go, and do likewise" (v. 37). Love is validated by action, and being a true neighbor is expressed by charitable action toward a person in need.

This is one of several parables unique to Luke included in the travel narrative. Many of these parables, in continuity with Old Testament law, illustrate God's deep concern for outcasts in society and the great reversal taking place through Jesus's ministry: humble outsiders are welcomed and blessed, while arrogant insiders are rebuked and left out. Throughout this section, we see the following parables reinforce and resonate with this theme of reversal.

Mary and Martha (10:38–42)

After Jesus tells his parable, he and his followers, "as they [go] on their way," enter a village where a woman named Martha welcomes him (v. 38). Mary, Martha's younger sister, takes the posture of a disciple, humbly sitting at Jesus's feet and listening to him. You'll recall the Father's words to Peter, John, and James on the Mount of Transfiguration: "Listen to him!" This is exactly what Mary does. Her example stands in contrast to the lack of compassion shown by the priest and the Levite in the parable of the good Samaritan, not to mention the scribe who questioned Jesus, all of whom failed to understand and heed God's word.

What's more, in the story, Mary's quiet, devoted listening stance stands in contrast to her action-oriented older sister Martha, who asks Jesus to tell Mary to help her serve. This may appear to be a reasonable request, and Martha seems certain Jesus will join her in shaming Mary for not helping. But there is an unexpected reversal of expectations. Jesus refuses to rebuke Mary and instead commends her for doing the "one thing" that is truly "necessary" (v. 42). Martha isn't wrong for serving, but she is wrong for chiding Mary for listening to Jesus. Listening has priority over serving, and serving must flow out of listening rather than being a substitute for it.

Jesus's Teaching on Prayer (11:1–13)

The story of Martha and Mary is followed by yet another reference to Jesus's life of prayer: "Now Jesus was praying in a certain place" (11:1). Luke previously mentioned how Jesus

- prayed at his baptism—when the heavens opened, the Spirit descended on him, and the Father commended him as his beloved Son (3:21–22);
- would regularly "withdraw to desolate places and pray" (5:16);
- went to a mountain to pray and "all night . . . continued in prayer to God," before appointing the Twelve the following morning (6:12);
- told his followers to pray for those who abused them, something Jesus did himself (6:28);
- prayed alone before asking his disciples who they and the crowds thought he was (9:18–20); and
- took Peter, James, and John to the Mount of Transfiguration to pray (9:28).

This is an impressive list of Jesus's commitment to prayer throughout his earthly ministry, especially before making important decisions. What's truly impressive is that Jesus is the Son of God and yet feels an acute and consistent need to pray. This shows that Jesus, in his humanity, goes about his messianic mission with a keen sense of dependence on God, which drives him to prayer. Prayer thus becomes an important means by which Jesus overcomes spiritual challenges and opposition and by which he achieves significant milestones and breakthroughs in his ministry. He knows that it is God who has to reveal his true identity to his followers, and he continually and persistently prays for God to do so until they understand that he is the suffering *and* glorious Messiah who gives his life on the cross so sinners can be saved and lost people be found.

In keeping with Luke's theology of prayer centered on Jesus, the next three units all deal with prayer:

1. The Lord's Prayer (11:1–4)
2. The parable of the reluctant neighbor (vv. 5–10)
3. The parable of the father who gives what his child needs (vv. 11–13)

In contrast to the religious leaders who are long on talk and short on action, Jesus is the opposite. He lives by example, and his prayer life is no exception. Jesus is praying apparently within earshot of his disciples, and when he finishes, his disciples ask him, "Lord, teach us to pray, as John taught his disciples" (v. 1). Elsewhere, Jesus tells the disciples not to make many words or offer flowery prayers like pagans do. In keeping with this maxim, the Lord's Prayer is a model of concision.

The first two petitions focus on God, plainly addressing him as "Father": "May your name be honored. May your kingdom come" (v. 2; my paraphrase). This teaches us to be God-centered rather than self-centered. Rather than frame our prayers in terms of *self*-interest, we're called to frame them in terms of *God's* interests, which are bound up with the greater glory of his name and the advancement of his kingdom. In this way, Jesus teaches his followers to discipline themselves to think about their needs in the context of God's larger purposes in this world. Within this context, they can trust God to supply what they need to carry out their God-given mission.

Only after making these God-centered requests should Jesus's followers humbly ask God to supply their daily needs; to forgive their sins, as they forgive the sins of others; and to deliver them from temptation. These requests fittingly describe human existence in this fallen world, which entails a concern for material provision, a need for forgiveness, and a recognition of human sinfulness and weakness that render us susceptible to temptation. Notice how this prayer expresses humble dependence on God. In this model prayer, Jesus teaches us to look to God to meet all our needs, so that he may be glorified and his spiritual reign be advanced on this earth.

Earlier, we learned about the Father entrusting all things to the Son; here, we learn about his goodness and graciousness toward his children. Jesus drives this truth home through the illustration of a man and his friend, who knocks at his door at midnight and asks him to lend him three loaves of bread. At first, the man says his children are with him in bed, but eventually he gets up and grants his friend's request simply to get rid of him, because he is so persistent! Jesus adds, "If you then, who are evil, know how to give good gifts to your children, how much more will the heavenly Father give the Holy Spirit to those who ask him!" (v. 13). The Holy Spirit is the Father's most precious gift.

The True Source of Jesus's Power (11:14–26)

Part of Jesus's ministry entails exercising divine authority by casting out evil spirits. However, many people wonder: What is the true source of Jesus's power? In the next scene, Jesus drives out a demon, which triggers a series of controversies regarding his ministry. While the crowds marvel at Jesus's authority, some allege that the source of his power is none other than Satan. Perhaps he is some sort of medium! Jesus masterfully parries the argument and shows its flawed logic. A kingdom divided against itself cannot stand. If Satan is divided against himself, how can he prevail? Anyone wanting to plunder a house must first overcome the one who guards it. Jesus concludes, "But if it is by the finger of God that I cast out demons, then the kingdom of God has come upon you" (v. 20).

True Blessedness and the Sign of Jonah (11:27–32)

At this, a woman in the crowd calls Jesus's mother blessed; but Jesus retorts that blessed rather are those who hear God's word and keep it. This continues Jesus's emphasis on discipleship, which transcends flesh-and-blood ties (cf. 9:59–62). As the crowds swell, Jesus denounces this "evil generation" for seeking a sign from him to prove the legitimacy of his messianic claim (11:29; cf. v. 16). He flatly refuses to give any sign "except the sign of Jonah" (v. 29; cf. Jonah 3:4–10). Ironically, people have already received the sign they are seeking. As it is, both the queen of Sheba (a Gentile ruler who came to pay homage to King Solomon) and the people of Nineveh (who repented at Jonah's preaching) will rise up to testify against Jesus's contemporaries at the final judgment. People should recognize that "something greater than Jonah is here" (Luke 11:32).

What Truly Defiles a Person (11:33–54)

Jesus's teaching on the eye being the lamp of the body sets up the next scene. When a Pharisee asks him to dine with him, he is astonished that Jesus doesn't wash his hands before dinner. At this, Jesus denounces the Pharisees' preoccupation with external appearances and their neglect of their inner lives. They have attempted to clean house through religious reforms, but in the end, the house's condition is worse than before. They are full of darkness, not light. Consequently, Jesus pronounces a series of woes against them for their hypocrisy. After the first three woes, a lawyer tells Jesus he is offended—at which Jesus adds three more woes! This predictably does little to ease the growing tension between Jesus and the Jewish leaders. They begin to apply added pressure, hoping to trap him by his own words.

The Rich Fool and the Importance of Being Ready (12:1–13:9)

Be Guarded but Not Afraid (12:1–12)

Incredibly, Jesus's popularity is still growing; Luke tells us that "so many thousands" gathered "that they were trampling one another" (12:1). In view of the Pharisees' hostility, Jesus warns his followers to be on their guard and to face opposition with faith rather than fear. This section alternates between Jesus addressing his disciples and the large crowd. He warns his followers of three specific obstacles to hearing and keeping his word: religious hypocrisy, greed, and sluggishness.

Avoid Improper Attachments and Don't Be Anxious (12:13–31)

When asked to mediate in an inheritance dispute, Jesus teaches that "one's life does not consist in the abundance of his possessions" (v. 15). Any disciple of Jesus must renounce improper flesh-and-blood ties and worldly possessions and hold these with an open hand. In keeping with the request in the Lord's Prayer for one's daily bread, his disciples should not be anxious about material needs. If people seek God's kingdom, they can trust him to provide for all their needs. Jesus's followers put God and his interests first, even though this means putting self-interest aside:

"Fear not, little flock, for it is your Father's good pleasure to give you the kingdom" (v. 32).

Be Alert and Ready (12:32–59)

At the same time, Jesus's followers must remain faithful—acknowledging him before others, trusting in God's providential care, and remaining vigilant until the end. Jesus seeks to impress this need for continual vigilance on his followers through a lengthy parable in which servants are put in charge of a household and their master's return is delayed. Faithful servants will be rewarded in the end, while faithless ones will be "cut . . . in pieces" (v. 46). There is a pronounced sense of urgency in Jesus's tone. He must undergo a "baptism" (his crucifixion) and is in great distress until it is accomplished (v. 50). Rather than bring peace, his coming has divided entire families, in keeping with the words of the prophet Micah (Mic. 7:6). Sadly, while Jesus's hearers can forecast the weather, they're unable to discern the significance of his coming.

Importance of Repentance and Bearing Fruit (13:1–9)

After this, some tell Jesus about "the Galileans whose blood Pilate had mingled with their sacrifices," a cruel act that has left many with raw emotions questioning God's sovereignty (Luke 13:1). How could God allow this kind of suffering? Did these people somehow deserve this? Jesus is quick to dispel such a notion: "Do you think that these Galileans were worse sinners than all the other Galileans, because they suffered in this way? No, I tell you; but unless you repent, you will all likewise perish" (vv. 2–3). He mentions a similar incident in which eighteen people were killed when the Siloam tower fell on them. Rather than lead to speculation, such reports should put the fear of God into people and cause them to repent. What's more, as John the Baptist noted, people must produce fruit in keeping with repentance, as Jesus underscores by telling a mini-parable about a barren fig tree.

The Mustard Seed, the Narrow Gate, and the Trilogy of Lost Things (13:10–15:32)

Healing on the Sabbath (13:10–17)

The next phase of the journey contains a long thread of Jesus's teachings. Another round of controversies ensues, triggered by Jesus's healing ministry. This time, the dispute surrounds the timing of the healings—on the Sabbath. Just as the Sabbath recalls God's deliverance from the bondage of slavery, so Jesus sets a woman free on the Sabbath who has been disabled for eighteen years. Yet in their hypocrisy, the Jewish leaders fail to recognize the work of God in their midst, and the synagogue ruler objects: "There are six days in which work ought to be done. Come on those days and be healed, and not on the Sabbath day" (v. 14).

Jesus pointedly replies, "You hypocrites! Does not each of you on the Sabbath untie his ox or his donkey from the manger and lead it away to water it? And ought not this woman, a daughter of Abraham whom Satan bound for eighteen years, be loosed from this bond on the Sabbath day?" (vv. 15–16). Jesus's words expose that, in their maze of Sabbath traditions, the Jewish leaders have no heart. They care more about upholding their tradition than about helping this poor woman and alleviating her suffering. Jesus's adversaries are "put to shame," while the crowds rejoice at all the "glorious things" Jesus does (v. 17).

Teaching in Parables and More Healings (13:18–15:32)

At this, Jesus resumes his teaching on the nature of God's kingdom by telling people the parables of

- the mustard seed (13:18–19);
- the leaven (vv. 20–21);
- the wedding guest (14:7–11);
- the great banquet (vv. 12–24); and
- the lost sheep, coin, and son (15:1–32).

In between these parables, Jesus provides other instructions to his followers, as discussed below.

The Parables of the Mustard Seed and the Leaven (13:18–21). The parable of the mustard seed makes the simple point that the kingdom will grow from inconspicuous beginnings until it is expansive. The parable of the leaven similarly asserts that the kingdom will gradually grow until it fills the entire world.

Enter Through the Narrow Gate (13:22–30). Luke's introductory remark, "He went on his way through towns and villages, teaching and journeying toward Jerusalem" (13:22), reminds the reader that Jesus is still on his way to Jerusalem. The question "Lord, will those who are saved be few?" leads Jesus to affirm that those who would be saved must enter through the "narrow door" (vv. 23–24). Jesus hints that many Gentiles will dine in God's kingdom with the patriarchs and the prophets, while many of his Jewish contemporaries will be shut out. Thus, some who are last will be first, and some who are first will be last.

Jesus Laments over Jerusalem (13:31–35). At this, some warn Jesus that Herod Antipas is out to kill him. He replies that they should go tell "that fox" that he will continue to cast out demons and heal because no prophet should perish outside Jerusalem (vv. 32–33). He also laments, "O Jerusalem, Jerusalem, the city that kills the prophets and stones those who are sent to it!" (v. 34). In this way, Jesus reiterates his resolve to go to Jerusalem to finish his work. This shows that the cross has been Jesus's destiny all along and that Jerusalem, represented by her leaders, has been bent on rejecting her Messiah. The leaders reject Jesus not only when putting him on the cross but throughout his ministry—with ever-escalating hostility. This shows the extent to which human hearts are hardened toward the Messiah and his salvation; there is nothing Jesus could have done to overcome such opposition. The cross has been inevitable.

Another Sabbath Healing (14:1–6). Jesus performs another Sabbath healing. His argument is almost identical to the previous one. His opponents have no reply, though one senses that their hearts harden even more.

The Parables of the Wedding Guest and the Great Banquet (14:7–24). These parables continue Jesus's instruction about the nature of God's kingdom. The parable of the wedding guest makes the point that humility is prized highly in the kingdom, so people should choose to "sit in the lowest place" (v. 10). In the parable of the great banquet, those who are invited to the banquet all make excuses, so servants are sent out to invite "the poor and crippled and blind and lame" and even people from the "highways and hedges" to fill the banquet hall for the feast (vv. 21, 23).

Again, Luke strikes the note of reversal in God's kingdom. The tables will be turned; those exalted in society will be brought low, and the lowly will be exalted. This is tremendously encouraging for those who are powerless and lack recognition in this world, yet it poses an enormous challenge to the rich and powerful. It's no wonder that Luke's gospel has been a favorite among advocates of justice. However, while socioeconomic and political justice does matter, a concern for justice must be balanced with a recognition that, ultimately, people are saved only by believing in Jesus and the gospel.

The Cost of Discipleship (14:25–35). Great crowds continue to follow Jesus, so he takes the opportunity to teach them another lesson on discipleship: "If anyone comes to me and does not hate his own father and mother and wife and children and brothers and sisters, yes, and even his own life, he cannot be my disciple. Whoever does not bear his own cross and come after me cannot be my disciple" (vv. 26–27). This is an incredible disclaimer for anyone who thinks following Jesus is easy. No one can accuse him of sugarcoating the gospel or of luring people into following him without having them read the fine print first.

Following Jesus is hard! Therefore, Jesus urges people to count the cost, just like the builder of a tower or a king sending his army into war. If they don't have the resources and the stomach to complete what they've finished, they'll be everybody's laughingstock and suffer great loss: "So therefore, any one of you who does not renounce all that he has cannot be my disciple" (v. 33). Tasteless salt is good for nothing, except the trash heap. If anyone, after deciding to follow Jesus, turns back in view of the cost, he is like salt that has lost its taste. Such a shallow profession of faith is utterly worthless. These are stern words, but they're true. Also, it's equally true that while following Jesus is hard, it's also infinitely rewarding in the end; conversely, not following Jesus comes at a terrible price—a Christless eternity.

The Parables of the Lost Sheep, Coin, and Son (15:1–32). The parables of the lost sheep, coin, and son continue the banquet theme, each ending with a joyful feast. The three parables form a single unit, moving from the lesser to the greater. Notice that the value of what is lost increases exponentially with each parable—one of ninety-nine sheep, one of ten coins, and one of two sons. If a shepherd, woman, and father will search assiduously for what they've lost, how much more will God seek after lost people! This is exactly what God is doing through Jesus's ministry.

However, some are too self-righteous to recognize their need for God's grace. The parables are specifically directed toward the Pharisees and scribes who, like the older brother in the parable of the prodigal son, are unable to rejoice in Jesus's gracious welcome of sinners. The Pharisees' opposition to Jesus's fraternizing with so-called sinners (as if they aren't sinners too!) triggers this unique trilogy of parables. The three parables are mutually reinforcing, packing a triple punch in Jesus's powerful response to the Pharisees' objections.

Jesus opens the first parable with a question: "What man of you, having a hundred sheep, if he has lost one of them, does not leave the ninety-nine in the open country, and go after the one that is lost, until he finds it?" (15:4). Sure enough, when the lost sheep is found, the man calls his friends and neighbors together to tell them the joyful news. The clincher is this: "Just so, I tell you, there will be more joy in heaven over one sinner who repents than over ninety-nine righteous persons who need no repentance" (v. 7). The joyless, even reproachful, attitude of the Pharisees regarding Jesus's efforts to seek and save the lost stands exposed and corrected.

The second parable in the trilogy—the shortest of the three—has a woman as the main character, who has lost a coin. She lights a lamp, sweeps the house, and searches diligently until she finds it. As in the previous parable, the focus is on the joy that accompanies finding what was lost. Similarly, "there is joy before the angels of God over one sinner who repents" (v. 10). Just as in the previous parable, a lost item represents a repentant sinner, and in both cases, there is great joy in heaven. Salvation is what it's all about! Meanwhile, the Pharisees jockey for position while laying religious burdens on people and caring little for their spiritual well-being.

Finally, Jesus tells the third parable in the trilogy, which is so well developed that it seems to relegate the first two parables to mere preambles. The opening of the parable is innocuous enough: "There was a man who had two sons" (v. 11). The younger son comes to his father and asks for his inheritance. Normally, people don't receive their inheritance until the person from whom they receive it has actually died. Yet here we have a son who asks for his inheritance during his father's lifetime! The father in the story, however, is very gracious and does as his son has requested, and soon the young man is off with his share of the inheritance to a faraway country. There, he "squander[s] his property in reckless living" (v. 13). At this, a famine arises, so the young man takes a job feeding pigs. He longs to eat the pods he is feeding to the pigs, but "no one [gives] him anything" (v. 16).

Then the miracle happens, and the story turns around radically: the young man comes to his senses and repents! This represents his spiritual conversion, which leads him to return to his father's house. He swallows his pride and decides to go back to his father and admit his mistake. The emotional high point of the story comes when the son approaches the father's house: "while he was still a long way off, his father saw him and felt compassion, and ran and embraced him and kissed him" (v. 20). The son says to his father, "Father, I have sinned against heaven and before you. I am no longer worthy to be called your son" (v. 21). The father, though, cuts the son's apology short and honors him with a big feast celebrating his return: "For this my son was dead, and is alive again; he was lost, and is found" (v. 24). The parable has a happy ending—but wait! The story isn't over yet.

When the older son arrives at the scene, hears the music and dancing, and asks what all the fuss is about, he is told that it's a party to celebrate the return of his (previously rebellious) younger brother. At this, he is filled with self-righteous indignation and bitterly complains to his father: "It's not fair! I've never done anything wrong," he says in effect, "but you never even gave me a young goat to celebrate with my friends! Yet when my brother returns, you slaughter the fattened calf so he can have a feast!" The father gently tries to console his son and pleads with him to join in the festivities: "Son, you are always with me, and all that is mine is yours. It was fitting to celebrate and be glad, for this your brother was dead, and is alive; he was lost, and is found" (vv. 31–32).

In many ways, this parable is the emotional high point of the entire gospel. It's here that we see Jesus's heart on display, which in turn is a reflection of the very heart of God. It's a heart full of love for wayward sinners, with a gracious willingness to forgive and to celebrate true repentance and conversion. What's more, not only does Jesus through this parable plead with the Pharisees to join in his joy over lost (Gentile) sinners; he tries to reassure them that they continue to be welcome in his Father's house. Despite Jesus's gentleness in issuing this invitation, it falls on deaf ears.

The Dishonest Steward, the Rich Man and Lazarus, and Unworthy Servants (16:1–17:10)

The Parable of the Dishonest Manager (16:1–13)

In the next parable, a manager is fired by his master due to a mismanagement of funds. Before his employment ends, however, he summons his master's debtors and reduces their debts to curry their favor for when he'll be out of a job. The twist comes when the master commends the manager for his shrewdness. The lesson is this: "Make friends for yourselves by means of unrighteous wealth, so that when it fails they may receive you into the eternal dwellings" (16:9). Money is a tool rather than an object of worship; therefore, use that tool effectively: "For the sons of this world are more shrewd in dealing with their own generation than the sons of light" (v. 8).

Jesus doesn't commend dishonesty; he simply advocates dealing shrewdly with "unrighteous wealth." His charge for his followers is to be faithful in little things. Otherwise, they won't be entrusted with spiritual wealth of their own. What's more, they must make up their mind about whom they will serve, God or money, because no one can serve two masters. This speaks to the heart attitude of a disciple when it comes to stewardship. Do we use our possessions wisely, even shrewdly, for the advancement of God's kingdom? And do we realize that what we own is just a tool to accomplish his purposes?

Addressing the Pharisees (16:14–18)

Again, the Pharisees serve as a foil because they are "lovers of money" (v. 14). And Luke tells us that they ridicule Jesus for his teaching! Yet as Jesus is quick to point out, God knows their hearts: "For what is exalted among men is an abomination in the sight of God" (v. 15). God knows our hearts. He even knows that people may ignorantly praise those who present their greed as generosity! In his kingdom, hearts will be revealed, and God will effect a dramatic reversal of the injustices and patterns of pretense that run rampant in this world.

The Parable of the Rich Man and Lazarus (16:19–31)

After a brief interlude, Jesus continues his teaching on wealth and poverty with the parable of the rich man and Lazarus. This is the only parable in all the Gospels with a named character—Lazarus (not to be confused with the Lazarus Jesus raises from the dead)—and Abraham, the Old Testament patriarch, is featured in the parable as well. Here, Jesus paints a vivid picture of the rich man feasting every day, while poor Lazarus languishes miserably at the rich man's gate, longing "to be fed with what fell from the rich man's table" (v. 21). Both men die and are transported to their eternal destiny. In hades (hell), the rich man catches a glimpse of Lazarus, who now is at the side of Abraham, the patriarch.

Now the roles are strangely reversed, with the rich man in deep anguish, begging Lazarus to dip the end of his finger in water to cool his tongue. Yet Abraham informs him that a great chasm has been fixed between them that no one can cross. This is yet another powerful parable that impresses on Jesus's listeners, as well as Luke's readers, the importance of fearing God in this life—one's eternal destiny depends on it. In a sort of epilogue, the rich man asks Abraham to send Lazarus to warn his five brothers who are still living, lest they end up in the same horrible place. Abraham refuses, saying they have Moses and the Prophets. When the rich man insists, Abraham retorts that if they don't listen to the Scriptures, they won't be convinced if someone were to rise from the dead.

With this, Jesus predicts his own resurrection and once again highlights the stubborn unbelief of the Jewish leaders, for whom no evidence is compelling enough to change their minds about Jesus. While we should take care not to build our entire theology of the afterlife on this parable, it nonetheless conveys powerful spiritual truths. We must respond to the ample evidence we have about Jesus rather than always demanding more. Also, our wealth can't save us. If we live our lives for the sake of accumulating material possessions and enjoying life in the present apart from God, our wealth will rot when we die, and our only prospect will be to spend eternity apart from God in hell. And no one can say Jesus didn't warn us.

The Need for Faith and Humble Servanthood (17:1–10)

With the self-righteous Pharisees still in the background, Jesus continues to instruct his followers: "Temptations to sin are sure to come, but woe to the one through whom they come!" (17:1). You'll be tempted, but make sure you're not the source of temptation for others. In fact, it would be better for such a person "if a millstone were hung around his neck and he were cast into the sea" than for him to "cause one of these little ones to sin" (v. 2). Clearly, Jesus is talking about the Jewish leaders who, rather than gently leading their flock, have put unbearable burdens on their followers. By contrast, Jesus's disciples must forgive those who sin against them if they truly repent.

All they need is the tiniest amount of faith. Jesus goes on to tell a story of a servant who is working in the field or tending sheep. When he returns to the house, does his master invite him to join him at the dinner table? No; he tells him to go prepare supper! He may not even thank the servant for the work he has done, because it is expected of him. In the same way, Jesus's followers should be content with being God's servants. They should be humble and obedient and let their privilege of working for their Master be enough. Our motivation for serving shouldn't be to be recognized and praised by others.

The Ten Lepers, the Persistent Widow, the Rich Ruler, and Zacchaeus (17:11–19:27)

Cleansing Ten Samaritan Lepers (17:11–19)

In case some of his readers have forgotten, Luke reminds them that Jesus is "on the way to Jerusalem" (v. 11). The final portion of his journey to Jerusalem (no surprise here) focuses on the topics of faith and the kingdom. These are the topics that Jesus has tried to hammer home to his followers throughout his entire ministry, and he continues to do so in order to impress on them the importance of faith and the preeminence of God's kingdom. While Jesus has told several powerful parables, Luke now shifts to narrative to impress on his readers some of the same lessons.

As Jesus passes through the region between Samaria and Galilee, he enters a village and heals ten lepers. He tells them to go to the priests, but only one—a Samaritan—thanks Jesus. Jesus rightly asks: "Where are the [other] nine?" (v. 17). As in the parable of the good Samaritan, a Samaritan is the hero of the story, indicating the great reversal taking place in God's kingdom. Jesus goes on to tell the one who has returned to thank him, "Your faith has made you well" (v. 19). The other nine lepers are merely cleansed physically; the Samaritan is made whole spiritually as well.

The Arrival of the Kingdom (17:20–37)

When asked by the Pharisees when the kingdom of God will come, Jesus declares that it is already in their midst. Clearly, he is speaking about himself, the King who has already come to proclaim the good news of the arrival of God's kingdom. Tragically, by refusing the King, the Jewish leaders will be shut out of God's kingdom. Turning to his disciples, Jesus goes on to predict a time when he will no longer be in their midst—until, one day, he will return as a lightning flash. Jesus's return will be highly public and visible: "But first he must suffer many things and be rejected by this generation" (v. 25).

Conditions at Jesus's return will be as in the days of Noah (the flood) and Lot (Sodom and Gomorrah; cf. Gen. 6:9–22; 19:1–26). People will go about their daily lives, unsuspecting that "today is the day." Yet "in that night," two will be sleeping in one bed; one will be taken, and the other left behind (the rapture; Luke 17:34; cf. 1 Thess. 4:13–17). Jesus teaches his followers that there are two aspects of his kingdom. On the one hand, the kingdom is a *present* reality, even though many are oblivious to the signs of its arrival. On the other hand, the kingdom has a *future* dimension, which climaxes in Jesus's second coming and the judgment that will ensue.

The Parable of the Unrighteous Judge and the Persistent Widow (18:1–8)

Jesus continues to highlight the issues of faith and the kingdom with the parable of the persistent widow. Luke states the moral of the parable at the outset: Jesus's followers "ought always to pray and not lose heart" (Luke 18:1). While the judge doesn't care about the justice the widow is seeking, in the end he gives in to her persistent pleas, simply to get her off his back. If this unrighteous judge gives the widow the justice she persistently seeks, Jesus asks, "will not God give justice to his elect, who cry to him day and night?" (v. 7). He concludes the parable by querying, "[W]hen the Son of Man comes, will he find faith on earth?" (v. 8). Jesus's return will be preceded by a period of great tribulation, in which believers' faith will be severely tested and many will be martyred. This is a great challenge to pray persistently and not to give up, because in the end God will vindicate those who put their faith in him and answer their prayers for justice.

The Parable of the Pharisee and the Tax Collector (18:9–14)

One vital ingredient of Jesus's parables is that they often aim to address heart attitudes in need of correction. Jesus tells the next parable "to some who trusted in themselves that they were righteous, and treated others with contempt" (v. 9). In the parable, Jesus pits a self-righteous Pharisee, who is proud of all his religious accomplishments, against a humble tax collector, who cries out to God for mercy; yet only the latter goes home justified. Again, we see a stunning reversal in common expectations. As Jesus concludes, "Everyone who exalts himself will be humbled, but the one who humbles himself will be exalted" (v. 14).

The Little Children and the Rich Young Ruler (18:15–30)

Jesus reinforces his lesson on humility by welcoming little children. In the process, he rebukes his own disciples, who had rebuked those who were trying to bring the children to Jesus. "Let the children come to me," Jesus tells them, "for to such belongs the kingdom of God" (v. 16). In fact, "whoever does not receive the kingdom of God like a child shall not enter it" (v. 17). Those who would enter God's kingdom must admit that they have nothing to offer him. They must be willing to humble themselves to receive his free gift of salvation in the Messiah.

The episode featuring little children is juxtaposed with the story of the rich young ruler, who had obeyed all of God's commandments from his youth but was unwilling to give away his wealth to the poor. Jesus observes, "How difficult it is for those who have wealth to enter the kingdom of God!" (v. 24). At the same time, he reassures Peter and the others, "There is no one who has left house or wife or brothers or parents or children, for the sake of the kingdom of God, who will not receive many times more in this time, and in the age to come eternal life" (vv. 29–30). Following Jesus has great rewards.

The Third Passion Prediction (18:31–34)

Momentum continues to build as Jesus is getting closer to Jerusalem. At this juncture, Jesus predicts his suffering for the third and last time. In this final prediction, he declares his reason for going to Jerusalem—namely, to be handed over to the Gentiles and to be beaten, killed, and raised on the third day, in keeping with the message of the Prophets. Jesus is going to Jerusalem to accomplish God's predetermined plan of salvation. He is a man on a mission—and is in the process of executing it in faithfulness to God and in fulfillment of Old Testament expectations. The disciples, however, still don't understand that Jesus must die, because this spiritual truth has been "hidden from them" (v. 34).

In this regard, Luke is in complete alignment with the other gospel writers, all of whom go to great lengths to show that until the resurrection, Jesus's followers didn't believe that the Messiah had to suffer and be crucified in order to accomplish salvation. This furnishes powerful proof that the story of Jesus wasn't fabricated by his followers. Jesus's three passion predictions serve this very purpose: to show that Jesus knew what would happen to him and walked willingly into his death.

Healing a Blind Man on the Road to Jericho (18:35–43)

Undaunted, Jesus continues on his way, misunderstood by those closest to him yet confident in God's plan and assured of his presence and approval. As Jesus approaches Jericho, now within striking distance of Jerusalem, a blind man sitting by the road wonders what the commotion is about. When told that "Jesus of Nazareth is passing by," he cries, "Jesus, Son of David, have mercy on me!" (vv. 37–38). As in the case of the children brought to Jesus earlier, people tell him to be quiet and not to bother Jesus. After all, Jesus is a prophet embarking on an important mission! Yet the blind man cries even louder: "Son of David, have mercy on me!" (v. 39).

At this, Jesus stops and asks that the blind man be brought to him. He speaks a word of healing and tells him that his faith has made him well. Immediately, the man is healed and follows Jesus, praising God, as do all those who see the amazing miracle. In this way, Jesus continues to furnish proofs of his messianic identity. Again, it is those who are desperate for healing—those who come to Jesus with empty hands, crying out for mercy and recognizing him as the Son of David—who receive healing. Conversely, others continue to misconstrue Jesus's identity because it doesn't conform to their own misguided expectations about the Messiah.

Zacchaeus the Tax Collector (19:1–10)

Next, Jesus enters Jericho on his way to Jerusalem. There, he encounters a man named Zacchaeus, a chief tax collector, who has used his position to enrich himself greatly. This Zacchaeus wants to catch a glimpse of Jesus passing through town but can't because he is too short. So he runs ahead and climbs onto a sycamore tree. When Jesus notices him, he tells him to come down. Not only had Jesus previously called Matthew to join the ranks of the Twelve; he had recently told a parable involving a tax collector. Now, he is calling another tax collector to salvation!

While Jesus's opponents grumble, Zacchaeus shows active repentance by giving away half of his fortune and promising to repay those whom he has defrauded. In this way, Zacchaeus serves as a role model. When the rich young ruler had come to Jesus and had been unwilling to part with his wealth, Jesus noted that it's difficult for the rich to be saved, but all things are possible with God. Zacchaeus demonstrates that Jesus's words are true. Following his act of repentance, Jesus declares, "Today salvation has come to this house" (19:9). For Jesus has come "to seek and to save the lost" (v. 10).

The Parable of the Ten Minas (19:11–27)

Finally, as he nears Jerusalem, Jesus again seizes the moment because he knows that his followers expect him to usher in the kingdom upon his entrance into the city. This reflects widespread Jewish expectations that the Messiah would come as a national deliverer for Israel—to restore David's kingdom and to overthrow Israel's political enemies. Luke writes to correct these expectations, both in terms of the scope of God's kingdom (it's not merely for Israel but includes believing Gentiles as well) and in terms of the nature of Jesus's kingship (he's not a national, earthly messiah but the suffering and risen Savior and Son of God).

In the parable of the ten minas, therefore, Jesus addresses the expectations of those who think the kingdom will appear immediately upon his entrance into Jerusalem. The story revolves around a nobleman (representing Jesus) who goes away to receive a kingdom. Upon his return, he calls his servants to account for their stewardship, rewarding those who have been faithful, while punishing the servant who makes excuses for failing to invest his money. The bottom line is this: What matters most is that Jesus's followers remain faithful with what they've been entrusted; they can safely trust God to bring about his kingdom at his appointed time.

DISCUSSION QUESTIONS

1. Do you enjoy traveling? What is the longest or most memorable journey you've ever taken?

2. Luke frequently depicts Jesus in prayer. How is your prayer life?

3. What is the main lesson of the parable of the prodigal son and how is it relevant to your life?

4. Jesus had a lot to say about stewardship and dealing with money. How do you manage your resources in relation to God's kingdom?

As the time approached for him to be taken up to heaven, Jesus resolutely set out for Jerusalem. And he sent messengers on ahead, who went into a Samaritan village to get things ready for him; but the people there did not welcome him, because he was heading for Jerusalem. When the disciples James and John saw this, they asked, "Lord, do you want us to call fire down from heaven to destroy them?" But Jesus turned and rebuked them.

—Luke 9:51–55 NIV

As followers of Christ, one of the things we have to learn is how to properly deal with opposition to the gospel. Not everyone will receive our message with open arms. In fact, many will reject it. How will we respond? James and John, the Zebedee brothers, invoked Elijah who called down fire from heaven when dealing with the prophets of Baal in Old Testament times. Surely Jesus would want to destroy the Samaritans who refused passage to them! But Jesus, nicknaming them "sons of thunder," instead rebuked them. He preferred to use not shock and awe-inspiring power, but gentle persuasion. He engaged others in spiritual conversation and offered his works as evidence that his claims regarding himself were true.

CHAPTER 10—LUKE

FINAL DAYS AND ASCENSION

MINISTRY IN JERUSALEM, PASSION, AND ASCENSION (19:28–24:53)
Jesus's Entry and Final Ministry in Jerusalem (19:28–21:38)
The Last Supper, Arrest, Crucifixion, and Resurrection (22:1–24:49)
The Ascension (24:50–53)

MINISTRY IN JERUSALEM, PASSION, AND ASCENSION (19:28–24:53)

After the lengthy buildup in Luke's travel narrative, we now enter the final, decisive phase in Jesus's mission. Preparations are made for his final Passover, and he enters Jerusalem hailed by the crowds. But he laments the city's fate and cleanses the corrupt temple. In response to a challenge to his authority, he tells a parable that predicts his imminent rejection by the Jewish authorities. Various other disputes follow, showing the rising degree of animosity toward Jesus by the leaders. In the Olivet Discourse, Jesus predicts the destruction of Jerusalem and the temple in greater detail. The Last Supper and the final events of Jesus's earthly ministry ensue in rapid succession, culminating in his resurrection, final commission, and ascension.

Jesus's Entry and Final Ministry in Jerusalem (19:28–21:38)

The Entry and Jerusalem's Future Destruction (19:28–44)

In Jesus's preparations for his arrival, we're given the first of many indications that all the various events are taking place in keeping with God's sovereign, predetermined plan. Everything turns out to be exactly as Jesus has told his disciples, who are to fetch a colt and bring it to Jesus so that he can mount it and ride into Jerusalem as the humble King and Savior. As Jesus approaches the Holy City, his disciples are brimming with messianic hope. Descending from the Mount of Olives, Jesus arrives in Jerusalem in humility and peace, in fulfillment of Zechariah's prophecy (Zech. 9:9; cf. 14:4).

Luke's account focuses on the reaction of the crowd of disciples, who recognize the significance of the event by announcing: "Blessed is the King who comes in the name of the Lord! Peace in heaven and glory in the highest!" (Luke 19:38; cf. Ps. 118:26). The reader has no trouble recognizing the allusion to Jesus's birth narrative, in which a multitude of angels hailed the infant Messiah by exclaiming, "Glory to God in the highest, and on earth peace among those with whom he is pleased!" (Luke 2:14). Note, however, that the rejoicing "multitude" of angels is now replaced by a rejoicing "multitude" of Jesus's disciples!

The exuberant reception by the disciples contrasts with the disparaging reaction of the Pharisees, who urge Jesus (calling him a mere "teacher") to rebuke his disciples (19:39). Jesus's response is pointed: if his followers are silent, the very stones will cry out! In many ways, therefore, Jerusalem epitomizes the polarized response to Jesus. Fully aware of what will happen to him, Jesus mourns the city's fate. At the very beginning of the gospel, John the Baptist's father, Zechariah, spoke of God "visiting" his people to provide redemption (1:68). Decades later, Jesus begins his final approach to the Holy City and laments because, as he says, "[Jerusalem] did not know the time of [its] visitation" (19:44).

In entering Jerusalem, Jesus again displays great prophetic foresight, declaring that Jerusalem has failed to recognize him as its messianic king. As a result, the city won't know peace, but instead its enemies will lay siege to it and raze it to the ground, decimating its population. Jesus presents these future events as God's judgment on the city and its people for rejecting him as their messianic King. This represents a heart-wrenching failure to recognize God's saving purposes for his people. It's like when, as a parent, you go through great expense and trouble to give one of your children a precious gift, and they throw it in the trash.

Similarly, God's people, represented by their religious leadership, would treat the Messiah with contempt and trample God's magnificent gift underfoot. Notice that Jesus is saying these things when a multitude of disciples hails him as the messianic King foretold in the Psalms and the Prophets. This makes clear that even his disciples don't truly understand who Jesus is and that their acclaim is not to be trusted. Jesus knows that he will end up on the cross in just a few short days. Yet Jesus's followers speak better than they know, and Jesus really is the Davidic King—and yet a different kind of Messiah than they expect.

Cleansing the Temple (19:45–48)

In the next scene, in a fairly terse account, Jesus enters the temple area and drives out the merchants. He had just predicted the destruction of Jerusalem; now, he acts out God's judgment on the temple by cleansing it. Explaining the significance of his action, Jesus tells the merchants—conflating the words of the prophets Isaiah and Jeremiah—"It is written, 'My house shall be a house of prayer,' but you have made it a den of robbers" (v. 46; cf. Isa. 56:7; Jer. 7:11). Jesus has acted with messianic authority in keeping with the words of Israel's prophets. The merchants, sanctioned by the corrupt, ungodly leadership, had utterly perverted God's purpose for Israel's central sanctuary. Rather than being a site of worship, the temple had become a place of greedy commerce. After cleansing the temple of activities unworthy of the true God, Jesus sets up shop (so to speak) in the temple area himself and begins teaching there daily. Jesus continues to be a thorn in the side of the religious leaders, who are out to destroy him; but there is as of yet nothing they can do because the people are hanging on his every word.

A Challenge to Jesus's Authority (20:1–8)

After this, Luke elaborates on Jesus's teaching "and preaching the gospel" in the temple area (Luke 20:1). In so doing, he directs our attention to the escalating opposition of the Jewish leaders as representative of Israel's rejection of Jesus. Promptly the Jewish leaders challenge his authority to cleanse the temple. This is a pointed challenge, as they're in charge of what happens in the temple area. In effect, by cleansing the temple, Jesus has invaded what they consider to be their turf. Jesus, of course, as the Messiah and Son of God, has a higher spiritual authority, conferred on him by God the Father himself, which transcends any human authority, such as that of the Jewish leaders and temple authorities.

In his response, Jesus poses a counterquestion. Aligning himself with John the Baptist, he asks his opponents whether they think John's baptism was "from heaven" (divinely authorized) or "from man" (self-appointed) (v. 4). Since people commonly think that John was a prophet (a spokesman for God), the Jewish leaders know they're between a rock and a hard place: if they say "from heaven," they concede Jesus's point that he stands in the prophetic tradition of John the Baptist; but if they say "from man," they find themselves in conflict with the common people. So they say they don't know. Jesus replies, "Neither will I tell you by what authority I do these things" (v. 8). The reader knows that Jesus's authority is from heaven.

The Parable of the Wicked Tenants (20:9–47)

As a sort of allegorical commentary, Jesus goes on to tell people the parable of the wicked tenants. The parable occupies a pivotal place in Luke's gospel as a climactic indictment of the Jewish leaders who are about to kill Jesus, their Messiah. The owner of a vineyard rents it out to tenant farmers and at harvest time sends a series of servants to collect the harvest. The tenants abuse them all, until at last, the owner sends his beloved son, thinking that "perhaps they will respect him" (v. 13). It's easy to see that the owner of the vineyard, the servants, and the beloved son represent God, the Old Testament prophets, and Jesus, respectively, while the tenants represent Israel, which is frequently in the Old Testament depicted as God's vineyard (e.g., Isa. 5).

Outrageously, the tenants kill the son, surmising that now the inheritance will be theirs. Jesus poignantly asks, "What then will the owner of the vineyard do to them?" (Luke 20:15). The answer is obvious: he'll destroy them (i.e., the Jewish religious leaders and even Jerusalem and the temple) and give the vineyard to others (i.e., the Twelve, the believing Jewish remnant, a group that will eventually also include believing Gentiles). The people who hear this story are aghast, but Jesus looks straight at them and cites a well-known Old Testament passage: "The stone that the builders rejected has become the cornerstone" (v. 17; cf. Ps. 118:22). Jesus—the stone the builders (the Jews) rejected—has become the cornerstone in God's plan of salvation, and those who have rejected him will be destroyed, "broken to pieces," and utterly crushed (Luke

20:18). Just as Israel had persecuted the prophets, so the Jews are about to kill God's beloved Son and thus bring divine judgment on themselves.

In response, the scribes and chief priests are enraged. They seek to "lay hands on him," as they know full well that the parable is directed at them (v. 19). They put him under constant surveillance and even send spies to catch him in something he might say, so that they can report him to the Roman governor. In the next few scenes, they make their next attempt to corner Jesus by questioning him on now-familiar controversial issues, such as paying taxes to Caesar and marriage in the resurrection. In each case, Jesus responds impeccably and silences his opponents, demonstrating his superior wisdom and unmatched authority. The unit closes with Jesus's counterchallenge to his opponents—How can the Messiah be both David's son and his Lord? (cf. Ps. 110:1)—and his warning to his disciples concerning the scribes' pride and hypocrisy.

The Widow's Mite (21:1–4)

The warning is accentuated in the next scene, where Jesus observes a poor widow put two small copper coins into the offering box in the temple area. While the scribes "devour widows' houses" (Luke 20:47), Jesus commends this poor widow for her generosity, which allows Luke to highlight the theme of reversal in God's kingdom once again. Caring for widows and orphans was expected of God's people, as these groups were particularly needy and vulnerable. To take advantage of such weak individuals was heinous and despicable. And here, Jesus draws attention to a widow who, by her sacrificial giving, puts those to shame who put on a pious facade but whose hearts are far from God.

The Olivet Discourse (21:5–38)

With the time of his departure quickly drawing near, Jesus instructs his disciples concerning the end times. This is now the third time that Jesus has spoken of end-time events, each passage providing additional detail. Luke's version of the Olivet Discourse places particular emphasis on the imminent destruction of the temple and Jerusalem. The discourse gradually moves from the destruction of the temple to the demise of Jerusalem and, from there, to Christ's return.

In this discourse, Jesus prepares his disciples for the persecution that will take place in the decades following his ascension, still during their lifetime, and he also instructs them regarding the circumstances of his more distant return—the glorious return of "the Son of Man." Most gripping is the statement "When you see Jerusalem surrounded by armies, then know that [the temple's] desolation has come near" (21:20).

In prophetic fashion, the more imminent events surrounding the destruction of the temple and Jerusalem serve as a sort of lens through which to view the more distant events accompanying Jesus's return. Clearly, tumultuous times lie ahead, so Jesus exhorts his disciples to be discerning through the parable of the fig tree. They must constantly stay alert, so they'll be able "to escape all these things" and "to stand before the Son of Man" (v. 36).

The Last Supper, Arrest, Crucifixion, and Resurrection (22:1–24:49)

The Plot Against Jesus and Judas's Betrayal (22:1–6)

Luke opens the second major subsection of Jesus's ministry in Jerusalem with the following solemn declaration: "Now the Feast of Unleavened Bread drew near, which is called the Passover" (22:1). In what follows, Luke narrates the events leading up to Jesus's crucifixion in three parts: preparation, confrontation, and crucifixion. The opening scene is framed by the approach and arrival of Passover. The chief priests and scribes continue to seek an opportune time to put Jesus to death (with the help of the Romans), though such an occasion has yet to present itself. At this, Judas, one of the Twelve, arrives on the scene; chillingly, we're told that Satan enters him, and he confers with the chief priests.

Now, at last, the Jewish leaders have the breakthrough they've long been looking for. They've penetrated Jesus's inner circle, which will enable them to nab him discreetly without attracting undue attention. In this way, they will avoid stirring up a riot, which would rile the Roman authorities—especially during the Passover, when Jerusalem's population swelled to massive proportions. Passover was one of the "pilgrim festivals," and many made the trek to the Jewish capital to celebrate the feast there. The chief priests seal the deal with Judas by promising him money for his treachery. Now, it's no longer solely them who seek to arrest Jesus; Judas, too, is looking for an opportune moment to hand Jesus over to the authorities.

In this way, Luke shows that there is more in play than what appears on the surface—petty partisan politics, jockeying for position, or conflicting commercial, religious, and socioeconomic interests. As the time of

Jesus's suffering draws near, Luke highlights the cosmic significance of Jesus's journey to the cross by noting that Satan himself is actively working behind the scenes to bring about Jesus's demise. Judas's act of betrayal is ultimately orchestrated by Satan, who hatches his wicked schemes to destroy Jesus. Later, when predicting Peter's denials, Jesus will reveal that Satan has asked to "sift" him "like wheat" (22:31). At his arrest, Jesus will tell his opponents, "This is your hour, and the power of darkness" (v. 53). Jesus's impending death is not the result of mere human ploys but the outcome of a battle between God and Satan.

The Last Supper (22:7–38)

At one level, things are going almost perfectly. The preparations for celebrating the Passover are marked by God's providential ordering of even the smallest detail. As earlier when rounding up the donkey on which Jesus rode into Jerusalem, the disciples line up the upper room and prepare the Passover just as Jesus has instructed them to do. When the hour comes and Jesus reclines at table with the Twelve, the solemnity of the occasion is palpable. Jesus's last Passover with his disciples is also the first Lord's Supper, which marks the new covenant Jesus is establishing with them as a believing Jewish remnant and as representatives of the new messianic community.

In the context of Luke's narrative, the Last Supper represents the culmination of Jesus's ministry with his disciples. At this festive, solemn occasion, so pregnant with meaning, Jesus reveals to his disciples the purpose of his now-imminent death. His sacrifice will serve as an atonement for the forgiveness of sins, establishing a new covenant through his broken body and shed blood. In this way, the Passover meal is transformed from a commemoration of God's deliverance of the Israelites from bondage in Egypt to a memorial of Jesus's death for humanity's sins as God's ultimate Passover Lamb.

Jesus's Prayer and Arrest, and Peter's Denials (22:39–65)

After the meal, Jesus leads his disciples to the Mount of Olives, where he agonizes in prayer—dreading the impending suffering, in his humanity, yet resolved to do God's will. Jesus and his disciples have come to the end of a long road. The stage has been set for Jesus's death, burial, and resurrection. As the passion narrative unfolds, two significant themes emerge: (1) Jesus is in full control of the circumstances surrounding his death, and (2) he suffers while being innocent of all the charges brought against him. We see these two themes running throughout the narrative like two pearls on a string, with Jesus's innocence shining brightly.

In scriptural terms, Luke portrays Jesus as Israel's righteous Servant. The scene opens with the Jewish authorities coming to arrest him, armed with swords and clubs as if he were a criminal. Judas the traitor is leading them, betraying Jesus with the famous "Judas kiss." A disciple—John tells us it is Peter—draws his sword and cuts off the ear of the high priest's servant. Jesus stops the nonsense, quickly puts the ear back on, and asks the arresting officers why they come to seize him like a common criminal. Any unbiased reader of Luke's narrative will realize that treating Jesus in this way is grotesque, to say the least.

As Jesus himself points out, he has taught daily in the temple area in a very public forum. There was no need to track him down like this and insinuate that he has been eluding the authorities and would resist arrest. Nevertheless, Jesus hands himself over to the authorities, because this is their "hour." Peter follows at a distance; he ends up denying Jesus three times, just as Jesus has predicted. The men guarding Jesus proceed to mock and beat him.

The Jewish Trial (22:66–71)

The early morning witnesses a formal assembly of the Sanhedrin. Jesus is formally tried and asked point-blank if he is the Messiah. He refuses to answer the question directly, saying only that if he were to tell them, they wouldn't believe, as they've amply demonstrated by rejecting his claims throughout his entire ministry. Then, strikingly, Jesus identifies himself as "the Son of Man" who "shall be seated at the right hand of the power of God," referring to his vindication and enthronement with God (v. 69).

At this, the Sanhedrin asks Jesus, "Are you the Son of God, then?" But he only replies, "You say that I am" (v. 70). Jesus won't openly identify himself as the Messiah, only for the Jewish authorities to reject his claim. Yet they can easily read between the lines that, despite Jesus's evasive answers, he really does claim to be the Son of God, as well as the exalted, authoritative Son of Man. This is more than sufficient for them to charge him with blasphemy. In their eyes, Jesus must die.

The Roman Trial (23:1–25)

Next, the Jewish leaders rush Jesus over to Pontius Pilate, the Roman governor of Judea. Shrewdly, they frame their charges against Jesus in political terms, knowing that the Romans have kept a watchful eye on any potential Jewish rebellion. They tell Pilate that Jesus has been misleading their nation, has forbidden them to pay taxes to Caesar, and has claimed to be "Christ, a king" (23:2). Whereas they focused on theological charges (blasphemy) in their Sanhedrin meeting, when talking to Pilate they make Jesus out to be a threat to Roman rule, something they had to know was disingenuous and completely unfounded.

Despite the travesty of justice that is rapidly unfolding, Jesus maintains his composure. Acknowledging that Jesus, whose home is in Galilee, belongs to Herod Antipas's jurisdiction, Pilate sends him to Herod, who is glad to see Jesus. Herod questions him at length, but he says nothing. At the same time, the Jewish leaders are there, "vehemently accusing him" (v. 10). In the end, Herod and his soldiers treat him with contempt, putting a robe on him to mock his royal claims. This shows that unbelieving, sinful humanity has nothing but disdain for Jesus and the good news and salvation he has come to bring. In fact, the sinful response is to ridicule Jesus's claims and to despise his apparent weakness.

As Pilate is about to find out, you can't take a neutral stance regarding Jesus. You must be either for or against him. Ironically, as Luke notes, while Pilate and Herod had previously been enemies of one another, their common contempt for Jesus makes them allies. Nevertheless, Pilate realizes that despite the ferocity of the Jewish leaders' accusations, there are no objective grounds for indicting Jesus. So he calls the Jewish leaders together to inform them of the outcome of his investigation. As the Roman governor, he has the authority to release Jesus. In fact, the Jewish leaders need him to pronounce the death sentence, as this was the prerogative of the Romans. Will he oblige, despite his own better judgment?

Meanwhile, the crowd refuses to relent and ratchets up their demands. They even ask for the release of Barabbas, a murderer and rebel, in the place of Jesus. The irony here is that the crowd chooses to call for the release of a proven criminal while urging Pilate to convict an innocent man. Barnabas's release reinforces the unmistakable impression that a terrible injustice is being carried out. For a third time, Pilate asks, "What evil has he done?" (v. 22). Clearly, the implied answer is "Nothing at all!" But instead of taking command of the situation, Pilate is swayed by the rabid voices of the crowd. In the end, he takes the politically expedient route of pacifying the Jewish leaders and sentencing Jesus to be crucified.

Jesus's Crucifixion and Burial (23:26–56)

The hour of Jesus's crucifixion has arrived. Luke presents the events surrounding the crucifixion in five scenes: (1) the way to the cross (vv. 26–31); (2) the crucifixion (vv. 32–34); (3) mockery (vv. 35–43); (4) death (vv. 44–49); and (5) burial (vv. 50–56). In each section, Luke is careful to highlight Jesus's faithfulness in the face of death. In addition, Luke presents a full range of responses to Jesus's death.

On the way to the cross, we see a large crowd of people who lament Jesus's fate. Simon from Cyrene is enlisted to help Jesus carry the cross. He is depicted as a model disciple—one who takes up his cross to follow Jesus. Among the crowd of onlookers, a group of women follow Jesus in mourning. Jesus responds to them with a prophetic warning about the destruction of Jerusalem.

At the scene of Jesus's crucifixion, the reaction is drastically different, shifting from mourning to scoffing. The Jewish leaders ridicule Jesus: "He saved others; let him save himself, if he is the Christ of God, his Chosen One!" (v. 35). The Roman soldiers join in the mockery. The climax of humiliation comes when one of the criminals crucified with Jesus echoes the taunts of the leaders.

Despite the cruelty and abuse, Jesus is undaunted in fulfilling God's plan. Luke highlights Jesus's faithfulness to the very end in several ways. First, Jesus prays for the forgiveness of his enemies. Second, he ministers to the repentant criminal crucified next to him. He assures him with the promise, "today you will be with me in paradise" (v. 43). Third, Jesus's death is accompanied by several remarkable signs, including darkness at midday and the curtain in the temple being torn in two, which demonstrate that something far greater than a criminal's execution is taking place. In his final prayer, Jesus cries out, "Father, into your hands I commit my spirit!" (v. 46). The Jewish leaders wanted to lay hands on Jesus, but he commits his life into his Father's hands.

After Jesus's final breath, Luke makes note of three specific responses to his death. Upon seeing what has happened, the *centurion* gives glory to God, exclaiming, "Certainly this man was innocent!" (v. 47). The centurion's statement serves as the climax of a lengthy list of declarations of Jesus's innocence throughout the passion narrative. His verdict is reminiscent of Isaiah 53:11, where the prophet speaks of a suffering Servant who is "the righteous [i.e., innocent] one" and who will bear the sins of his people.

Next, Luke describes the reaction of the *crowd* that has gathered to witness Jesus's death. These people depart "beating their breasts," sensing the gravity of what has taken place (Luke 23:48). In addition, Luke highlights "all his *acquaintances*" (i.e., a group of disciples larger than the Twelve) and "the *women* who had followed him from Galilee" (v. 49, emphasis added; cf. 8:1–3). These women stand at a distance to separate themselves from the crowd, yet they remain with Jesus until the very end.

Finally, Luke makes special note of *Joseph of Arimathea*. While a member of the Sanhedrin, Joseph was not involved in the plot and decision to kill Jesus. He is depicted as a faithful disciple who honors Jesus with a proper burial. The women also honor Jesus by anointing his body with spices for burial. Each of the burial preparations is done in accordance with Jewish law before the Sabbath. The day of rest serves as a segue to the next scene.

The Empty Tomb and Resurrection Appearances (24:1–49)

Following Jesus's crucifixion and burial, he is vindicated by God through his resurrection. Luke records three separate resurrection appearances on "the first day of the week" (i.e., Sunday; 24:1): (1) to the women at the tomb (vv. 1–12), (2) to the two disciples on the road to Emmaus (vv. 13–35), and (3) to the eleven apostles in Jerusalem (vv. 36–49).

The Women at the Tomb (24:1–12). The women are first to arrive at Jesus's tomb early that morning. They come to bring the spices they have prepared, with no expectation that Jesus would be raised from the dead. They're perplexed to find the body of Jesus missing. They're greeted by two angels, who announce, "He is not here, but has risen" (v. 6). In the mind of the readers of Luke's gospel, this triggers the memory of Jesus's words during his ministry that he would rise on the third day (cf. 9:21–22; 18:33). The women remember his words and relay the message to the apostles. Peter responds and goes to see the empty tomb for himself.

Two Disciples on the Road to Emmaus (24:13–35). In the next scene, Jesus appears to two disciples on the road to Emmaus, a village about seven miles outside Jerusalem. Like the women, the two disciples—one unnamed, one named (Cleopas)—have no expectation of Jesus's resurrection as they leave Jerusalem for the nearby village of Emmaus. Upon meeting Jesus on the road—with his identity hidden from them—they express their profound disappointment at his tragic death. Jesus responds by rebuking them for their hardness of heart and points them back to the Scriptures. The two disciples invite Jesus to their home to share a meal with them. When they break bread together, their eyes are opened, and they recognize Jesus.

At this, they respond exuberantly, saying, “Did not our hearts burn within us while he talked to us on the road, while he opened to us the Scriptures?” (24:32). They proceed to find the apostles already announcing, “The Lord has risen indeed, and has appeared to Simon!” (v. 34). This is yet another report of a resurrection appearance that clearly was totally unexpected and certainly not imagined or invented (see the chart listing Jesus's resurrection appearances in all four gospels below).

The Eleven Disciples in Jerusalem (24:36–49). In the final episode, Jesus appears to the Eleven. The disciples are initially startled and frightened by his appearance, but Jesus seeks to allay their fears by issuing an invitation: “See my hands and my feet, that it is I myself” (v. 39). Throughout the scene, Luke emphasizes the reality of Jesus's bodily resurrection. He is not a spirit or ghost; he even eats a piece of broiled fish in the presence of his followers! Jesus proceeds to remind them that everything has happened in accordance with his words and Old Testament Scripture. This reiterates his message to the Emmaus disciples: it was “necessary” for him to suffer, that the Scriptures might be fulfilled (v. 26). As in the case of the Emmaus disciples, Jesus “opened their minds to understand the Scriptures” (v. 45; cf. v. 27). Jesus began his public ministry by reading Scripture and announcing its fulfillment. Now, at the end of his ministry, he explains how the Scriptures have all been fulfilled.

JESUS'S RESURRECTION APPEARANCES IN ALL FOUR GOSPELS

Recipients and Location	Time	Matt.	Mark	Luke	John	Acts	1 Cor.
FIRST SUNDAY							
1. The empty tomb	Early morning	28:1–10	16:1–8	24:1–12	20:1–9		
2. Mary Magdalene at the tomb	Early morning				20:11–18		

JESUS'S RESURRECTION APPEARANCES IN ALL FOUR GOSPELS							
Recipients and Location	**Time**	**Matt.**	**Mark**	**Luke**	**John**	**Acts**	**1 Cor.**
FIRST SUNDAY							
3. Peter in Jerusalem	Late morning?			24:34			15:5
4. Two disciples on the Emmaus road	Midday/ afternoon			24:13–32			
5. Ten disciples in the upper room	Evening			24:36–43	20:19–25		
SECOND SUNDAY (ONE WEEK LATER)							
6. The Eleven in the upper room	Evening				20:26–29		15:5
SUBSEQUENTLY (PRIOR TO PENTECOST)							
7. Seven disciples by the Sea of Galilee	Daybreak				21:1–23		
8. The Eleven on a mountain in Galilee	Sometime later	28:16–20					
9. More than five hundred at an unknown location	Sometime later						15:6
10. James at an unknown location	Sometime later						15:7
11. The Disciples on the Mount of Olives	Forty days later			24:44–49		1:3–8	

JESUS'S RESURRECTION APPEARANCES IN ALL FOUR GOSPELS							
Recipients and Location	**Time**	**Matt.**	**Mark**	**Luke**	**John**	**Acts**	**1 Cor.**
LATER							
12. Saul on the road to Damascus						9:1–19	

Seeing the great variety and large number of resurrection appearances of Jesus can strengthen our faith considerably, as it's highly unlikely that all of them are fictional or mere figments of imagination. This is yet another example of why we can be glad that we have four gospels rather than only one.

Throughout the resurrection narrative, Luke highlights the process by which one comes to recognize the risen Lord. An essential step is understanding the Scriptures in light of Christ's fulfillment. Jesus summarizes the basic content of Scripture by way of three verbs: Christ would "suffer," he would "rise," and repentance for the forgiveness of sins would "be proclaimed" to all nations (vv. 46–47). Many of the details in this last scene anticipate themes that will be picked up in the book of Acts. The disciples are "witnesses" to the things Jesus has done and taught. Jesus also promises to send the promised Holy Spirit (v. 48). He directs his followers to stay in Jerusalem until the outpouring of the Spirit.

The Ascension (24:50–53)

The gospel ends with a brief epilogue. In an unusual, distinctive scene, Jesus is shown to ascend to heaven from Bethany outside Jerusalem. The disciples return to Jerusalem, praising God with boundless joy. This ending prepares the reader for the opening scene of Acts and all that Jesus will continue to do through his apostles and the community of believers in the years following his ascension.

DISCUSSION QUESTIONS

1. Jesus was betrayed by one in his inner circle. Did you ever experience betrayal? If so, what happened?

2. Pilate tried to remain neutral regarding Jesus. Why is it ultimately impossible to do so?

3. How is it significant that Jesus appeared to multiple groups of people after the resurrection?

4. How does Luke prepare his readers for the book of Acts, the sequel of the gospel of Luke?

While all the people were listening, Jesus said to his disciples, "Beware of the teachers of the law. They like to walk around in flowing robes and love to be greeted with respect in the marketplaces and have the most important seats in the synagogues and the places of honor at banquets. They devour widows' houses and for a show make lengthy prayers. These men will be punished most severely."

—Luke 20:45–47 NIV

One thing I learned early in my Christian life is the difference between religion and a personal relationship with God through faith in the Lord Jesus Christ. I grew up in a tradition with plenty of ritual and liturgy, but Christ was depicted as still on the cross, and I had no idea why he was hanging there, much less about his resurrection. When I was told I could have a personal relationship with God in Christ, I first had a hard time understanding how that could be possible; but over time, I began to see that Christianity is at heart not a religion but a relationship, and I gladly entered that relationship by repenting of my sin and trusting in Christ. Over the years, I've grown in that relationship, which is very precious to me. Conversely, as Jesus told his followers, beware of people who, like the Jewish leaders in Jesus's day, use religion as a means to achieve status and prestige, displaying their religious "piety" before others, while taking advantage of the weak and vulnerable they are supposed to help.

PART 4

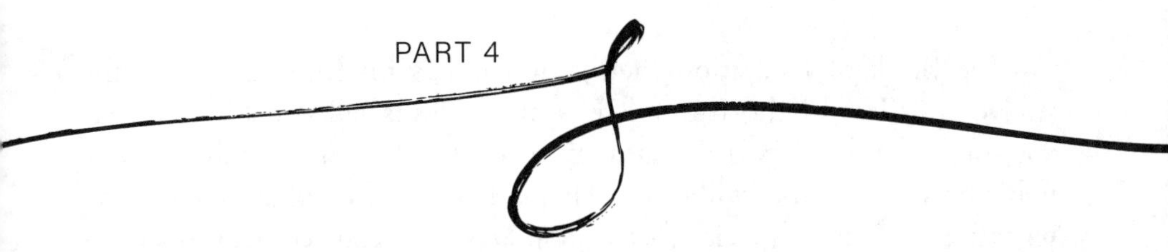

THE GOSPEL ACCORDING TO JOHN: JESUS, THE GOD-MAN

WHO WAS JOHN?

John, the son of Zebedee, was a member of the twelve apostles and one of the first followers of Jesus. What's more, he was a member of Jesus's inner circle, consisting of Peter; John's brother, James; and John himself. As such, John was privileged to witness momentous events, such as the raising of Jairus's twelve-year-old daughter, Jesus's glorious transfiguration, and Jesus's agonizing prayer in the garden of Gethsemane.

In his gospel, John stakes a bold claim of eyewitness testimony (see esp. John 19:35; 21:24–25). A Galilean fisherman, he may have been the youngest member of the Twelve and the only apostle to live to a ripe old age, without being martyred for his faith. In his gospel, John modestly calls himself "the disciple whom Jesus loved" (21:20; cf., e.g., 13:23). Without a doubt, John was one of the greatest theologians the world has ever known.

WHAT IS DISTINCTIVE ABOUT JOHN'S GOSPEL?

Like the other evangelists, John writes a gospel—a narrative centered on Jesus's life and earthly ministry, culminating in his crucifixion, burial, resurrection, and commissioning of his followers. There is a nice symmetry to John's gospel, as he begins with a lengthy prologue and concludes with an extended epilogue. In between these, John presents the life of Jesus in the form of a two-part drama: the Book of Signs (chaps. 2–12) and the Book of Exaltation (chaps. 13–20). The backbone of the Book of Signs are seven selected messianic signs performed by Jesus. The Book of Signs ends with a lament over the Jewish rejection of Jesus (12:36b–50).

The Book of Exaltation then shows Jesus's final instruction of the twelve apostles. In the Farewell Discourse, Jesus talks to his followers about life after his departure, the coming of the Holy Spirit, and the inevitable persecution that will ensue (chaps. 13–17). The Johannine passion narrative exhibits a special focus on Jesus's sovereign control of events and provides a detailed account of his Roman trial before Pontius Pilate (chaps. 18–20). The account of Jesus's crucifixion, burial, and resurrection is followed by a narration of the risen Jesus's appearances to Mary Magdalene and three groups of disciples and an account of Jesus's final words to Peter and the author himself, the apostle John (chap. 21).

WHAT ARE SOME OF JOHN'S MAJOR EMPHASES?

Writing a generation after the other three gospels, John penned a gospel that climaxes and completes the fourfold gospel in our New Testament. While the Synoptic Gospels—Matthew, Mark, and Luke—resemble each other in many ways, John breaks new ground. This is even more remarkable, as the three evangelists preceding him include a large amount of material in their accounts of Jesus's three-and-a-half-year ministry. John, it seems, is determined not merely to repeat what has already been covered (though he does, of course, include indispensable material, such as the passion narrative). Instead, he is going out of his way to present fresh information. What's more, where he does overlap with the earlier gospels, he significantly deepens our understanding of the theological significance of events in Jesus's life, a fact that has earned his work the epithet "the spiritual gospel."

John starts out his gospel with a magnificent prologue that sets Jesus's coming into this world into an eternal, cosmic perspective. John begins his prologue with the startling assertion of Jesus's (the Word's) deity. He ends the prologue with the equally startling claim that while "no one has ever seen God," "the one and only Son, who is himself God and is in closest relationship with the Father [Jesus], has made him known" (1:18 NIV). In this way, John's prologue sets up the following account of Jesus's life and ministry as a narration of how Jesus has made God the Father known in both word and deed.

In comparison to the Synoptic Gospels (i.e., Matthew, Mark, and Luke), John's worldview is rather unique. John sees the world in polarities or opposites: above and below, light and darkness, love and hate. John's favorite Old Testament theologian is the prophet Isaiah, from whom he derives his presentation of Jesus as the Word sent by God to accomplish his mission on earth and to return to his sender once the mission is accomplished (Isa. 55:10–11). He also borrows from Isaiah the depiction of Jesus as "lifted up"—physically lifted up in crucifixion and spiritually exalted by God in resurrection. Also, in a dual quotation from both major portions of Isaiah (i.e., Isa. 1–39 and Isa. 40–66), John closes his Book of Signs to show that Israel's rejection of Jesus's messianic mission has fulfilled Old Testament prophecy. Another unique feature of John's gospel is his realized eschatology—his belief that we can experience Jesus's presence and an abundant life already in the here and now.

CHAPTER 11—JOHN

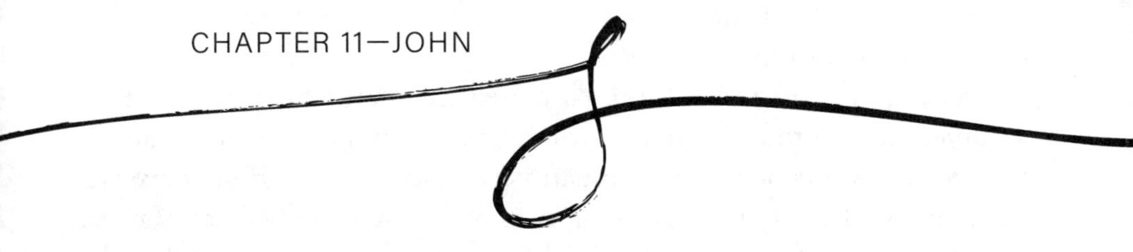

SIGNS OF THE MESSIAH: WATER INTO WINE, CLEANSING THE TEMPLE

INTRODUCTION AND THE CANA CYCLE (1:1–4:54)
Introduction (1:1–51)
The Cana Cycle (2:1–4:54)

INTRODUCTION AND THE CANA CYCLE (1:1–4:54)

Introduction (1:1–51)

The Word Became Flesh (1:1–18)

As Lewis Carroll once wrote in *Alice's Adventures in Wonderland*, "'Begin at the beginning,' the King said, very gravely, 'and go on till you come to the end: then stop.'"[1] John starts at the beginning—but not, as the other gospels have done before him, at the beginning of Jesus's human existence (i.e., his birth as a baby in a Bethlehem manger). Instead, he reaches all the way back into eternity and observes that in the very beginning Jesus—the Word—was already there: "In the beginning was the Word, and the Word was with God, *and the Word was God*" (John 1:1, emphasis added). Thus, John peels back the layers of time and shows that

1. Lewis Carroll, *Alice's Adventures in Wonderland* (New York: Macmillan, 1898), 182.

Jesus's birth as a human child didn't mark the beginning of his existence; it merely constituted the momentous event when the preexistent Word took on human form.

Yet John doesn't present himself merely as an armchair theologian or an objective, neutral historian. Rather, he identifies himself as a participant in the events he is about to narrate; in fact, he is a primary eyewitness: "and we have seen his glory, glory as of the only Son from the Father, full of grace and truth" (v. 14). "We" here refers to the apostle John, the author of this gospel, and the other members of the Twelve who accompanied Jesus throughout his earthly ministry, witnessed his messianic signs, and heard his extended discourses that revealed his true nature and unique relationship with God. As John continues, "For from his fullness we have all received, grace instead of grace. . . . No one has ever seen God; the only God, who is at the Father's side, he has made him known" (vv. 16, 18 ESV, slightly revised).

In between, in verses 6–8 and again in verse 15, the evangelist introduces another John, who will turn out to be a significant character in the story of Jesus—namely, John the Baptist. (To avoid confusion, the evangelist calls himself "the disciple whom Jesus loved.") This John, as Jesus's forerunner, bears witness to Jesus as the first of a series of witnesses to Jesus throughout the gospel. In this way, the evangelist assembles a veritable cloud of witnesses attesting to Jesus's true messianic identity, which will put the world on trial for its rejection of Jesus. While later the Jewish high priest and the Roman governor put *Jesus* on trial, the evangelist pointedly observes that it is in fact *they* who are on trial for rejecting Jesus. What a powerful way of turning the tables on those who put Jesus on the cross!

At the heart of the prologue, in verses 9–14, John highlights the incarnation of the Word and extols the privilege of becoming a child of God through faith in him. Take a closer look at the staircase-like structure of the prologue:

- The Word's activity in creation (vv. 1–5)
  - John's witness regarding Jesus (vv. 6–8)
    - The Word's incarnation and the privilege of becoming God's children (vv. 9–14)
  - John's witness regarding Jesus (v. 15)
- The final word in the revelation of God the Father (vv. 16–18)

In the above diagram, you can see that verses 9–14, on the Word's incarnation and the privilege of becoming God's children, epitomize the good news John has for his readers. Starting in verse 10, we read: "He was in the world, and the world was made through him, yet the world did not know him. He came to his own, and his own people did not receive him. But to all who did receive him, who believed in his name, he gave the right to become children of God" (vv. 10–12).

In these verses, John strikes an ominous note: the rejection of the Word by the world he has made. There is profound irony—even tragedy—in this: How could the world disavow its Creator? How could people reject the very one who made them? This seems utterly preposterous and inconceivable. Yet this is exactly what has happened, as the remaining narrative will show. At the climax of the escalating conflict between Jesus and the Jewish authorities, Jesus is put on a cross. He is buried, and on the third day, he rises from the dead—the gospel in a nutshell! The eternal Word in the flesh—Jesus, the God-Man—dies a real human death, so that everyone who believes in him can receive eternal life and become a child of God.

Finally, the evangelist relates the coming of Jesus to the role of Moses, asserting that while the law was given through Moses, grace and truth come through Jesus Christ (v. 17). The law, to be sure, furnishes evidence of God's gracious self-disclosure, for in it he reveals a glimpse of his righteous and holy character and lays down his expectations for how his people should live. And yet, in Jesus, God's self-revelation has reached new, unprecedented heights. For as we read in the book of Exodus, Moses, while serving as the vehicle of God's revelation at the giving of the law, couldn't see God and live. By contrast, Jesus not only has seen God but is continually present with him at his side; thus, he can make him known in an infinitely greater and more definitive way than Moses ever could.

This, then, is how the evangelist wants us to read the rest of his gospel. Jesus is the eternal Word, who had been active in creation and has now become flesh in Jesus. In what follows, the evangelist completely skips over Jesus's human birth and starts immediately with the testimony of John the Baptist. If you've read through the first three gospels already and are about to embark on your reading of the fourth and final gospel, you're well equipped for the journey. John won't duplicate much material from the others. There's inevitable overlap, but John will add significantly to your understanding of who Jesus is and what he said and did. You'll see that John, like a laser, focuses on Jesus's claim to deity, which is amply borne out by his messianic signs—but which is also, unfortunately, rejected by the Jewish leaders. You'll also learn more about different kinds of faith—both temporary and abiding—through a series of representative characters.

The Voice in the Wilderness and a Promise of Greater Things (1:19–51)

Now that John has set the stage with his carefully crafted prologue, he jumps right into the action, fast-forwarding to the days of John the Baptist. We've already seen that the evangelist draws a connection between the Word's role in creation and Jesus's taking up residence among his people in the recent past (from the evangelist's vantage point). Now, he takes this "new creation theology" a step farther, narrating the first week of Jesus's ministry in a way that mirrors the seven days of creation.

Day 1: John's Witness Regarding Himself (1:19–28) Verses 19–28 narrate "the testimony of John" (v. 19) that the fourth evangelist has anticipated in the prologue. Yet before he tells us who he is, John emphatically makes clear who he is not:

- He is not *the Messiah*. While the word "Messiah" is surprisingly rare in the Old Testament, the expectation is clear there that this figure will one day come and deliver his people.
- Nor is John *Elijah*. Some Jews expected Elijah—who never died but was taken up to heaven—to return.
- Nor, finally, is John *the Prophet*. On the basis of Moses's prediction that God would send a prophet like himself, many expected "the Prophet like Moses" (cf. Deut. 18:15).

From the very start, John makes clear that he is neither the Messiah nor Elijah nor the Prophet. Then who is he? Says John: "I am the voice of one crying out in the wilderness, 'Make straight the way of the Lord,' as the prophet Isaiah said" (John 1:23; cf. Isa. 40:3). Well then, the people ask John, "Why are you baptizing, if you are neither the Christ, nor Elijah, nor the Prophet?" (John 1:25). Fair question. John's answer is this: he's baptizing in order to prepare the way for the coming Messiah, yet he is "not worthy to untie" even "the strap of [his] sandal" (v. 27).

In this gospel and the others, John serves as the epitome of humility, whom all of us would do well to emulate. He is content to play second fiddle to Jesus and does so with distinction. As Jesus later teaches, God will bring about a reversal in which those who are first in this world will be last and those who are last will be first. The Baptist serves as a perennial example of one who knows his vital, supportive role and embraces it wholeheartedly.

Day 2: John's Witness Regarding Jesus (1:29–34) "The next day," John calls Jesus "the Lamb of God, who takes away the sin of the world," and says the reason he has been baptizing people is "that [Jesus] might be revealed to Israel" (vv. 29, 31). This shows that Jesus has come first to the Jews, God's chosen Old Testament people, who were promised that a Messiah would come to lead and deliver them. The Baptist humbly acknowledges that he could identify Jesus as the Messiah only because the Holy Spirit descended from heaven like a dove and rested on him.

Days 3–4: Jesus's Call of His First Disciples (1:35–42) Then, on "the next day," John points two of his own disciples to Jesus, "the Lamb of God," and they begin following him (vv. 35–37). One of them is Andrew, who is here identified as "Simon Peter's brother" (v. 40), even though Peter himself hasn't yet been mentioned in the gospel. Apparently John, writing a generation later than the other gospels, expects his readers to know who Peter is already. The other disciple remains unnamed, but he may have been none other than the apostle John, the author of the gospel.

Day 5: Jesus's Call of More Disciples and a Promise of "Greater Things" (1:43–51) In what follows, the evangelist highlights a pattern of pointing others to the Messiah:

- Andrew finds his brother, Simon (Peter), and brings him to Jesus.
  - Andrew says to him, "We have found the Messiah" (v. 41).
  - No response is recorded, but it is implied that Peter follows Jesus.
- Philip finds Nathanael and tells him to come to Jesus.
  - Philip claims, "We have found him of whom Moses in the Law and also the prophets wrote" (v. 45).
  - Upon meeting Jesus, Nathaniel exclaims, "Rabbi, you are the Son of God! You are the King of Israel!" (v. 49).

When Nathaniel is amazed at Jesus's supernatural knowledge—Jesus tells him he saw him under a fig tree—Jesus in effect replies, "You ain't seen nothin' yet!" Alluding to Jacob the patriarch, whom God later renamed "Israel," Jesus asserts that he—the Son of Man—will be the source of even more amazing revelation. Those who follow him "will see heaven opened" (v. 51). What a teaser at this early stage in the gospel!

The Cana Cycle (2:1–4:54)

Sign 1: Turning Water into Wine (2:1–12)

We've already seen how John has organized the inception of Jesus's ministry in the form of a week of activity. The week culminates "on the third day" with a wedding in a village called Cana (2:1), not far from Jesus's hometown of Nazareth in Galilee, and at which Jesus performs the first of his seven signs recorded in this gospel. Not only do we see the conclusion of Jesus's first week of ministry, therefore; we also witness the beginning of Jesus's signs, which will span the remainder of the first half of John's gospel—the Book of Signs (see table "The Seven Signs of Jesus" below).

John organizes this early stage of Jesus's ministry in the form of the "Cana Cycle," showing Jesus's movement from Cana (attending the wedding at the beginning of chap. 2) to Jerusalem, Judea, Samaria, and back to Cana (healing an official's son at the end of chap. 4). Thus, John shows how Jesus comes full circle, going on a circuit that leads him from Cana in the Galilean north to Jerusalem (where he clears the temple, celebrates the Passover, and engages in conversation with Nicodemus), to Judea and Samaria (where he converses with a woman at a historic well, again evoking memories of Jacob the patriarch), all the way back to Cana. As with Jesus's "creation week" of ministry, the Cana Cycle thus exhibits a nice pattern of symmetry, which makes Jesus's early movements appear coherent and well ordered, unfolding according to the divine plan.

First, then, we witness a wedding. Many commentators believe that the family of the bride or groom may have been friends with Jesus's mother, who features prominently in the story. When the wedding hosts run out of wine—considered to be a major faux pas in the ancient world—Jesus's mother gently goads her son to help. Does she know that he can create new wine because he has performed miracles previously? When Mary approaches him and asks him to help the family out of their predicament, Jesus's response is remarkably pointed: his hour, he tells his mother, has not yet come. This statement represents a common feature in John's narrative—a misunderstanding of Jesus's identity, of the purpose of his messianic mission, and (in the present case) specifically of his timing. He will not be revealed as the Messiah until a later time.

THE SEVEN SIGNS OF JESUS		
THE CANA CYCLE (2:1–4:54)		
Sign 1: Turning water into wine	Galilee (Cana)	2:1–11
Sign 2: Clearing the temple	Jerusalem	2:13–22
Sign 3: Healing the official's son	Galilee (Cana)	4:46–54
THE FESTIVAL CYCLE (5:1–10:42)		
Sign 4: Healing an invalid	Jerusalem	5:1–15
Sign 5: Feeding the multitude	Galilee	6:1–15
Sign 6: Healing a man born blind	Jerusalem	9:1–41
THE LAZARUS CYCLE (11:1–12:50)		
Sign 7: Raising Lazarus	Bethany (near Jerusalem)	11:1–44

Unperturbed, Jesus's mother tells those helping at the wedding, "Do whatever he tells you" (2:5). At this, Jesus miraculously turns a large amount of water into wine, entirely behind the scenes. This makes clear that the purpose of Jesus's miracles—or "signs," as John prefers to call them—is not primarily to wow his audience but to reveal himself to his followers as the Messiah. When John tells us at the end of this account that by performing this sign Jesus "manifested his glory" to his disciples—and that they "believed in him" (v. 11)—he signals that Jesus's purpose for performing his sign had been fulfilled: his followers had come to see a glimpse of his messianic identity and had placed their faith in him. Plus, he had helped the family save face and done a very nice thing for the young couple!

The First Passover and Sign 2: Clearing the Temple (2:13–22)

After spending a few days in nearby Capernaum with his mother, brothers, and disciples, Jesus travels to Jerusalem for Passover. Passover commemorated the occasion just prior to Israel's exodus from Egypt when the death angel "passed over" those who had smeared blood on their doorposts as a sign of their trust in God (Exod. 12). Ever since, the Israelites celebrated God's miraculous deliverance with a festive meal and a subsequent week of festivities, the Feast of Unleavened Bread (Exod. 13:1–16; Lev. 23:5–8; Deut. 16:1–8).

At this, his first Passover during his public ministry, Jesus goes straight to the temple and finds it to be a place of irreverent commercialism. In passionate zeal for God's glory and in righteous indignation at the scene he witnesses—money changers making a handsome profit providing worshipers with the right currency, dove sellers offering pigeons for the poor to sacrifice, presumably at inflated prices—Jesus clears the temple area to purify his "Father's house" for worship, the temple's God-intended purpose (John 2:16). Now, it is the Jewish authorities' turn to be indignant, pressing Jesus to present a sign of his authority. Ironically, however, Jesus had just performed the sign they are asking for—the temple clearing.

Jesus's action of confronting these merchants symbolizes God's judgment on the temple. It will soon be destroyed, and Jesus's broken and raised body will take its place as the proper realm of worship. "Destroy this temple," Jesus dares his detractors, "and in three days I will raise it up" (v. 19). In other words, they will try to destroy Jesus's body, but three days later he will rise. In this way, the temple clearing furnishes a second messianic sign, though the Jewish authorities tragically fail to understand the true meaning of Jesus's words and are unable to perceive the significance of his actions.

Jerusalem: Jesus's Conversation with Nicodemus (2:23–3:21)

Still in Jerusalem, Jesus receives a nightly visitor, a Pharisee named Nicodemus, "a ruler of the Jews"—that is, a member of the powerful supreme council called the Sanhedrin. This "man of the Pharisees" (3:1) is one of the men regarding whom Jesus needs no witness—he knows people can't be trusted because of their sin nature. Jesus tells Nicodemus that he lacks one very important thing—spiritual rebirth: "You must be born again" (v. 7). Nicodemus should have realized from reading Scripture that Israel must be restored and revitalized, which entails a real spiritual awakening.

John depicts Nicodemus as a representative of official Judaism, which scrupulously observed the law but lacked true spiritual life and vitality, so much so that when the long-awaited Messiah finally came to the Holy City, those who were supposed to recognize and welcome him with open arms had no use for him and missed out on benefiting from his coming altogether. What's more, they found him to be an inconvenient nuisance who kept them from engaging in business as usual, threatened their powerful positions and livelihood, and rivaled their sway over the common people.

Nicodemus doesn't understand the mysterious operation of the Spirit, though Jesus tries to explain it to him by using the analogy of the wind. Neither does he understand Jesus's statement that "as Moses lifted up the serpent in the wilderness, so must the Son of Man be lifted up" (v. 14). Jesus here refers to an incident during the exodus in which people were dying of snakebites and God told Moses to make a bronze serpent and raise it in plain view of the people; everyone who looked at the serpent in faith would live (Num. 21:4–9). It would be the same with Jesus: God would "raise" him up on the cross, and everyone who looked at him in faith would live and receive eternal life.

At this point, the narrative transitions from the story of Jesus and Nicodemus to the evangelist's commentary (contra the ESV): "For God so loved the world . . ." John's point here is that God's great love for sinful humanity is revealed at the cross, at great sacrifice to himself: "he gave his only Son" (John 3:16). This recalls Abraham's giving of Isaac, his "only son," at a critical juncture in his journey of faith (Gen. 22; see esp. vv. 2, 12, 16). But now, John explains, God himself gives his only Son for the life of the entire world—not merely for the Jewish people.

Judea: John's Continued Witness (3:22–36)

At this, Jesus and the disciples travel to the Judean countryside, where they perform baptisms as John the Baptist has done. The evangelist's parenthetical remark, "for John had not yet been put in prison" (John 3:24), suggests that he expects his readers to be familiar with the basic gospel story already. Once again, the Baptist clarifies his role in relation to Jesus. This time, he uses the illustration of a bridegroom's friend. Just as this friend is content to assist the groom on his special day, so the Baptist is happy to point people to Jesus: "He must increase, but I must decrease" (v. 30). The rest of the chapter contains additional commentary by the Baptist, pointing people to Jesus.

Samaria: Jesus's Conversation with a Samaritan Woman (4:1–42)

On his way back to Galilee, Jesus, John tells us, "had to pass through Samaria" (4:4). In fact, there was a shorter way, but John is here speaking of

God's sovereign will. God had wanted Jesus to go through Samaria because he had a special mission for him there. The place is historic—Jacob's well. As Jesus sits down by the well, thirsty and tired (not only God in the flesh but also fully human), a Samaritan woman comes to the well at noon to draw water. What ensues is a remarkable conversation in which Jesus engages the woman about her sin, spiritual thirst, and need for a savior.

The evangelist juxtaposes this story with the Nicodemus narrative as a study in contrasts. Nicodemus is a man—a Jew, a member of the Sanhedrin, and a "teacher of Israel," who comes to Jesus at night. The woman—who, unlike the highly prominent Nicodemus, remains unnamed—is a Samaritan, part of a people the Jewish people don't associate with because they consider them racially and ritually unclean, a mixed race with heretical views, including the view that people ought to worship God on Mount Gerizim in Samaria rather than in the temple in Jerusalem. She meets Jesus in broad daylight, at noon.

While these two characters couldn't be more different, what they both have in common is their need for a savior. But while Nicodemus is left speechless, the Samaritan is willing to be engaged and grows increasingly animated. She first recognizes Jesus as a Jew, then calls him a prophet, and finally asks hopefully, "Can this be the Christ?" (v. 29). In the end, she turns into an evangelist, bringing her entire town to Jesus. God is no respecter of persons. He so loves the world that whoever believes in him can have eternal life—even an immoral woman from an "impure" race! That's grace.

Sign 3: Healing the Official's Son (4:43–54)

After staying in Samaria for two days, Jesus returns to Galilee and arrives back in Cana, where he started his journey. Upon his arrival in Cana, Jesus receives a visit from an official from the nearby town of Capernaum. His son has fallen ill, and he asks Jesus to come and heal him. Jesus does in fact heal his son, but not by going to Capernaum; rather, he heals him simply by speaking the word!

John closes out the Cana Cycle by writing that "This was now the second sign that Jesus did" in Cana of Galilee (v. 54), reminding the reader of Jesus's first Cana sign, when he turned water into wine at the wedding. If the temple clearing in Jerusalem constitutes a sign as well, this means that Jesus has now manifested his messianic identity both in Galilee and in Judea—and, for good measure, in Samaria as well.

DISCUSSION QUESTIONS

1. Which one is your favorite gospel, and why?

2. What is unique about John's gospel when compared to the other three New Testament gospels?

3. Does identifying Jesus as God in the first verse of the gospel rob it of all suspense? Discuss.

4. What is the Cana Cycle, and what is its significance in the gospel of John as a whole?

Once more he visited Cana in Galilee, where he had turned the water into wine. And there was a certain royal official whose son lay sick at Capernaum. When this man heard that Jesus had arrived in Galilee from Judea, he went to him and begged him to come and heal his son, who was close to death. "Unless you people see signs and wonders," Jesus told him, "you will never believe." The royal official said, "Sir, come down before my child dies." "Go," Jesus replied, "your son will live." The man took Jesus at his word and departed

—John 4:46–50 NIV

John tells the story of a royal official, most likely a Roman Gentile, whose son was close to death. So this desperate father made the trek from Capernaum to Cana, a day's journey of about sixteen miles. Upon his arrival, the man begged Jesus to come and heal his son. Even when Jesus gave what appeared to be a discouraging initial response, the man didn't relent but pleaded with Jesus to come and heal his son before he died. Stunningly, Jesus simply stated that the man's son would live. Rather than come with him, as the man had asked, Jesus healed his son long-distance! Now, what's amazing is the official's response: he "took Jesus at his word" and went on his way. This is the kind of faith that pleases God!

CHAPTER 12—JOHN

SIGNS OF THE MESSIAH: HEALING THE SICK, FEEDING THE PEOPLE

THE FESTIVAL CYCLE (5:1–10:42)
Sign 4: Healing an Invalid (5:1–17)
The Sabbath Controversy (5:18–47)
Sign 5: Feeding the Five Thousand (6:1–15)
Jesus Walks on Water (6:16–21)
The Bread of Life Discourse (6:22–71)
The Feast of Tabernacles (7:1–8:59)
Sign 6: Healing a Man Born Blind (9:1–41)
The Good Shepherd Discourse (10:1–21)
The Feast of Dedication (10:22–42)

THE FESTIVAL CYCLE (5:1–10:42)

The next cycle of Jesus's activities is often called the Festival Cycle, spanning chapters 5–10. During this critical phase of his ministry, Jesus encounters increasing opposition from the Jewish authorities as he attends various Jewish festivals—an unnamed feast in Jerusalem (John 5); Passover in Galilee (chap. 6); Tabernacles, also called the Feast of Booths (chaps. 7–8, plus the aftermath in 9:1–10:21); and the Feast of Dedication, also called Hanukkah (10:22–39). As in the Cana Cycle, Jesus is shown to perform three messianic signs: (1) the healing of an invalid (chap. 5), (2) the feeding of the five thousand (chap. 6), and (3) the healing of a man born blind (chap. 9). In this manner, Jesus manifests his messianic identity to the Jewish people in tangible and ever more powerful ways.

Sign 4: Healing an Invalid (5:1–17)

The healing of an invalid—Jesus's fourth messianic sign in this gospel—triggers a significant wave of opposition and persecution. The fact that Jesus heals the man on the Sabbath makes him a breaker of God's law in the eyes of the authorities, who take the commandment to keep the Sabbath day holy with utmost seriousness and observe it scrupulously. Yet while their zeal is commendable, they fail to realize that as God's Son—himself divine—Jesus has authority over the Sabbath. Not that Jesus brazenly disregards scriptural Sabbath regulations. Rather, he interprets the Sabbath in light of God's underlying purpose. What's more, he himself fulfills the Sabbath by giving people abiding rest (Matt. 11:28–29; Heb. 3–4).

In fact, Jesus uses the occasion to affirm his unity with God the Father, which makes the Jewish leaders even more furious, because "not only was he breaking the Sabbath [at least in their eyes], but he was even calling God his own Father, making himself equal with God" (John 5:18). In this way, the evangelist keeps his narrative's single-minded focus on what he believes is the central issue in the entire story of Jesus: his claim to be none other than God in the flesh. As a matter of fact, the Festival Cycle will end exactly as it began, with Jesus claiming oneness with God the Father—"I and the Father are one"—and the Jews picking up stones to kill him because of perceived blasphemy (10:30–33).

The Sabbath Controversy (5:18–47)

The remainder of the unit is given to a close narration of the controversy surrounding the Sabbath between Jesus and the authorities. In the process, Jesus not only claims authority over the Sabbath but also affirms that as the Son of Man, he has authority to execute judgment on the last day. In addition, he calls several witnesses to the stand, who attest to the truthfulness of his claims, including John the Baptist (5:33–35), the works Jesus is performing (v. 36), God the Father (vv. 37–38), and Moses and the Scriptures (vv. 39–47). The unit ends with Jesus's parting challenge: "If you do not believe [Moses's] writings, how will you believe my words?" (v. 47).

Sign 5: Feeding the Five Thousand (6:1–15)

The next unit finds Jesus in Galilee. (The previous unit took place in Jerusalem.) This is now the second Passover Jesus observes in this gospel, yet this time Jesus stays in Galilee. There, Jesus miraculously feeds five thousand men, plus women and children—Jesus's fifth messianic sign. Philip and Andrew (Peter's brother) emerge as characters in the buildup to the miracle. Jesus is shown to take the initiative by asking Philip, "Where are we to buy bread, so that these people may eat?" (v. 5). As John tells us, "he said this to test him, for he himself knew what he would do" (v. 6).

It's interesting that Jesus here involves his followers in the miracle at all, as he could have simply performed it by himself. Philip assesses the situation realistically: "Two hundred denarii would not buy enough bread for each of them to get a little" (v. 7). (A denarius was a day's wage.) Thus, Jesus's idea of feeding all these people was completely beyond the realm of human possibility. At this, a second disciple, Andrew, ventures a longshot suggestion: "There is a boy here who has five barley loaves and two fish, but what are they for so many?" (v. 9).

Jesus simply tells his followers to have people sit down. Then he takes the loaves, gives thanks, and has the disciples distribute them and also the fish. And miraculously, there's enough to feed all the people! He even has the disciples gather twelve basketfuls of leftovers. When people see Jesus's sign, they exclaim that Jesus is the Prophet like Moses (who John the Baptist denied being) and want to compel him to be their king. But Jesus withdraws to a mountain by himself.

Jesus Walks on Water (6:16–21)

Meanwhile, his disciples embark on a boat on their own to cross the Sea of Galilee to Capernaum. Even though several of them are fishermen (and thus should be used to the stormy weather), they get scared when a gust comes up and the sea gets very rough. At this, Jesus walks toward them on the surface of the large lake, and now they get really scared and think Jesus is a ghost. When they recognize him and take him into the boat, a second miracle occurs—the boat immediately reaches the shore! Again, Jesus displays an attribute of deity—walking on the water—and identifies himself as "I am," the name with which God identified himself to Moses in the burning bush and which is also used repeatedly by Isaiah with reference to Yahweh.

The Bread of Life Discourse (6:22–71)

As soon as Jesus and the disciples land on the other side of the lake, people track them down, but Jesus says to them, "Truly, truly, I say to you, you are seeking me, not because you saw signs, but because you ate your fill of the loaves. Do not labor for the food that perishes, but for the food that endures to eternal life" (vv. 26–27). The people reply, "What must we do, to be doing the works of God?" (v. 28). Jesus's response is profound: "This is the work of God, that you believe in him whom he has sent" (v. 29). In other words, you don't need to do anything except believe! And even that is really God's doing, as no one can come to Jesus unless the Father draws him.

Sadly, people fail to understand. In the ensuing interchange, they again ask Jesus for a sign, revealing that they've failed to perceive the sign he has just performed when feeding the multitudes. Will Jesus provide yet another sign? No. Instead, he proceeds to explain the significance of the sign he has just performed. The crowd wants Jesus to duplicate Moses's feeding miracle of providing the Israelites in the wilderness with the mysterious manna, the "bread from heaven." They even pit Jesus against Moses: "Moses fed us with manna from heaven. What are you going to do?" (cf. vv. 30–31). What they ignore, however, is that when Moses gave people the manna, they complained. In response, Jesus explains that he himself is the heavenly bread that gives life—and this not merely to the Jews but to the entire world! This is truly a breathtaking claim, putting Jesus way above Moses to an elevated status otherwise occupied only by God the Father.

Just like their ancestors, the Jews grumble at Jesus's words and take offense at his language that people must eat his flesh and drink his blood. (The scene now takes place in the synagogue at Capernaum.) As it turns out, this occasion becomes a watershed moment in Jesus's ministry, because many of his close followers abandon him at this point; so offended are they at his teaching. Only the Twelve remain, represented by Peter, who at Jesus's challenge responds, "Lord, to whom shall we go? You have the words of eternal life" (v. 68). Judas, on the other hand, will betray Jesus. John unveils the identity of the betrayer early in the narrative, so his readers can track his movements and actions in light of this fact (even though his fellow disciples seem to be in the dark about his devious designs until the end).

The Feast of Tabernacles (7:1–8:59)

Opposition to Jesus is not limited to his disciples, however. Rejection and misunderstanding meet him at every turn, even with his own family.

We've already seen how earlier, at the Cana wedding, Jesus's own mother didn't understand his messianic timing. His brothers were mentioned right after that occasion, but nothing was said about their stance toward Jesus's messianic mission. Now, we see them urging Jesus to come out into the open so that he can show himself to the world, because not even they believe in him. As you might expect, just as Jesus had earlier refused his mother, he now reiterates to his brothers that his time has not yet come.

This being part of the Festival Cycle, it's now the Feast of Booths or Tabernacles, at which the Jewish people celebrate their dwelling in tents during the exodus in the wilderness. In keeping with Jesus's reluctance to reveal himself openly as the Messiah before his time has come, we witness no sign here but instead are treated to a smorgasbord of messianic expectations that swirl around Jesus's appearance at the feast, in conjunction with Jesus's claim that, in fulfillment of Tabernacles symbolism, he is "the light of the world" (8:12).

In fact, there was considerable uncertainty and much confusion surrounding the exact person, time, and circumstances of the Messiah's coming. Would he come to suffer and die or to rule and reign? (Most thought the latter.) Would he come just for Israel or for Gentiles as well? (Most thought just for Israel.) Where would the Messiah come from—would he be of mysterious origin or be born in Bethlehem in keeping with biblical prophecy? (Many, though not all, believed the latter.) This is the kind of matrix against which people compared anyone who claimed to be the Messiah—and there were several false messianic claimants in the first century—to see whether they fit the bill. (See "Opinions Regarding Jesus" below.)

John structures his account of Jesus's appearance at the Feast of Tabernacles as follows. Starting in 7:14, Jesus teaches at "about the middle of the feast." Then, in verse 37, Jesus teaches again "on the last day of the feast." At the former occasion, Jesus revisits the Sabbath healing of the lame man in chapter 5, pointing out that even the Jewish rabbis conceded that baby boys may be circumcised on the Sabbath. So why not heal a man on the Sabbath? At the latter occasion—at Tabernacles, a feast known for its water-pouring ceremonies—Jesus invites spiritually thirsty people to come to him, the one through whom the Holy Spirit will be given not many days later.

At this, multiple opinions regarding Jesus surface again. These conversations are sandwiched between the reference to the Jewish authorities sending officers to arrest Jesus in verse 32 and the return of these officers to the chief priests and Pharisees in verse 45—without Jesus! It appears even the officers have fallen under the spell of Jesus's teaching. What's more, even among the Sanhedrin—the Jewish ruling council—are those like Nicodemus who defend him and urge that he be treated fairly.

Opinions Regarding Jesus:

- "He is a good man" (v. 12).
- "He is leading the people astray" (v. 12).
- The Messiah will be of mysterious origin (v. 27).
- Will the Messiah perform more signs than Jesus? (v. 31).
- "This really is the Prophet" (v. 40).
- "This is the Christ" (v. 41).
- The Messiah was to be born in Bethlehem, yet Jesus came from Galilee (v. 41).

Continuing his teaching at the feast, Jesus now boldly states, "I am the light of the world" (8:12). The Pharisees promptly challenge him, objecting that a person's witness regarding himself cannot be accepted without additional witnesses (Deut. 19:15). Jesus retorts that his testimony is true, but it doesn't stand alone; God the Father attests to Jesus's messianic identity and divine commission as well. This moves discussion to Jesus's relationship with the Father which, as the readers of the gospel already know, is unique. In fact, the Festival Cycle is pervaded by Jesus's repeated and explicit claims to deity. This sets him on an inevitable collision course with the Jewish authorities, who tenaciously defend monotheism, the belief in one and only one God. In this way, John makes his entire gospel a referendum on Jesus's deity.

The Jewish authorities believe he is a mere man whose origin and family background they know. In fact, Jesus came from heaven as the God-sent Messiah to accomplish his mission (attested by his messianic signs). Upon completing his mission, he will return to his divine glory by way of the cross, where he will be "lifted up" both physically and spiritually—crucified by humans but exalted by God. Earlier, Jesus presented his own "lifting up" in analogy with the bronze serpent Moses had "lifted up" in the wilderness (John 3:14). Here, we find the second such reference: "When you have lifted up the Son of Man, then you will know that I am he" (8:28). This shows that Jesus's crucifixion is inescapable, that it is part of God's sovereign plan, and that Jesus is consciously and deliberately moving toward the cross. While the Jewish and Roman authorities are dead set on destroying him, and while Satan will use Judas as a human instrument of betrayal, God will use human evil to accomplish his good and sovereign purposes. He won't allow crucifixion to be the last word but will overrule it by raising Jesus from the dead.

The remainder of the unit finds an astonishing dynamic at work: the same "Jews who had believed" Jesus (v. 31), when challenged to continue in his word to prove that they're really his disciples, turn out at closer scrutiny to be slaves to sin and children of the devil! In this way, Jesus confronts the Jewish people's presumption that just because they are Jews ethnically, this means they are also God's children spiritually. Yet while they are God's chosen people and God had indeed entered into covenant with Abraham, they are still sinners and in need of God's grace. Merely affirming, as they do, "Abraham is our father" is inadequate, because, as Jesus points out, "If you were Abraham's children, you would be doing the works Abraham did" (v. 30). James and Paul later address this same issue, as does the Jerusalem Council in the early days of the church.

The debate between Jesus and the Jewish leaders gets increasingly heated. They accuse him of demon possession, while he points out that their true father is not Abraham but the devil. The interchange culminates in Jesus's claim, "Before Abraham was, I am"—affirming that Jesus has existed even prior to Abraham—at which the Jews once again pick up stones to throw at Jesus because of perceived blasphemy (vv. 58–59). This is an incredibly climactic moment in John's gospel, because it continues the string of references to Jesus's claim to deity that proves deeply offensive to his monotheistic Jewish contemporaries. In fact, the entire Festival Cycle is framed by references to Jesus's deity and his Jewish opponents' attempt to stone him on account of blasphemy.

Sign 6: Healing a Man Born Blind (9:1–41)

With the merest of transitions ("As he passed by"; 9:1), John continues the narrative by recounting Jesus's healing of a man born blind, another astonishing messianic sign performed by Jesus. At the outset, Jesus is addressing some false notions about the nature of suffering—namely, that suffering is always a result of a person's sin or at least that of his parents. In the present case, at least—the predicament of the man having been born blind—the man's blindness is to serve to reveal the glory of God in Jesus, "the light of the world" (vv. 3, 5).

The story is told in some detail. First, John records the actual healing (vv. 1–12). Then he features the Pharisees' initial interrogation of the formerly blind man (vv. 13–17). After this, he narrates the Pharisees' interrogation of the man's parents (vv. 18–23). This is followed by a second round of questioning of the healed man by the Pharisees (vv. 24–34). Finally, John uses the event as a sort of real-life parable illustrating the spiritual blindness of the Pharisees (vv. 35–41). It's as if John is saying Jesus can open the eyes of those who are physically blind, but he can't help those who claim to see while being spiritually blind!

The healed blind man provides a striking contrast with the healed invalid at the beginning of the Festival Cycle in chapter 5. While the invalid reports Jesus to the authorities, the healed blind man defends Jesus and ultimately worships him. This again illustrates the importance of responding to Jesus in faith, discerning the way in which his messianic signs reveal his identity as the Messiah and Son of God. In this way, this sign becomes the vehicle of his message that undergirds his entire gospel. His burning desire is that people believe in Jesus and as a result have eternal life in him.

The Good Shepherd Discourse (10:1–21)

Chapter 10 picks up seamlessly where chapter 9 left off, starting with an authoritative pronouncement of Jesus regarding legitimate and illegitimate shepherds of God's sheep. The Good Shepherd Discourse by Jesus contained in this chapter is one of two sustained symbolic discourses in this gospel, the other being the discourse on the vine and the branches in chapter 15. Both highlight corporate metaphors for God's people: God's flock and God's vineyard. Both metaphors are used for Israel in the Old Testament but are now applied by Jesus to his new messianic community made up of all believers in him, both Jews and Gentiles.

The Good Shepherd Discourse contains two of the seven "I am" sayings of Jesus in this gospel: "I am the door [or gate]" (10:7, 9) and "I am the good shepherd" (vv. 11, 14). How can Jesus be both the gate to the sheep and their shepherd? This shows the fluidity that one often finds in these kinds of symbolic discourses. The fact is that Jesus is both: he is the only legitimate way of access to God's flock—he is "the way" (14:6); and he is also the divinely appointed shepherd of God's flock, in contrast to Israel's faithless shepherds who, as Ezekiel lamented, have used their sacred office only to enrich themselves at the sheep's expense.

All of this makes clear that Jesus is still talking about the Pharisees who have opposed his healing of the blind man. The connection with the preceding chapter is underscored by the renewed charge of demon possession hurled toward Jesus, as well as the people's response: "These are not the words of one who is oppressed by a demon. Can a demon open the eyes of the blind?" (10:21).

The Feast of Dedication (10:22–42)

With this, the scene transitions to yet another feast, the last one mentioned in the Festival Cycle, which is slowly but surely drawing to a close—namely, the Feast of Dedication. This festival is not mentioned in the Old Testament, because it was instituted only in the intertestamental period, amid a Jewish revolutionary movement led by the Maccabees in the second century BC. While the locale is different than before—Jesus is now moving about in the temple area, in a place called Solomon's Colonnade (v. 23)—and it is now winter (v. 22), the topic is much the same as earlier in the chapter: Jesus's rightful authority over God's flock and his role as the Good Shepherd.

Reassuring his followers, Jesus insists that no one can snatch his sheep (i.e., believers) out of his hand, because God the Father, who has given him these sheep, is greater than all. Jesus proceeds to depict God the Father and himself—God the Son—as working in tandem throughout his messianic mission, boldly asserting, "I and the Father are one" (v. 30). For the third time in the Festival Cycle, the Jews are picking up stones to throw at Jesus because of alleged blasphemy. At this, Jesus engages them in a rather technical rabbinic debate about whether it is ever appropriate to call someone other than God "Son of God." The implied answer is yes—but the Jews aren't convinced.

For now, though, Jesus continues to elude their grasp and returns to the place where John the Baptist had started his baptizing ministry. This is the last time the evangelist refers to the Baptist. This portion of the gospel thus ends the same way it began: with Jesus's forerunner. As the evangelist points out, unlike Jesus, John performed no sign, yet everything he said regarding Jesus was true. He was the foundational witness to Jesus, the Messiah.

DISCUSSION QUESTIONS

1. What is your favorite holiday?
2. What is your favorite sign in John's gospel, and why?
3. What is the Festival Cycle, and what is its significance in the gospel of John as a whole?
4. What were some of the opinions people had regarding Jesus, and what is your opinion?

When evening came, his disciples went down to the lake, where they got into a boat and set off across the lake for Capernaum. By now it was dark, and Jesus had not yet joined them. A strong wind was blowing and the waters grew rough. When they had rowed about three or four miles, they saw Jesus approaching the boat, walking on the water; and they were frightened. But he said to them, "It is I; don't be afraid."

—John 6:16–20 NIV

Some of Jesus's disciples were rugged fisherman, like Peter, but one night when they were rowing across the Sea of Galilee and the wind was howling and the waves were high, they were gripped by fear. They had already rowed three or four miles (a considerable distance, especially in those rough conditions) when at last they saw Jesus coming toward them, walking on the water. Now they were even more afraid! But he reassured them that it was him; there was no need to fear. What are you afraid of? Failure? Sickness? Or even death? If you trust Jesus, he'll come alongside you and walk with you. Jesus is no mere man; he is the God-man. Trust in his supernatural presence as you go through the rough waters of life.

CHAPTER 13—JOHN

THE GREATEST SIGN AND JESUS'S FAREWELL

THE LAZARUS CYCLE AND THE FAREWELL DISCOURSE (11:1–17:26)
The Lazarus Cycle (11:1–12:50)
The Last Supper, the Farewell Discourse, and Jesus's Final Prayer (13:1–17:26)

THE LAZARUS CYCLE AND THE FAREWELL DISCOURSE (11:1–17:26)

Following the Cana Cycle (John 2–4) and the Festival Cycle (chaps. 5–10), each of which features three of Jesus's messianic signs, a bridge section, spanning chapters 11–12, narrates the seventh, climactic sign—the raising of Lazarus—and closes the Book of Signs. While two chapters remain in this book, Jesus's public ministry has all but come to a close with the third and final attempt to stone him at the end of chapter 10. All that's left for Jesus to do is perform his final sign.

The Lazarus Cycle (11:1–12:50)

Sign 7: Raising Lazarus (11:1–44)

Lazarus is the brother of Mary and Martha, a pair of sisters also featured in Luke's gospel, where Jesus defends Mary against Martha's complaint that she should help her host instead of sitting at his feet to learn from him (Luke 10:38–42). John expects his readers to be already familiar with Mary, as he mentions at the beginning of chapter 11 that it was Mary who anointed Jesus's feet with perfume and wiped his feet with her hair—even though he doesn't recount this story until the next chapter in his gospel (12:1–8)! As at the healing of the blind man, Jesus notes at the outset that Lazarus's illness has occurred so that the glory of God could be manifested in and through Jesus (cf. 9:5).

There is a dramatic delay in that Jesus, when hearing of Lazarus's illness, stays "two days longer in the place where he was" (11:6). In the interim, Lazarus dies. When Jesus arrives on the scene, Lazarus has already been in the tomb for four days. Jesus is met by Lazarus's older sister, Martha, and assures her that her brother will rise again. Martha replies that yes, she knows Lazarus will rise again "in the resurrection on the last day" (v. 24). Yet Jesus, declaring, "I am the resurrection and the life," makes clear that he has the power to raise Lazarus right now (v. 25). When he challenges Martha and asks if she believes this, she responds, "Yes, Lord; I believe that you are the Christ, the Son of God, who is coming into the world" (v. 27). In this way, Martha anticipates John's purpose statement at the end of his gospel.

Next, Jesus meets up with Lazarus's younger sister, Mary. Heartbroken yet full of confident faith in Jesus, she simply tells him, "Lord, if you had been here, my brother would not have died" (v. 32). Like her sister, Mary has enough faith to believe Jesus could have kept Lazarus from dying, but perhaps not enough faith to believe, now that her brother is dead, that Jesus can raise him from the dead—at least not right now. When Jesus sees Mary and others weep, he too bursts into tears. How touching! As at previous occasions, John helps his readers connect the present event with the preceding sign when he quotes some Jews as saying, "Could not he who opened the eyes of the blind man also have kept this man from dying?" (v. 37). Like Mary, these Jews fall short of believing that, now that Lazarus is dead, Jesus can do anything about it, much less raise him from the dead.

The remainder of the narrative is told rather tersely, with great economy of words. Jesus arrives at the tomb, directing the people, "Take away the stone" (v. 39). Martha's protestations notwithstanding (i.e., that Lazarus would exude an odor of death, as he has already been in the tomb for four days), they take away the stone. Jesus utters a short prayer and commands with a loud voice, "Lazarus, come out" (v. 43). At this, the dead man walks out of the tomb, still bound with linen strips and a face cloth! Jesus says simply, "Unbind him, and let him go" (v. 44), at which the scene shifts abruptly from Lazarus's tomb to a Sanhedrin meeting.

The raising of Lazarus is Jesus's climactic, seventh messianic sign in the Book of Signs, which makes up the first half of his gospel. In this first half, John depicts Jesus's mission to the Jews as their Messiah. Tragically, they reject him, despite the abundant proof he furnishes in keeping with the messianic expectations voiced by the Old Testament Prophets, especially Isaiah. As a raising from the dead, the raising of Lazarus—even more than the other signs—points to Jesus's own resurrection, proving that he is indeed "the resurrection and the life" in his very being. If people don't believe in Jesus when he raises people from the dead, how will they believe in the resurrected Jesus?

The Sanhedrin's Plot Against Jesus (11:45–57)

In their meeting, the chief priests and Pharisees are exasperated. What can they do? Jesus's popularity is meteorically on the rise. Then Caiaphas, the high priest, speaks up, arguing that "it is better for you that one man should die for the people, not that the whole nation should perish" (v. 50). John astutely observes that Caiaphas here unwittingly prophesies that Jesus will die on the cross for people's sins—not only for Jews but also for Gentiles. The chapter ends on the ominous note that the third Passover recorded in John's gospel is at hand and that orders are out for Jesus's arrest. Will he even come to the feast?

Jesus's Anointing at Bethany (12:1–11)

Chapter 12 opens with a remarkable scene: a dinner given in Lazarus's honor, the very one whom Jesus had raised from the dead. As anticipated in the previous chapter, Mary anoints Jesus's feet with precious, expensive perfume, intuitively sensing that Jesus's crucifixion and burial are imminent. While the other gospels don't reveal the identity of the one who objects to this "extravagant waste," John notes that the anointing serves as an occasion for Judas's antagonism to be revealed, as pious posturing masks the fact that he is a thief.

The Sanhedrin's desperation is underscored by the fact that they are now resolved to kill not only Jesus but Lazarus as well, because his very presence constitutes incontrovertible proof that Jesus has the power to raise the dead. It's hard to argue with a dead man come to life! John here provides us with both a positive example of devotion to Jesus

(Mary) and a negative example of antagonism toward Jesus (Judas). This shows how people must either pledge to follow Jesus in loyalty and faith or reject him and suffer the consequences. There's simply no middle ground.

Jesus's Entry into Jerusalem (12:12–19)

Jesus's final week has now begun. It's Palm Sunday, and Jesus is about to enter Jerusalem. Throngs of people welcome him into the city, waving palm branches from nearby Jericho, the "City of Palms," a symbol found on coins celebrating Jewish national pride in the face of foreign oppression and occupation. By riding into the city on a lowly donkey, Jesus not only emulates King Solomon's mode of entry into the city; he also evokes the memory of the coming lowly King envisioned in Zechariah's prophecy: "behold, your king is coming, sitting on a donkey's colt!" (12:15; cf. Zech. 9:9; cf. also 1 Kings 1:33, 38, 44). Again, John connects an event to what had happened previously—in the present case, the raising of Lazarus. It's deeply tragic and ironic that people here acclaim Jesus on the basis of a shallow notion of who the Messiah was going to be. Later the same week, they will shout, "Crucify! Crucify!" This shows that Jesus was right when he chose not to entrust himself to anyone. Public adulation is extremely fickle.

The Dawning Era of the Gentiles (12:20–36a)

Jesus's popularity is further underscored by the fact that some Greeks (i.e., Gentiles) ask to see him. This triggers Jesus's pronouncement that "the hour has come for the Son of Man to be glorified" (John 12:23). As we've seen, Jesus has repeatedly affirmed that the time at which he will publicly reveal his messianic identity has not yet come. But now, it appears, it is approaching Gentiles who signal to Jesus that his "hour"—his saving cross death—is near. Jesus likens himself to a grain of wheat that must fall into the ground and die in order to bring much fruit—apparently, including many Gentiles—and speaks of losing his life.

When a heavenly voice promises to glorify God's name, Jesus utters his third "lifted up" saying in this gospel: "And I, when I am lifted up from the earth, will draw all people to myself" (v. 32). Doubtless, by "all people" Jesus means "both Jews and Gentiles." And yet John doesn't say whether the Gentiles who ask to see Jesus get their wish. You surmise that they don't, as Jesus has not yet been "lifted up" on the cross. At the end of the Book of Signs, this gives a heads-up to the reader that Jesus's death will open the door of salvation to all. People might reject him, but God will accept his sacrifice on our behalf.

Concluding Indictment of Jewish Unbelief (12:36b–50)

At this, Jesus hides himself, conveying God's judgment and hiddenness for those who are about to reject him as Messiah and God-sent King. John draws the somber spiritual conclusion: "Though [Jesus] had done so many signs before them, they still did not believe in him" (v. 37). Even this unbelief, however, John points out, fulfills biblical prophecy. As in Isaiah's day, God's message through Jesus has largely fallen on deaf ears. As the prophet lamented, "Lord, who has believed what he heard from us, and to whom has the arm of the Lord been revealed?" (v. 38; cf. Isa. 53:1). "The arm of the Lord" refers to God's power, which has been on ample display in Jesus's powerful works. Tellingly, this first of two Isaianic passages John quotes is part of the Song of the Suffering Servant, which is fulfilled in Jesus.

The second passage is one of the most frequently cited in the entire New Testament. In it, Isaiah proclaims, "He has blinded their eyes and hardened their heart, lest they see with their eyes, and understand with their heart, and turn, and I would heal them" (John 12:40; cf. Isa. 6:10). Remarkably, this passage immediately follows Isaiah's throne room vision of the holy God. John introduces this second passage from Isaiah, which speaks of the people's hardening toward God's message and work among them by commenting, "Therefore they could not believe" (John 12:39). Notice he doesn't say "*did* not" but "*could* not," which raises all kinds of complex theological questions regarding the relationship between God's sovereignty and human responsibility. Essentially, people must believe to be saved, but ultimately God is still sovereign.

The Book of Signs closes with a monologue by Jesus. It's as if all the other actors have left the stage; only Jesus remains. Jesus reiterates that he has "come into the world as light," so that those who believe in him "may not remain in darkness" (v. 46). With that, the curtain closes. Act 1 of the Johannine drama has come to an end. After a brief intermission, act 2 will begin.

The Last Supper, the Farewell Discourse, and Jesus's Final Prayer (13:1–17:26)

The Book of Signs (chaps. 1–12) is now followed by act 2 in John's two-part drama, the Book of Exaltation. The Book of Signs narrated Jesus's performance of seven signs to demonstrate to the Jewish people that he is the expected Messiah. However, their rejection of him is signaled at the end of the Book of Signs, so the Book of Exaltation starts out with Jesus's preparation of a believing remnant, the Twelve. In the Farewell Discourse, Jesus celebrates the Last Supper with his new messianic community. After Judas's departure, Jesus instructs the Eleven about his imminent departure and the coming of the Holy Spirit. The passion narrative ensues, including Jesus's arrest, trials, crucifixion, resurrection appearances, and final commissioning.

The Foot Washing and the Last Supper (13:1–30)

Moving from the end of chapter 12 to the beginning of chapter 13, it's as if you're starting to read a new book, complete with a new introduction. While the focus in the first half of John's gospel was on Jesus's public performance of striking messianic signs, the focus now shifts to Jesus's private instruction of his new messianic community, the Twelve. This community is cleansed, first literally (the foot washing) and then figuratively (by the removal of Judas, the betrayer). Jesus himself, it appears, is no longer engaged in acrimonious debate with his opponents. Rather, he anticipates that he will shortly die on the cross and subsequently return to his heavenly glory.

The main need now is to provide final instruction to his followers. In typical rabbinic fashion, Jesus engages in a didactic action: washing his disciples' feet in order to demonstrate their need to serve one another humbly in love. It's almost as if, for John, the foot washing serves as an anticipatory commentary on the meaning of the cross. The lesson of the foot washing, then, is this: "If I then, your Lord and Teacher, have washed your feet, you also ought to wash one another's feet. For I have given you an example" (13:14–15).

In that day, people would walk for miles in sandals on dusty roads; when they arrived at their host's house, a household servant would greet them at the door and wash their feet, so that when they reclined to eat, resting on one elbow, the person beside them didn't have to smell their stinky feet! At the Last Supper, though, the problem is that the disciples have rented an upper room, but apparently the household servant wasn't included! So who would rise to the task? No one—except for Jesus. The disciples are aghast—how could their Master condescend to the lowly stature of a slave? John tells us the reason is love: "Having loved his own who were in the world, he loved them to the end" (v. 1).

The touching foot-washing scene gives way to Jesus's gentle but pointed exposure of Judas, the betrayer. The reader was told a while back that in due course Judas would betray Jesus. It appears, however, that at the time the other apostles are completely unaware. At the anointing of Jesus, Judas's antagonism reared its ugly head, but his two-faced nature was lost on the disciples. During the Last Supper, Jesus tells the "beloved disciple" (John, the author) that the betrayer is Judas (vv. 23–26). This is the first self-reference of the fourth evangelist, the apostle John, in this gospel. Since "John" in this gospel refers to the Baptist (e.g., 1:6), and in order to avoid confusion the apostle John chose to identify himself as the "beloved disciple," emphasizing the fact that he knew himself to be loved by Jesus. The scene ends with Judas stepping out of the room into the night, ominously foreshadowing the hour when darkness would reign (cf. Luke 22:47–48, 53).

The Farewell Discourse (13:31–16:33)

Now that his inner circle of followers has been cleansed—not merely physically by the foot washing, but also spiritually by the removal of the betrayer—Jesus begins to instruct his followers. He first gives them "a new commandment"—namely, "that you love one another: just as I have loved you, you also are to love one another" (John 13:34). This is how people will know that they are Jesus's disciples. At this, Peter pledges undying loyalty, but Jesus predicts that Peter, the apostles' unquestioned leader, will shortly deny him three times. It's interesting that Jesus speaks first and foremost of love and loyalty. In the face of Judas's defection and the prospect of Peter's denials, Jesus unconditionally loves his followers all the way to the cross and talks to them about selfless love.

The next three chapters contain what is commonly referred to as the Farewell Discourse. It consists of two teaching cycles on the topic of life after Jesus's departure. The first cycle spans from 13:31 to 14:31, and the second comprises chapters 15 and 16. In this material, unique to John, Jesus engages in a sort of Q and A with his followers, who are deeply troubled at the prospect of his imminent departure and the accompanying loss they will suffer. The following disciples take turns asking questions or making a request:

- Thomas: "How can we know the way?" (14:5).
- Philip: "Lord, show us the Father, and it is enough for us" (v. 8).

- Judas (not Iscariot): "Lord, how is it that you will manifest yourself to us, and not to the world?" (v. 22).

Read this portion with a healthy dose of historical imagination and put yourself in the disciples' shoes: How would you feel if you were in their place? They had put their lives, family ties, and possessions on the line for Jesus; now, it seems, all their investments are going to be reduced to zero in a matter of days. Have they made the wrong decision? And what will life be like without Jesus? These are the kinds of questions Jesus addresses in the last few hours before his betrayal, arrest, Jewish and Roman trials, and crucifixion.

Jesus's main burden here seems to be to convince his disciples that, contrary to their own expectations, his departure in fact will benefit them, because once he is exalted with God, he and the Father will send the Spirit. What's more, Jesus has been *with* them—the Spirit will be *in* them. Using the illustration of a vine's close connection with its branches, Jesus explains the way in which the disciples will be able to remain connected with him and the Father through the Spirit. These are truths familiar to us, but they were all news to the disciples!

Jesus also prepares his followers for upcoming persecution and reassures them that the Spirit will bear witness alongside them. Not only does Jesus instruct his disciples about the work of the coming Holy Spirit; he also equips them for the "little while" during which they will no longer see him—the interim between his burial and resurrection—and the time following the resurrection, when they will see him again before he is exalted with God (the ascension and exaltation). Their emotional roller-coaster ride will compare to that of a woman giving birth.

Jesus's Final Prayer (17:1–26)

After this, Jesus prays to the Father—for himself (17:1–5), his followers (vv. 6–19), and even later generations of believers (vv. 20–26). Essentially, this is the report of the Word who has come into the world, has accomplished his mission, and is about to return to his sender: "Mission accomplished!" In this, as in so many other ways, John seems strongly dependent on the theology of the Old Testament prophet Isaiah, who had memorably written,

> For as the rain and the snow come down from heaven
> and do not return there but water the earth,

making it bring forth and sprout,
giving seed to the sower and bread to the eater,
so shall my word be that goes out from my mouth;
it shall not return to me empty,
but it shall accomplish that which I purpose,
and shall succeed in the thing for which I sent it. (Isa. 55:10–11)

Doesn't this sound very similar to John's portrayal of Jesus's mission? Jesus, the Word, has been sent by God to earth and won't return to him empty; he accomplishes all that God has intended and succeeds in the thing for which God has sent him. Thus, he will cry on the cross, "It is finished" (19:30). This mission, in turn, is bound up with those whom the Father has given Jesus out of the world—his disciples—who will serve as his representatives and pass on the good news of salvation in him to later generations.

Here, Jesus's three-pronged vision comes into sharp focus: (1) setting apart believers from the world, (2) helping them grow in the truth, and (3) sending them back into the world to proclaim the saving message of Christ: "They are not of the world, just as I am not of the world. Sanctify them in the truth; your word is truth. As you sent me into the world, so I have sent them into the world" (17:16–18). Three chapters—and three days—later, this vision will become a reality.

DISCUSSION QUESTIONS

1. If someone were to say that the raising of Lazarus is the greatest sign in John's gospel, would they be wrong, and why or why not?

2. What is the purpose of Jesus's farewell discourse, and what is the primary message Jesus is trying to impress on his followers?

3. What does it mean to "abide" in Jesus, and how do you make sure that you abide in him?

4. What are two or three major requests Jesus makes in his final prayer to the Father in John 17?

I am the true vine, and my Father is the gardener. He cuts off every branch in me that bears no fruit, while every branch that does bear fruit he prunes so that it will be even more fruitful. . . . Remain in me, as I also remain in you. No branch can bear fruit by itself; it must remain in the vine. Neither can you bear fruit unless you remain in me. I am the vine; you are the branches. If you remain in me and I in you, you will bear much fruit; apart from me you can do nothing.

—John 15:1–2, 4–5 NIV

Jesus was a master teacher. His use of illustrations, many of them echoing Old Testament language, is unsurpassed. The night before the crucifixion, Jesus sought to impress on his followers their need to remain connected to him once he had departed from this earth. To do so, he told them the allegory of the vine and the branches. Jesus's main point is that to bear fruit, believers must remain connected to him through prayer and the indwelling Holy Spirit. He bluntly stated, "apart from me you can do nothing." Are you trying to accomplish something in your life? If so, are you trying to do so apart from Jesus? Don't be deceived; Jesus's words are true. Apart from him, we can accomplish nothing of abiding value.

CHAPTER 14—JOHN

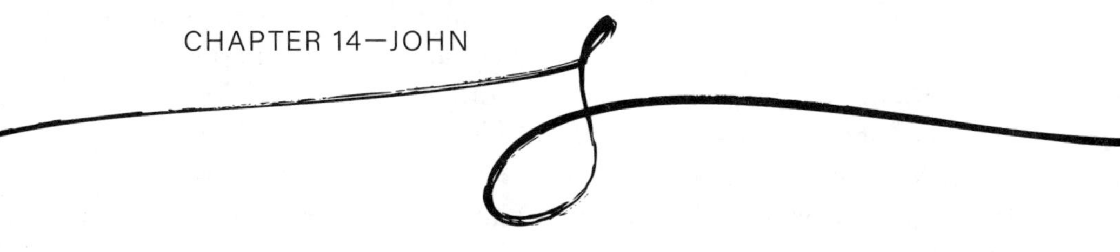

SUFFERING AND EXALTATION

THE PASSION NARRATIVE AND THE EPILOGUE (18:1–21:25)
The Passion Narrative (18:1–20:31)
The Epilogue (21:1–25)

THE PASSION NARRATIVE AND THE EPILOGUE (18:1–21:25)

The Passion Narrative (18:1–20:31)

The passion narrative in John's gospel—John's account of Jesus's arrest, trials, crucifixion, burial, and resurrection—in many ways resembles that of the other three gospels. This is to be expected, as Jesus's entire earthly ministry culminates in his saving mission at the cross, and all of the gospels are firmly grounded in actual history. And yet there are ways in which John emphasizes particular aspects of Jesus's passion, in many cases filling in certain gaps left by the other gospels.

John, more than the other gospels, stresses Jesus's sovereignty throughout the proceedings against him. We've seen this already in the preamble to the Book of Exaltation, where John stressed that Jesus knew where he had come from and where he was going. The arrest and crucifixion don't take Jesus by surprise! He isn't ambushed by Judas's betrayal; neither is he a messianic pretender who miscalculates the extent of opposition to him and is swept away by a wave of popularity that suddenly turns into rejection. To stress this, John emphasizes Jesus being in control of his surroundings at every turn. At his arrest, it is Jesus who asks the soldiers, "Whom do you seek?" (John 18:4). When they tell him, "Jesus of Nazareth," he fearlessly replies, "I am he," at which they draw back and fall to the ground, as in response to a manifestation of God, whose name he had just invoked (vv. 5–6). Then Jesus tells those who are about to arrest him to let his disciples go; and when Peter draws a sword to defend him, he tells him to put his sword away. He must "drink the cup that the Father has given" him (v. 11). You marvel at such courage, composure, and sovereign handling of a very trying situation.

Second, John focuses less on the suffering of Jesus and more on the glory of the cross. While no one can deny that Jesus suffered excruciating pain for us when he endured countless humiliations and the most inhumane form of execution, John presents the cross as nothing but a station on Jesus's return to the Father and to the glory he had before the world began. A representative statement is as follows: "I came from the Father and have come into the world, and now I am leaving the world and going to the Father" (16:28). Or consider Jesus's prayer: "But now I am coming to you. . . . Father, I desire that they also . . . may be with me where I am, to see my glory that you have given me because you loved me before the foundation of the world" (17:13, 24). Then, when hanging on the cross, Jesus's last statement in this gospel is "It is finished" (19:30). Mission accomplished! It's a cry of triumph, not defeat. Jesus has completed his redemptive mission. After dying a real death, his body will be buried, and then, three days later, he will rise and never die again.

Third, John all but presupposes Jesus's Jewish trial before Caiaphas and supplements the accounts in the other gospels in two ways. First, he records an informal hearing before Annas, the high-priestly patriarch and father-in-law of Caiaphas. And second, he recounts Jesus's interrogation by Pontius Pilate, the Roman governor, in considerably more detail than do the other gospels.

Jesus's Arrest, Hearing Before Annas, and Peter's Denials (18:1–27)

In the first part of John's passion narrative, he covers familiar ground. He narrates Jesus's arrest, his hearing before Annas, his transport to Caiaphas, and his interrogation before Pilate. In essence, all of the action is building up to Jesus's Roman trial, which climaxes the proceedings against

Jesus and culminates in the death sentence by crucifixion. By way of overview, John's account is structured like this:

- Jesus's arrest (18:1–11)
- Jesus's hearing before Annas (vv. 12–14, 19–24; sandwiched in between is Peter's first denial: vv. 15–18)
- Annas's sending of Jesus to Caiaphas (v. 24)
- Caiaphas's sending of Jesus to Pilate (v. 28; sandwiched in between are Peter's second and third denials: vv. 25–27; note that John doesn't narrate the Jewish trial before Caiaphas at all)
- Jesus's interrogation before Pilate (18:28–19:16)

Note how John devotes nine verses to the informal hearing before Annas, skips the formal Jewish trial before Caiaphas and the Sanhedrin, and devotes twenty-nine verses to Jesus's Roman trial.

The Roman Trial Before Pilate (18:28–19:16a)

The trial before Pilate, for its part, is structured in the form of alternating outside and inside episodes:

- outside (18:29–32)
- inside (vv. 33–38a)
- outside (vv. 38b–40)
- inside (19:1–3)
- outside (vv. 4–7)
- inside (vv. 8–11)
- outside (vv. 12–15)

In this way, John graphically depicts the dramatic back-and-forth between Pilate and the Jewish leaders who accuse Jesus before the Roman governor. Notice also that the Jewish leaders initially try to sway Pilate by bringing against Jesus a vague criminal charge—he is an "evildoer." They also seem to hint at a political charge, knowing that Rome has been very sensitive to any threats to its rule. Therefore, the next round of interrogation before Pilate revolves around the question of whether Jesus is King of the Jews. In response, Jesus pointedly tells the Roman governor that his kingdom is not of this world. Pilate has nothing to worry about; Jesus is no threat to Roman imperial power.

When neither the general nor the political charge sways Pilate, the Jewish leaders move to the heart of the matter: "We have a law, and according to that law he ought to die because he has made himself the Son of God" (v. 7). In this way too John sharpens the focus of the other gospels: at the core, what gets Jesus on the cross is a theological charge, alleged blasphemy—his claim to be God. The entire narrative has been building up to this moment. Repeatedly, the Jews have picked up stones to throw at Jesus because of perceived blasphemy. Now, they press their case before the Roman governor, and at last Pilate succumbs to the political pressure and—against his better judgment—condemns Jesus to die.

Jesus's Crucifixion and Burial (19:16b–42)

The crucifixion itself is narrated in terse and somber tones: "So they took Jesus, and he went out, bearing his own cross. . . . There they crucified him" (vv. 16b–18). After entrusting the care of his mother to the "beloved disciple" (none other than the author, the apostle John), Jesus says, "It is finished," bows his head, and dies (v. 30). Beyond this, John records several ways in which minor details surrounding the crucifixion fulfill biblical prophecy, again underscoring the fact that this has been God's plan all along. An equally respectful and somber account of the burial rounds out John's passion narrative. Two "secret disciples" of Jesus from among the Sanhedrin, Joseph of Arimathea and Nicodemus (mentioned only in John's gospel), ask Pilate for Jesus's body and, with his permission, take Jesus's body down from the cross and hastily prepare it for burial, as the Sabbath, on which no work is to be done, is about to begin.

The Empty Tomb and Resurrection Appearances (20:1–29)

On the "first day of the week" (20:1), Mary Magdalene goes to Jesus's tomb early, no doubt to complete the work that had remained unfinished because of the inbreaking Sabbath. She is surprised to find that the stone has been rolled away from the tomb and tells John and Peter, who promptly rush to the tomb and find it empty. They find the linen cloths with which Jesus's body had been wrapped lying there, as well as his face cloth neatly folded up by itself. Even this, apparently, is not enough for them to understand that Jesus is risen from the dead.

Then we find Mary back outside the tomb, crying. She sees two angels and turns around and sees Jesus but fails to recognize him at first. Thinking he's the gardener, she asks him where he has put Jesus's body. Historically, this suggests that neither the disciples nor the women were looking for a *risen* Jesus; for them, the cross and burial of Jesus were the end. At this, Jesus calls her by name: "Mary." She recognizes him at once, exclaiming "'Rabboni!' (which means Teacher)" (v. 16). Just as she was the first witness of the empty tomb, so now she becomes the first witness of the resurrection.

After this, the risen Jesus appears to the disciples on three separate occasions:

1. On the evening of that first Sunday, to ten of the apostles (without Judas and Thomas; vv. 19–23)
2. Eight days later, to the eleven apostles (including Thomas; vv. 26–29)
3. Sometime later, to seven disciples, who go fishing by the Sea of Galilee (21:1–14)

On the first occasion, Jesus commissions the disciples in the power of the Spirit: "As the Father has sent me, even so I am sending you. . . . Receive the Holy Spirit" (20:21–22). This is a pivotal point in the narrative, as thus far it has always been Jesus who is sent by the Father; now, Jesus is sending his new messianic community. Verse 21 is the center of John's trinitarian mission theology: the Father has sent Jesus; now, Jesus sends his disciples in the power of the Spirit.

On the second occasion, Thomas (who for some reason was missing the first time) is with the rest of the Eleven. When the other disciples tell him about Jesus's first appearance among them, Thomas is skeptical. Displaying divine knowledge, Jesus tells him to put his finger in his wounds and look at his nail-scarred hands. At this, "doubting Thomas" surrenders and believes, exclaiming, "My Lord and my God!" (v. 28).

Just as John had affirmed Jesus's deity at the very outset of his gospel, he concludes it with an unequivocal affirmation of Jesus's deity. What's more, now it is one of the Twelve, a character in the narrative, who has arrived at the same conclusion (despite considerable skepticism) that Jesus is Lord and God (even *his* Lord and *his* God). In this way, Thomas is the Johannine equivalent of the Roman centurion in the other gospels.

Jesus's response to Thomas's expression of worship seamlessly transitions from Thomas to the readers of the gospel, who have never had the opportunity to see Jesus in the flesh: "Have you believed because you have seen me? Blessed are those who have not seen and yet have believed" (v. 29). Jesus thus pronounces a blessing on those who, unlike Thomas, haven't seen him and yet have believed. Thomas's confession of Jesus as his Lord and God therefore provides a fitting climax to the gospel.

John's Purpose Statement (20:30–31)

With this, we've come to the end of the Book of Exaltation and the entire gospel. Wrapping up the gospel, John acknowledges that "Jesus did many other signs in the presence of the disciples, which are not written in this book" (v. 30). This is certainly a proper disclaimer, especially when one thinks of all the material included in the Synoptic Gospels that John has chosen not to include: the Sermon on the Mount (including the Lord's Prayer), the transfiguration, the Olivet Discourse, Jesus's numerous kingdom parables, demon exorcisms—the list goes on and on. Clearly, John has been extremely selective in what he includes.

He continues: "But these [signs] are written so that you may believe that Jesus is the Christ, the Son of God, and that by believing you may have life in his name" (v. 31). The first thing one notices is the highly unusual direct address: "that *you* may believe" (emphasis added). It is virtually unprecedented for a gospel writer to address his audience directly, but this is what John does here! He is not writing an impersonal treatise; he is writing for the purpose of leading his readers to Christ, whether directly (evangelizing them himself) or, more likely, indirectly (supplying believers with an evangelistic tool to use with unbelievers). One surmises that the other gospel writers pursued a similar purpose.

In his concluding purpose statement, the John conveniently touches on virtually all of the key emphases throughout his gospel. Pride of place goes to Jesus's messianic signs. As we've seen, John records seven particularly striking signs, including the raising of Lazarus as the seventh, climactic sign, which remarkably is not featured in the first three gospels. Also, John is writing to encourage his readers to believe that Jesus is the Christ, the Son of God. In this, he is very much in line with the other gospels. Throughout his gospel, he has used representative characters to lead his readers to this intended conclusion. Finally, those who believe in Christ will have eternal life.

The Epilogue (21:1–25)

Two resurrection appearances to his disciples have already been recorded, in addition to Jesus's encounter with Mary Magdalene. The gospel closes with a third appearance and Jesus's final instructions to Peter and John, the disciple whom Jesus loved and author of the gospel.

The Third Resurrection Appearance (21:1–14)

At his third resurrection appearance, Jesus shows himself to seven of his disciples, who, following Peter's lead, have gone fishing. They stay out all night but catch nothing. At daybreak, Jesus, standing at the shore, directs them to cast their net on the right side of the boat. The result is a huge haul of 153 fish. At that moment, John recognizes Jesus, at which point Peter jumps into the water and swims toward Jesus. Again on land, the disciples discover a charcoal fire, reminiscent of the charcoal fire burning in the high priest's courtyard, when Peter had denied Jesus three times. Shortly, Jesus will recommission Peter, asking him three times if he loves him. But first, the risen Jesus prepares breakfast for these men and, in customary fashion, breaks bread and gives it to them, together with the fish.

Jesus's Final Words to Peter and the Disciple Whom Jesus Loved (21:15–23)

After the meal, Jesus spends some one-on-one (or one-on-two) time with Peter and John. In the course of the conversation, he predicts Peter's martyrdom. When Peter inquires as to the fate of his fellow disciple, Jesus essentially tells him to mind his own business—he must follow Jesus! This final interchange highlights the fact that while all of Jesus's followers must bear witness to him, there will be different individual callings within this general responsibility. Some, such as Peter, will be called to give their very lives in martyrdom as an outflow of that witness. Others, such as John, will be called on to bear witness through writing or proclamation. In John's case, he will have the unique privilege of writing the fourth and final gospel included in the New Testament.

Conclusion (21:24–25)

The gospel closes with an acknowledgment that John, of necessity, has had to be highly selective in what he has recorded, as the entire world could not contain the books that would need to be written if everything Jesus had said and done were recorded. This, in fact, is a fitting ending not just to John's gospel but to the entire fourfold gospel witness in our New Testament. We aren't given an exhaustive account of Jesus's words and deeds, but only a selection, and yet what we do have is more than enough to make an informed decision about who Jesus truly is and what the significance is of his first coming.

DISCUSSION QUESTIONS

1. Have you experienced any significant suffering, and if so, what was it?

2. Why did Jesus suffer and die? Discuss.

3. What is significant about Jesus's resurrection? If Jesus had died but not risen from the dead, would we still be saved?

4. Was Thomas's demand to see the risen Jesus legitimate? Why or why not?

Peter turned and saw that the disciple whom Jesus loved was following them. (This was the one who had leaned back against Jesus at the supper and had said, "Lord, who is going to betray you?") When Peter saw him, he asked, "Lord, what about him?" Jesus answered, "If I want him to remain alive until I return, what is that to you? You must follow me."

—John 21:20–22 NIV

Many of us have the sinful desire to compare ourselves to others. We are competitive, and even envious or jealous of others at times who seem to have given a more attractive assignment in God's kingdom. Jesus has just told Peter that one day he would be called to die a martyr's death. So when Peter saw "the beloved disciple" (the apostle John), he couldn't help but ask Jesus, "Lord, what about him?" Jesus, in effect, replied, "Peter, none of your business"; following Jesus must be enough for him. We must take up our own cross and follow Jesus, not the cross of others. Others may have an easier life, but appearances may be deceiving. It must be enough for us to follow Jesus and fulfill the calling we received from him.

APPENDIX A

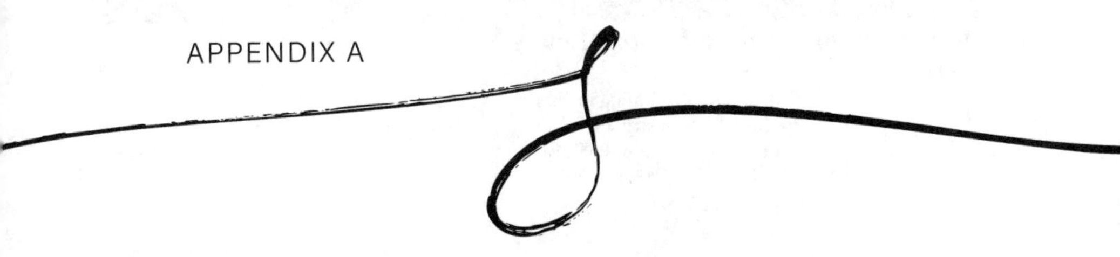

CHARTS OF THE GOSPELS

<table>
<tr><th colspan="9">THE GOSPEL ACCORDING TO MATTHEW</th></tr>
<tr><th>Preface</th><th colspan="8">Ministry in Galilee (4:17–18:35)</th></tr>
<tr><td>Jesus the Messiah, Descendant of Abraham and David (1:1–4:16)</td><td>Galilee, Part 1 (4:17–25)</td><td>BOOK 1: Sermon on the Mount (5–7)</td><td>Galilee, Part 2 (8–9)</td><td>BOOK 2: Commissioning of the Twelve (10)</td><td>Galilee, Part 3 (11–12)</td><td>BOOK 3: Kingdom Parables (13:1–53)</td><td>Farther North (13:54–17:27)</td><td>BOOK 4: Kingdom Parables (18)</td></tr>
<tr><th colspan="9">Ministry in Judea, Death, Burial, and Resurrection (19–28)</th></tr>
<tr><td colspan="3">Ministry in Judea and Jerusalem (19–23)</td><td colspan="3">BOOK 5: Kingdom Parables (24–25)</td><td colspan="3">Death, Burial, and Resurrection, the Great Commission (26–28)</td></tr>
</table>

<table>
<tr><th colspan="4">THE GOSPEL ACCORDING TO MARK</th></tr>
<tr><th colspan="4">Jesus the Messiah and Son of God (1:1–8:26)</th></tr>
<tr><td>Beginning of the Gospel (1:1–13)</td><td>Initial Ministry in Galilee (1:14–3:6)</td><td>Later Ministry in Galilee (3:7–6:6a)</td><td>Ministry beyond Galilee (6:6b–8:26)</td></tr>
<tr><th colspan="4">Jesus the Messiah and Suffering Servant (8:27–16:8)</th></tr>
<tr><td>Journey to Jerusalem (8:27–10:52)</td><td>Ministry in Jerusalem (11–13)</td><td colspan="2">Passion Narrative (14–16)</td></tr>
</table>

THE GOSPEL ACCORDING TO LUKE

Preface (1:1–4)	**Jesus's Birth and Preparation for Ministry (1:5–4:13)**			**Ministry in Galilee (4:14–9:50)**		
	Two Special Births (1:5–80)	Birth and Childhood of the Messiah (2:1–52)	Beginning of John's Ministry, Preparation for Jesus's Ministry (3:1–4:13)	Ministry in Galilee Part 1 (4:14–7:50)	Ministry in Galilee Part 2 (8:1–39)	Ministry in Galilee Part 3 (8:40–9:50)

Journey to Jerusalem (9:51–19:27)					**Ministry in Jerusalem (19:28–24:49)**		**Ascension (24:50–53)**
Lessons on Discipleship 1 (9:51–11:54)	Lessons on Discipleship 2 (12:1–13:9)	Lessons on Discipleship 3 (13:10–15:32)	Lessons on Discipleship 4 (16:1–17:10)	Closing in on Jerusalem (17:11–19:27)	Final Ministry in Jerusalem (19:28–21:38)	Last Supper, Arrest, Cross, Resurrection (22:1–24:49)	

THE GOSPEL ACCORDING TO JOHN

Prologue (1:1–18)	**John's Witness, First Disciples (1:19–51)**	**Book of Signs (2–12)**		
		Cana Cycle (2–4)	Festival Cycle (5–10)	Lazarus Cycle (11–12)
		SIGN 1: Water to Wine (2:1–11) SIGN 2: Clearing Temple (2:13–22) Nicodemus, Samaritan Woman (2:23–4:45) SIGN 3: Healing Official's Son (4:46–54)	SIGN 4: Healing an Invalid (5:1–15) SIGN 5: Feeding the 5,000 (6:1–15) Jesus at Feast of Tabernacles (7–8) SIGN 6: Opening Blind Man's Eyes (9) Good Shepherd, Feast of Dedication (10)	SIGN 7: Raising Lazarus (11) Anointing (12:1–11) Triumphal Entry (12:12–19) Approach of Gentiles (12:20–36a) Conclusion of Book of Signs (12:36b–50)

Book of Exaltation (13–20)		**Epilogue (21)**
Farewell Discourse (13–17)	Passion Narrative (18–20)	
Last Supper, Footwashing (13:1–30) Farewell Discourse Proper (13:31–16:33) First Teaching Cycle (13:31–14:31) Second Teaching Cycle (15–16) Jesus's Final Prayer (17)	Arrest and Jewish Trial Before Annas, Peter's Denials (18:1–27) Roman Trial Before Pilate (18:28–19:16a) Crucifixion and Burial (19:16b–42) Empty Tomb, Resurrection Appearances (20:1–29) Purpose Statement (20:30–31)	

ALSO BY THE AUTHOR

Growing in and Defending the Faith (Spiritual Formation and Apologetics)

- *The Heresy of Orthodoxy: How Contemporary Culture's Fascination with Diversity Has Reshaped Our Understanding of Early Christianity*
- *Truth in a Culture of Doubt: Engaging Skeptical Challenges to the Bible*
- *Truth Matters: Confident Faith in a Confusing World*

Studying the Bible (Hermeneutics)

- *For the Love of God's Word: An Introduction to Biblical Interpretation*
- *Inductive Bible Study: Observation, Interpretation, and Application through the Lenses of History, Literature, and Theology*
- *Invitation to Biblical Interpretation: Exploring the Hermeneutical Triad of History, Literature, and Theology,* 2nd ed.

Studying the Life of Jesus (Gospels Studies)

- *Jesus and the Future: Understanding What He Taught about the End Times*
- *The Final Days of Jesus: The Most Important Week of the Most Important Person Who Ever Lived*
- *The First Days of Jesus: The Story of the Incarnation*
- *The Jesus of the Gospels: An Introduction*

Studying the New Testament (New Testament Introduction)

- *The Cradle, the Cross, and the Crown: An Introduction to the New Testament,* 2nd ed.
- *The Lion and the Lamb: New Testament Essentials from* The Cradle, the Cross, and the Crown
- *Handbook on Hebrews through Revelation*

Studying the Theology of the Entire Bible (Biblical Theology)

- *Biblical Theology: A Canonical, Thematic, and Ethical Approach*

For a full list of Dr. Köstenberger's publications and additional resources, see https://biblicalfoundations.org.